A Tryst with
PARIS

Maret Jaks

The Jaks Group

Toronto, Ontario
CANADA

The Jaks Group
18 King Street East, Suite 1400
Toronto, Ontario M5C 1C4
Canada

Publisher's Note: This is a true and genuine memoir. To respect the privacy of the people involved in this book, we have changed the names and, at times, masked certain information about them.

A Tryst with Paris -- 1st ed.
ISBN 978-0-9918701-1-0

Book Cover by: xee_designs1 at Fiverr.com
Photograph by: Kipgodi at iStock.com

This book is dedicated to the lovely people
who share their lives with me
and to Olympe de Gouges.

.

After all these years, I see I was mistaken about Eve in the beginning; it is better to live outside the Garden with her than inside it without her.

—MARK TWAIN

CONTENTS

Part Three

About the Author

Some Basic Facts

Preface

··

Let me make one thing perfectly clear: this is a true story. To make the story flow, I did have to adjust some timelines (my editor told me to!) but the characters and all of our encounters are all real.

Completely.

Out of respect for their privacy, I have changed their names and, at times, masked certain information about them. I hope that if the people I've written about in *A Tryst with Paris* read this memoir, they will see that I have reflected their inner spirit both accurately and respectfully.

By the way, as you read this book you'll see that my first name is Maret. It's an Estonian name and it's pronounced Mah'-ret.

If you roll the "r," you'll be pronouncing my name just like an Estonian!

Part One

CHAPTER ONE

Sizing Things Up

Strong and feminine, soft and kind, a bit of an adventuress. Likes only the finest things in life: champagne, rich conversations, and the company of good friends and family. Looking for the right man for the rest of my life.

There. That should do it. I sat back, took a sip of champagne and admired the simplicity, the brevity of the profile. Unlike profiles I'd put up back home, this one was very much to the point. It had to be. It was about to go up on a French Internet dating site here in Paris. I needed words, simple words, that I could translate using my high school French.

There are plenty of nuances lurking there in that language. I suppose the same holds true for other languages. I knew of an American working in Indonesia who introduced the town's Chief of Police as the "Head of Coconuts." The Head of Coconuts enjoyed a good belly laugh, re-introduced himself, and all was well. But on a written profile, glaring out there in cyberspace, those translation mistakes can make you look childish or even rude and there'd be no Head of Coconuts to intercept the error.

That's why I kept the profile simple, crisp, easy to translate.

The site I chose is heavily advertised on TV here in Paris. The ads always close with a scene that scans across the same dating paraphernalia – a long-stemmed rose (red, of course) placed across a cute little evening purse, half open. Spilling out from the purse – lipstick, two used tickets for a show, a set of keys and a couple of packages of condoms. Always two condoms in every ad. Why two? I wondered this each time this scene flashed across the TV screen. Are the French taught to always have a backup in case one breaks or was one for night and the other for morning? Or was this a subliminal message to encourage women to believe they could get lucky enough, as I had once been back home, to find a lover who never failed to absolutely require two 'go rounds' before he could fall asleep?

I looked around the sweet little apartment I'd managed to rent in downtown Paris and figuratively patted myself on the back. It's not a simple thing to temporarily close up a life on one continent and get yourself organized on another, not when you're my age. At my age, with grown children back home, ex-husbands and a career in full throttle, people don't just pick up and go.

Not normally.

Speaking of age, should I be honest about it? I took another look at my profile. Forty-seven. A four and a seven. Looking fifty squarely in the eye . . . Indeed . . . Fifty . . . Nearly. Well, I thought to myself as I took an extra-long sip of champagne from the special flute I'd bought, well, when the four and the seven are the other way around, a seven and a four, you'll be looking back on 47 and thinking you were just a youngster.

But the question is, should I be honest about my age?

I'm compulsively honest.

I'm 47. My profile said I was 47. It's the truth. There.

I took another long sip, a gulp really, to compliment myself on the decision.

With the help of an online French-English dictionary, I crossed my fingers, translated my profile into French and managed to figure out how to save the translation by poking around at the buttons and tabs and stumbling into the online ads, all in French. At last, once saved, I opened the profile and reread the French part.

> Forte et feminine, gentile, un peu d'une aventureuse.
> Aimais seulement les choses les plus parfaites dans la
> vie : le champagne, les conversations riches et la com-
> pagnie de bons amis et de famille. Le fait de
> chercher l'homme juste pour le reste de ma vie.

"*Voilà!*" I said out loud. "The adventure begins."

I sat back and waited. It felt a bit like fishing, leaving the profile open and staying online to lure someone my way. Holding my glass up, I admired how the light from the cluster of candles huddled together in the fireplace made it seem like the champagne glowed from within. The apartment was quiet, serene. Three long windows here in this cozy living room, dark and tall, stood as sentinels protecting me from the cold night air.

Three decades ago I was a pregnant eighteen-year-old and alone and not sure if it was right to keep the baby. Back then, I drank ginger ale pretending it was champagne – not because I was pregnant and avoiding alcohol. It was just that ginger ale was all I could afford. But I've always been able to afford big dreams, so as I sipped the imaginary champagne, I would also force myself to imagine that when my baby was all grown up, I would find a way to live in Paris.

First, I had to find my way out of the nightmare that was my life: an uneducated, unskilled single teenaged mom with no idea how I was going to support the two of us.

∞

Outside, slicing the silence of the night, a French police siren hee-haw, hee-hawed past the apartment. For just a moment, each dark window flashed red.

Life is Good, I thought.

I drank a bit more champagne. Then a bit more. It felt like the tiny bubbles were now dancing in my head, doing the cha-cha. Should be doing the 'can can', I thought. Then I felt (imagined) 'can can' music all around me, making me want to get up and dance. I stood up and reached for the bottle, more than half empty, and was smart enough to walk it back to the teensy Parisian fridge. The rest would have to wait till tomorrow.

As I returned to my computer, I remembered that someone long ago in 1323 had written, "To be in Paris, is to be." To be. Ah, to be, to be, to be. To be here at my computer, to be here alone with the candles and the champagne and the dark Paris night pressed up against the windows. To be, just to be, felt precisely perfect at this moment.

I looked at my computer again. Yes, I had set the bait -- in pretty simple terms, I admit. Soon I'd have a nibble or two.

Oh. Already! That was fast.

I sat up. The instant message button was flashing. Hadn't thought of that, instant messaging in a foreign language. Could my fairly poor French handle it? With an email, there was always the French-English dictionary and a reasonable amount of time before one had to respond. But instant messaging? I'd type too slowly. I'd seem rude.

It's really wrong that so few people show common courtesies in cyberspace. In the real world I wouldn't for a moment flatly ignore a man who was speaking to me. Why would I do that in cyberspace? I mean, not answering an instant message is like walking right past a guy who smiles and says hello. In cyberspace it is still a human being who is reaching out, trying to communicate. Yes, I decided. It would be better to reply, and reply stupidly, than just look like I was ignoring him.

I clicked open the instant message button. Oh, not to worry. It was written in English.

"Do you like a big penis?" he asked.

"Depends on what it's attached to," I replied.

∞

OK, so the real answer is *bien sûr* (absolutely), a very clear *bien sûr* (capital letters, even), but tonight I decided to break my own rule. Tonight, after nearly half a bottle of champagne, after doing my best to be culturally sensitive and managing to put a mildly bilingual profile up on this site, I decided not to behave like my compulsively over polite cyber self. Normally, I gently reply to each and every person, even to a slightly rude statement, and when I'm not interested – even when the guy's a bit whacky – I always close politely and say, "I'm sorry, I don't think we're a match. Good luck to you." Then, he generally says good-bye and that's that.

Not this time. I looked at the fellow's question again, muttered *bien sûr* out loud (OK, by now it was the champagne talking) and then hit the *bloqué* button.

Just then another instant message flashed on my computer, this time from a different man.

Him: "*Bonsoir*, Madame. How are you this evening?"

Me: "Fine thank you."

See? *Bonsoir*. Good evening. Now that was polite.

Me: "And you?"

Him: "Fine, thank you."

Then nothing.

Then a bit more silence. And then the instant message button flashed again.

Him: "I have to warn you."

Oh, really? I sipped my champagne and waited.

Finally, Him: "I'm a nudy boy."

Nudy boy? Nudie boy. Oh.

Me: "I'm happy for you."

Him: "And I need to find a girl who likes coming with me to sex clubs to make love with people around is very exciting."

Me: "No, thank you."

Him: "OK do you like boys with very big sex."

Bloqué encore!

I signed off and closed up my computer. It was late anyway. The weird ones always lurk on the Internet late at night it seems. It had been the same back home. Well, not quite the same. Never such immediately direct 'come ons' like this, not right off the bat. But this was Paris, wasn't it?

Soon I was tucked in under the covers and cozied up to my pillow and muttering *bien sûr*. I began to doze off, weaving memories of the more athletic evenings I'd enjoyed. Yes, yes, I know that women are told that size shouldn't matter because it's supposed to all be about the man's skill etcetera, etcetera, but as a friend of mine once said, "If I had a choice between a good lover and a bad lover who was well endowed, I d'ruther the good lover. But if both were good lovers, I d'ruther the other."

I'm a woman fortunate enough to have had my share of lovers. Not only my share of lovers, but my share of French lovers. I hail from Canada and Canada has an entire province full of French people. With the exception of this odd couple of ducks I'd just *bloquéd*, I say *"Vivre la différence!"* and it's not the difference between men and women that I'm talking about, but the difference between French lovers and everyone else. For decades, now, studies keep finding that women would "d'ruther" have a French lover over all other nationalities.

Why?

The difference between a French lover and everyone else is that everyone else undresses a woman from the top, down. A French lover undresses her the other way around.

"Ah," said an American friend in response to this. "The French lover saves the best for last."

"No," I replied rather tersely. "That's precisely the point."

French lovers know that their own pleasure compounds immeasurably if they first make the woman sing . . . and they know the source of the song and how to play the music. Really, really well. My own French lovers would plead breathlessly for me to offer them 'a little prayer' and would hold back until I'd had my moment -- or even two -- before making their own peace with God. When on occasion I was too tired or distracted to offer up a prayer, my lover would move into his moment reluctantly and later tenderly complain that it is never good 'alone' and, rubbing his face against mine, softly request that perhaps I could still join him. It would make us both feel better, he would assure me.

He was often right.

∞

Now, just because I've always openly acknowledged my delight at the touch of a man, the smell of his skin, doesn't mean I go along with the current thinking about the so-called sexual revolution. Call me old-fashioned, but I still believe that men and women are equal. In a just society, both men and women would have the same privileges and obligations but I'm afraid that the outcome of the so-called sexual revolution isn't all that inspiring. When the West proclaims it has liberated sexual mores by insisting that a man has a natural born right to amuse himself with naked women he's purchased (either photographically or in real life), who wins? Nobody, and certainly not women.

I suppose this twisted logic is to be expected given that we're surfacing out of centuries sexual oppression. Yes, it's to be expected – but not accepted – and yet here we are in the 21st century where, incredibly, we keep being asked to believe that it is the height of a just and compassionate society to offer men lots of ways to buy women.

Revolution, indeed. Women have been able to take their clothes off for money for centuries. The new story, the real revolution, is that a woman can now earn a decent living and keep her clothes on.

William Blake, the 18th century poet and mystic, wrote, "Prisons are built with the stones of law; Brothels with bricks of Religion" so it's not so strange that I first started thinking about sex in church, when I was seven. After all, the world's major religions have a weird fixation on a woman's private parts and what she can and cannot do with them. Right smack dab into the 1970s, good Christian women (and menstruating girls) were told to keep their heads covered inside a church, thanks to Eve and all that. A boy was never expected to wear something to announce the fact that he had just sprouted his first pubic hair, but when a girl hit her first menstrual cycle, bam. She had to cover her head. There are still plenty of churches today – and, of course, entire Muslim countries – that expect a girl to cover her head once she enters puberty.

During my early years as a child in Toronto, I liked going to church – mostly because we got to dress up and I could wear my shiny patent leather shoes. At seven, I was too young to cover my head in church. I was also too young to be wearing the little white gloves that my grandmother had given me but my mother let me take the gloves out of my dress-up box on Sunday mornings and put them on for church. I would sit in the pew to one side of my mother, my little brother to the other side, and I'd fluff up my skirt and tug at my gloves the way I'd seen the other ladies do it and pretend I was grown up. It's true that I did like to try to figure out what the Anglican priest was saying but mostly I liked to admire all the beautiful hats and the lacey scarves on the women and the older girls.

One Sunday morning I finally got up the courage to ask my mother if maybe I, too, could wear a pretty lace scarf on my head the way the older girls did. "I have one in my dress-up box," I offered hopefully, showing it to her.

"Why do you want to cover your head in shame?" she snapped, taking the lace scarf from my hand and shoving it back in the dress-up box.

I don't know, I thought. What is shame?

But I didn't ask. We were late for church and my mother was in a mood.

CHAPTER TWO

The Perfect Kiss

As I got older, I began to understand why my mother was in such a huff about church and all that shame stuff. She was born in Estonia – that explained a lot. Given that there are hardly any Estonians in the world, not many people would understand what this means so I'll explain.

Estonia is a small Scandinavian country that hugs the Baltic Sea south of Finland. It and its tribal people (whom others had decided to call Estonians although they had called themselves *maarahvas* – People of the Land) were 'discovered' by some German merchants back in the 12th century. When reporting back to Catholic Headquarters, the German merchants said with some surprise they'd stumbled upon nature worshipping pagans who were refusing baptism and having sex without being married. Horror of horrors, thought the Pope. So he unleashed the last major Holy Crusade that targeted Europeans. The German Livonian Brothers of the Sword invaded this little country to subdue those European heathens. The Brothers won the battles but not the souls. Estonians begrudgingly showed up in church but also continued on with their own ways of worshipping nature and celebrating their own gods. More German soldiers were sent in to try to keep the natives under control but something kept happening that worried the priests so much that

Catholic Headquarters decreed that it was forbidden, absolutely forbidden, for a German to marry an Estonian, ever.

What was the problem? Well, the young German soldiers found that being pagan was a lot more fun and they kept abandoning their Catholic ways for the love and laughter of robust Estonian women, marrying them and dancing for joy at solstice celebrations and for their good fortune.

To this day, when you meet an Estonian – even those of us born outside of the country -- one of the first things they'll tell you is that they're the last pagans in Europe.

See? I just did it, myself.

My own Estonian step-grandfather called himself a sun-worshipper, not a pagan. He said he celebrated the dance between light and dark, good and evil. Born on a small island in the Baltic Sea, his religion focused on the movement of the sun, like so many other indigenous religions. Even today, the Estonian government's website highlights the fact that there are only really two major holidays in that country -- Winter Solstice and Summer Solstice (Christmas and *Jaanipäev*, respectively). Both are important, but of the two, Summer Solstice is considered the more sacred and important holiday. That's because it's the holy day that celebrates The Perfect Kiss.

With thousands of years of sunworshippers as ancestors, all rejoicing over The Perfect Kiss each and every June, it's not surprising that the concept of Sexual Shame was humiliating and unacceptable to my mother. I don't think that my mother, a new immigrant to Canada when she'd met my father, had fully appreciated what she'd walked into when she agreed to convert to his religion in order to marry him.

I remember my own Estonian grandmother would laugh out loud at Eve and Sin, disgusted that we women should be ashamed because we were women.

Life? Ashamed of Life? she'd ask.

Like Eve leaving The Garden, my grandmother had been forced from Estonia. It was toward the end of World War II. The Soviets had invaded for the second time in four years. During first Soviet occupation, my grandmother stood in the window of the farmhouse and witnessed Russians machinegun her brother to death as he was trying to run back home through the family's cabbage field. After it was done, my grandmother had to gather up the pieces of her brother and put them in a wheelbarrow. Then she and her mother washed his body parts clean and put the pieces back together as best they could and buried him.

With the second Soviet invasion poised to swallow up their tough but tiny country, my grandmother said good-bye to her family and to her *Emajõgi* (Mother River), to her friends and to her husband. He had agreed – against my grandmother's wishes – to go to the Russian Front and try to hold the Soviets back for as long as possible, to give other Estonians more time to escape. The way many Estonians say good-bye to someone they care about is to say *"ole tubli"* (live bravely) and this is what my grandmother had to do for her entire life. She fled with her little girl, my mother, and the two became refugees from the madness of Stalin, a madness that locked her homeland and those she loved behind the Iron Curtain for the rest of her life. She never saw her own mother, any of her friends, or her husband ever again.

After the war, she enjoyed her lovers, my grandmother did. And why not? She was young and beautiful and human and at the time she didn't know where her husband was or even if he was still alive. The war had long separated them. He was either dead or in the Soviet Gulag, she didn't know, but she knew she was alive and that their daughter was safe with her. They were refugees, yes, but they were alive. While waiting for a reunion that never came, she found refuge in foreign countries, first in Sweden, then Canada. In Sweden, she lived in a ghetto (yes, Sweden had ghettoes back then) and saved money so that she could take her daughter as far away from Russia as possible. When they got to Canada, the two had to learn yet another new language.

Life was hard, so hard, and sometimes my grandmother danced and drank and made love and made no apologies for it.

When she was finally granted the status of War Widow, my grandmother was living in Canada and had by then fallen in love with her second husband, Lembitu – the sun-worshipper. My grandmother had occasionally attended a Lutheran church back in Estonia, but I'd say that when it came to the attitudes about kissing and making love, she was really just Christian on the outside, for show. The Estonian women in my family leaned more toward Lembitu's way of life and, like any good Estonian during the past several thousand years, they robustly celebrated *Jaanipäev* – Summer Solstice.

∞

At *Jaanipäev*, Estonians shut everything right down, go off to the countryside, build big bonfires and celebrate The Perfect Kiss – the kiss of Dawn and Dusk. The story, as I was told it, starts with Twilight (female in Estonian folklore) taking The Big God's cattle down to the river in the evening so they could have a drink before she put them in the barn for the night. She leans over and admires her reflection in the river. Moon (male in Estonian Folklore) sees her reflection shining up at him and falls down from the sky to embrace her. She embraces him right back and in no time, the two get busy making love all night until Moon finally falls asleep on his lover's heart. When Twilight wakes up in the morning and finds Moon still fast asleep, she realizes that she plum forgot to put the cattle back in the barn the night before. Some are injured, others dead. Wolves had attacked in the dark. She rushes off to tell The Big God, the one who owned the cattle, to immediately let him know that she had neglected her duties because she and Moon were busy making love all night.

Does The Big God get angry with her, call her a whore? No. He thanks her for her honesty and tells her that she may marry Moon on the condition that she makes sure he awakens every night to do his duty and shine light on the earth.

So, the moral of Part One of the Summer Solstice story: Premarital sex is OK, just don't forget your farm duties.

As for Part Two, the Big God then turns to Dawn and Dusk, two passionate lovers, and asks them to keep a watch over light and dark, to make sure they keep a balance in the sky. Once a year on Summer Solstice, these two meet for a kiss, The Perfect Kiss. Year after year, the lovers meet like this until one day, The Big God offers to let them marry. Immediately, without consulting each other, they answer in unison, "No, thank you. We like it this way."

In other words, they like making love without being married – again, another story about premarital sex. Well, actually, another story about sexual love, about union, about two adults privately taking pleasure in each other on their own terms, without shame.

On the night of Summer Solstice, each and every year, Estonians all over the world still build huge bonfires, eat and drink too much, and send young people off into the woods on a wild goose chase, of a sort. These young people are sent in search of the sacred flower that blooms from a fern only one night a year, on this very night, it is said.

Ferns don't flower, of course. Every good pagan and *maarahvas* knows that.

"We Estonian Lutherans know we're all going to hell," said one man holding fast to his drink while sort of dancing around a Solstice fire in Canada. "But as long as there's plenty of vodka, we don't care."

Back in church in the late sixties, my Christian-on-the-Outside, Pagan-on-the-Inside family often sat in a pew fairly near the front of the church, my little brother to one side of my mother and me to the other. It was probably because I had been raised in the same house as my sun-worshipping step-grandfather and my lusty grandmother that I began to suspect something wasn't quite right in what the priest was telling us. On this particular day, the day my mother refused to let me cover my head in shame, I realized there were other things I didn't quite understand, either.

"Mom," I whispered rather loudly because I was beginning to feel a bit irritated, suspicious. "Mom, what's a whore, and what's a virgin?"

My mother's eyes widened and she pressed a white-gloved finger to her lips.

"Mom," I said even more loudly. "What's a whore and what's a virgin?"

"Not now, Maret!"

"Well," I snorted, crossing my arms and kicking out both legs, hitting the heels of my pretty patent leather shoes hard against the pew in front of me. "I don't care what the answer is, I'm not growing up to be either one!"

People around us laughed. I didn't know why. I just knew that something in church was wrong. In church, as I heard it, boys could grow up to be merchants and fishermen and rabbis and shepherds and soldiers and kings and carpenters and even God.

Girls could be whores or virgins.

That's not fair, I thought. Only two choices.

And these choices, when I was a girl of seven, were rather mysterious to me. But no matter. Right then and there I decided that I would grow up to be . . . to be . . . well, to be a Woman and as a Woman to be whatever I wanted to be and do whatever I wanted to do.

What a wise decision this turned out to be.

∞

This decision to grow up to be a Woman and claim my own place in the world, shamelessly, is what helped me hold tight to my baby back in the late 1970s when women were basically required to have a signed marriage license for permission to have sex.[i] People like to imagine that, at the simple flick of the so-called Sexual Revolution switch, thousands of years of sexual oppression had suddenly evaporated. Pardon? I knew women well into the 1980s who were pressured by their families to live out their 'illegitimate' pregnancies in hiding – in places often tended to by well-meaning nuns – and then give their babies up for adoption without ever holding them, without even seeing their tiny faces, not even once. Single women, especially girls just out of high school like I had been when I became pregnant, were still expected to hide the evidence of having had sex and just give their babies away.

During this time, when religious authorities were starting to muddle through the question of whether girls who hit puberty should still be expected to cover their heads in church, I got married, got divorced, and had a baby. In that order. It was California in the 1970s. My parents had moved our family to the U.S. from Canada when I was 10 and California in the 1970s was an "everything goes" sort of place but not quite. Teenagers with children weren't really a welcome sight and it was clear to everyone, especially me, that I had made a mess of my life.

The problem was, there was now another life that I needed to look after. I didn't know how to do this. I was terrified. Terrified of keeping my baby and terrified of losing her.

∞

Romance, when you're young, is fun to play around with and when I was 18 years old, I met a man who said he loved me and wanted to marry me. Yes, most people spend a lot more time thinking these things through but I didn't. He asked me to marry him and I said yes.

Plenty of people still ask me why I got married so young and, to tell you the truth, I can't answer that. I've always said, "Patience isn't my middle name," and I think I just impatiently wanted to get on with life. I had graduated from high school a year early, attended U.C.L.A. and then dropped out after one year, and was working as a secretary when I met my first husband. I suppose getting married made it seem I was making up for making a mess of my education.

But in short order, my first husband – a man in his midtwenties when we'd gotten married and very, very wealthy thanks to his father's money – wanted to blot us out of his memory, out of the story of his life. He was Jewish and I wasn't and, lest he be disinherited, he suddenly didn't want to admit to his parents that he'd eloped with a *schiksa*, a non-Jewish woman.

I need to make a special note to be clear about this. Seven years after that first disastrous marriage, I married again and had another child, again a daughter. By coincidence, my second husband, too, was Jewish. He and his very Jewish family from Brooklyn warm-heartedly embraced this *schiksa* and my first daughter, then the next daughter into their world. With me not being Jewish, this meant that neither child was Jewish, either. No one in my second husband's family cared. They loved us all.

The disgraceful behavior on my first husband's part was because he, a grown man, still felt he needed his father's permission to marry, given the family fortune and all that. We had eloped to Reno without his parents' knowledge. That was his idea, not mine. He thought it would be fun, and it was, but within six months, when I was five months pregnant, he decided this whole marriage thing wasn't fun anymore.

Well into my pregnancy, he offered me money to have an abortion. He offered me even more money to say I didn't know who the father was and a heck of a lot more money to give her up for adoption. A lot. But I said no. I wanted the baby. I knew who the father was. And I wanted the baby.

During the divorce, my first husband hid behind trust funds and, while driving a fancy new car (he alternated yearly between a new Porsche and a new Mercedes), promised that any child support I received would evaporate into legal fees. (He kept that promise, but that's another story entirely.)

Yes, it was true that I had absolutely no idea how my baby and I would make it in this world, me without an education and with legal bills piling up. No idea at all.

I do believe in choice. I could have had an abortion. I would have gotten a lot of cold, hard cash to do it, too. Given that I was an uneducated teenager, from the outside it looked like the logical choice. But it wasn't the choice for me. I wanted the baby and whenever anyone would ask me why on earth I would go through with all that, the fact was this: I wanted the baby. I didn't have to give an explanation, for God's sakes. She was my child. I've always been Pro-Choice and it was my Choice to keep her.

Yet, throughout the pregnancy and long after she was born, I felt guilty.

How could I sentence this poor little girl, such a precious little rosebud, to the life we were about to lead, a life of hopeless poverty? We couldn't live with my parents forever and what man would want me now, covered in stretch marks with a baby at my side? How would the two of us survive?

Survive? Well, I was sure we'd survive. My parents wouldn't ever let us starve. But I loved my beautiful baby and I wanted more for her than a life in cramped apartments in the wrong part of town with a mother grown weary fretting about the rent. Little girls deserve to grow up in a nice home, go to good schools and have pretty dresses and a toy-filled bedroom and a calm and happy mother, don't they?

At my parents' house, little Kaia and I shared a very tiny bedroom, me sleeping on a pullout couch, she in her crib next to me. I'd lie in bed and sing her to sleep, then cry. Each and every night, she'd wake up at 2:00 a.m. when the house was dark and still and we could have an hour alone together. I would walk her to the living room and sit on the only piece of furniture I owned – a wicker rocking chair – and rock her and wonder how we were going to make it. Sometimes I'd sing to her but most of the time, I'd worry and do my best not to cry. What should I do? I'd ask as we rocked together back and forth. Should I call her father and tell him I changed my mind, I'd give her up for adoption, after all? Wouldn't that be the loving thing to do, to give your child to someone who could give her a future, give her the kind of life that every child deserves, a life with a home and piano lessons and two parents to love her? Isn't love supposed to be true love when it's only the other person you think of, not yourself?

I held my little girl, who was cuddled up in blankets and only six months old, and rocked her back and forth and tried to find a way out of the nightmare. Worried that I might drop her, the sobbing had become so uncontrollable, I put my baby down on the floor gently, between my feet, with her little rosebud face looking up at me. What was I supposed to do? What should I do? I held my breath for a moment and tried to find an inner voice, a direction. Silence. There were no answers there in the dark. I was all alone. I put my face in my hands and dropped my head. I felt ashamed, selfish. I should give her up for adoption; give her a better home, a better mother.

When I opened my eyes I saw something a mother should never see, not in her own baby. Kaia was feeling sorry for me, worried. A tear rolled silently down her cheek and it seemed that if she could have moved her little arms out from the blanket she would have tried to reach to me, to comfort me, to ask me to stop crying.

"Oh, my poor baby," I said as I picked her up and tried to become bigger than who I was, more complete, more capable. "Oh, my poor baby," I said again, kissing away the tears on those chubby little cheeks. Holding her tight against my heart, I said, "I can't give you up. I'm sorry, I just can't."

It was at this point I made my promise to her – out loud, slowly, clearly, as if there were witnesses there in the dark with us and as if my little baby could understand. I held her in front of me, looked in her eyes and said, "I promise you this: I will give you a good life. You will have a nice home, piano lessons, good clothes, even a horse. I don't know how. But you will. I promise."

∞

To distract myself from the nightmare that was my life at that time, I read a lot. One of the books I read and re-read was Hemingway's *A Moveable Feast*, an ode to Paris in the 1920s and to the love and regrets he still held for his first wife. His way of capturing the spirit of Paris – its smells, its tastes, its mystery, its gifts to your soul – developed a lovely ache inside a dream that kept playing over and over in my head, a sweet impossible dream that pulled me through the terrifying darkness that was my life back then.

That famous line of his, "If you are lucky enough to have lived in Paris as a young man, then wherever you go for the rest of your life, it stays with you, for Paris is a moveable feast" buried itself inside me. I wanted to taste Paris. Hemingway's words stayed with me throughout those years of stretched-to-the-absolute-limit credit card bills and day care costs and struggling to pay the rent on time. One day, I kept saying to myself although I really didn't believe it, one day when my baby is all grown up and I have some money, I'll move to Paris and get back to my writing. That 'one day' was clearly a long way off and so it was safe to dream, wasn't it?

When we finally moved out of my parents' home, I took my daughter thousands of miles away back to Canada, where I'd been born. Why? Health care. It's healthier to be poor in Canada than poor in California because, like virtually all European countries, Canada has universal health care. I was a secretary at the time, hardly able to pay for rent along with day care costs. One doctor's bill was one doctor bill more than I could afford.

In a cramped one-bedroom apartment in Toronto, I slept on a mat on the living room floor because I couldn't afford a bed for myself (my daughter had one, of course, and the whole bedroom for herself and her toys). I constantly worried where I'd find the money for yet another pair of pants or another pair of shoes for my child, she was growing so fast. My own family didn't have any money to spare and, to be honest, I was too proud to ask for help.

One day, when my baby was nearly four years old and we were walking hand-in-hand through a nasty blizzard on our way to the subway, Kaia kept whining, "I want to take the car! We should take our car!"

"We don't have a car," I said calmly and kept dragging her forward, "so we're taking the subway."

"Wait!" she said and yanked at my arm, stopping us there in the midst of the snowstorm. Looking up, straight into my eyes, she asked accusingly, "Are we *poor*?"

"No," I said, "We're rich with love. We just don't happen to have any money right now."

"Oh," she said as if that made total sense (which it did, in a way) and turned to keep walking through the storm.

In a few years, it would be a lot harder to fool her. I never wanted my child to know we were poor, so each month, I put $5 or $10 away until I could afford one – just one! – computer course.

That decision of mine as a child, to be whatever I wanted to be and do whatever I wanted to do, helped me actually believe that I could work with computers, and somehow I did. From that one course and a lot of self-education, my skills blossomed into a business that allowed me to earn the kind of living that actually supported a child.

Later, I had a second daughter and, yes, I kept that promise of mine. Both of my girls grew up living in a small town just outside of Toronto, a university town called Guelph, because it was closer to their horses. Their horses! They also had piano lessons and pretty dresses and trips abroad and ate at some of the finest restaurants. My business even funded that impossible dream of mine.

But the dream?

It started out all wrong.

CHAPTER THREE

Twin Serpents

At a certain point in my life I had enough money to either live in Paris for seven months or pay off the mortgage.

I chose Paris.

At first.

I went online and found an apartment there (this was before AirBnB so you had to trust a foreign company's website), signed a contract and paid the rent, all seven months of it. It was a lot of money. A lot. The moment I paid the rent, I stopped sleeping. Each night, I'd wake up in a wild panic. Day after day, friends and family were congratulating me for actually doing it, for actually taking the steps to make that dream of mine actually happen. Most people, they were quick to point out, prefer to watch their dreams from a safe distance, always pushing them further and further into their own future until, at last, the dreams disappear. Friends and family said they envied me, they admired me, they were happy for me.

Me? I was becoming sleep deprived.

What had I done? Why would I just toss all that money – and interrupt my career – to go and chase a dream? I'd be all alone in Paris.

I would wake up four or five times in the night, worried about leaving. What would happen to my business? My clients? To add to my self-induced stress, I'd imagine that future bank account balance dwindling down, seeing all my money fading away for no good reason. What was I doing? Why? I started talking to myself in the middle of the night. Why can't you be normal like everyone else and have a normal mid-life crisis? You know, buy an expensive car or take ballet lessons or find a really young lover?

Gosh, Maret, I scolded myself, you don't have enough money to retire. Save for your retirement. Then go live in Paris for a while. That's what sane people do.

Night after night, I woke up with these thoughts spinning around, throwing me off balance.

Finally, I dragged myself out of bed and sat in the living room in the dark. The actual wire transfer of real money to rent a real apartment in a real city far away had suddenly coagulated my dream. It was now a reality, a small, but growing force that would prove to take on its own form and impact my life in ways I could not yet imagine but knew in my gut would happen. Things were beginning to slip out of my control and I was walking toward the end of a cliff, a cliff called Paris and I was about to tumble over. My dream was shimmering right there before me and instead of just being able to watch it like a movie playing in my head, I felt the dream almost physically pulling me forward, pulling with a powerful force that had been building over all those years of imaging that I would one day live in Paris.

But I didn't want to go. Not anymore.

∞

Love and Fear grew together silently alongside the dream, twin serpents, intertwined. The fear began to choke my love and longing for Paris. I was now completely melancholy about the idea of leaving home. I just absolutely didn't want to go at all.

Krishnamurti, one of the great spiritual leaders of the 20th century, said that there are only two emotions: Love and Fear. All other emotions and all of our actions are rooted in either Love or Fear. Life becomes much easier to manage when you understand that decisions based on Love are good and decisions based on Fear are not good. Decisions based on Fear just get us more jangled up, leading us in the direction of a messy, unfulfilled life.

This piece of wisdom had helped guide my actions as a young woman, helped me un-messy my life. Using this wisdom as a single mother with only a high school degree and a baby to raise, I could somehow always find the right place from which to make a decision. Well, not always but usually. This time, with both Love and Fear so strongly tangled up together, I was paralyzed.

That night, sitting alone in the dark, instead of berating myself or trying to give myself a pep talk or making an effort to locate some courage, I just spoke gently to myself. Out loud.

"OK, Maret," I said softly. "You're a grown woman. No one is making you go to Paris. You don't have to go if you don't want to. Yes, you'll lose all that rent money you just wired. It's gone, one way or the other. But you can stay right here, if you'd like. It's your right to change your mind. It's your life."

What would my daughters think? What kind of mother tells her children that life is meant to "Live! Live! Live!" (as Auntie

Mame in the movie of the same name always says) and then, embarrassingly enough, ignores her own sound advice?

"I don't care what you want to be when you grow up," I used to tell my children, "As long as you're happy."

Yes, follow your bliss, girls, but I'm too much of a coward to follow mine. Parents teach by example and I was fast collapsing in on my own dream, embarrassed to tell my children that I was afraid. Yes, that would be just too embarrassing. I probably should go to Paris, I thought.

Continuing to talk to myself, I said (rightly) that one shouldn't make any major life decision based on whether or not you'd be embarrassed, although it's such an easy thing to do. I've done it. As a teenager, before getting married to my first husband, I felt a wave of dread about it and thought, "I shouldn't marry him." Then I thought, "Oh, but I've already told people I'm getting married. It would be too embarrassing to call it off now."

Here's the stupid thing: We were eloping to Reno, Nevada and had told only a couple of friends. How easy would it have been to call off a fairly secret elopement?

But I didn't want to be embarrassed. As I said, that Reno marriage lasted 6 months, ending when I was left 5 months pregnant.

Now that was embarrassing.

Yes, I thought, I'll have to face my daughters because it would be better just to let all that rent money go and continue to make more money here, pay off the mortgage and get to my retirement faster.

Silence in the dark. I waited for an "aha" sense of relief from within myself, a little snap of clarity.

Nothing.

I now felt worse, trapped in what felt like a terrible riddle where no matter what you answer, it's wrong. It felt wrong to go off and live in Paris and it felt just as wrong to stay home.

So I tried a different approach. Imagine, Maret, I said to myself, that it is one year from now and for some horrible reason, you're on your death bed. Do you feel better or worse for having stayed?

Worse. So much worse.

You're still on your deathbed, Maret, but this time you've lived in Paris for those seven months before you died. Do you feel better or worse for having gone?

It was then that I knew that the mortgage was just going to have to wait. It would keep me company when I got back.

That night I slept very, very well.

The twin serpents remained intertwined. The fear didn't go away, not at all. But a decision had been made and even though I felt a gnawing in my gut as I stood at the airport, my daughters on each side of me, all of us smiling at the camera as my sister snapped the parting photos, I accepted it. I accepted that I would live with the fear and uncertainty and the pounding thrill of it all each day. This, along with the fortune I had already spent to rent the apartment, was just part of the price I would have to pay.

∞

I waved good-bye to the friends and family who had gathered at the airport to cheer me forward. They'd heard me talk about doing this for so long I suppose they were going to be relieved not to have to listen to sentences that started with, "When I'm living in Paris . . .". I turned to my daughters, young women who were now grown up and on their own and who were about to be living an ocean away from me.

"We're proud of you, Mom," said Kaia, my first child, and hugged me. My younger daughter just nodded and smiled, a bit too emotional to say anything.

My children – my beautiful girls – were proud of *me*. I'd learned so much from them just by being their mother and here they were, all grown up and here I was, still finding my way. Kaia and Anneli had somehow grown into such fine women.

"*Ole tubli,*" I whispered to each of them as I gave them a hug.

Back in the old days, reminding each other to live bravely at each parting helped my Estonian ancestors survive a never-ending series of brutal occupations, forced to live as serfs on their own land for nearly a thousand years. In the old days, German Barons bartered "their" Estonians, trading an Estonian child for a prize dog, for example.

Imagine the whispered "*ole tubli*" at that parting.

Me?

I had managed to screw up enough courage to get on a plane and go and eat croissants in Paris for a while. "Geesh," I thought a bit sheepishly as I waved good-bye. "What courage."

Boarding the plane, it was a relief to know that I was at least showing my daughters that I practiced what I'd preached about following your bliss. I knew that I was doing the right thing.

For me. For them.

Of course, I wasn't boarding the plane alone.

The twin serpents, Fear and the Love of a dream, had tagged along to keep me company.

CHAPTER FOUR

Landing With a Thud

At any given moment it's probably a good thing to recognize
that you've spent your whole life getting right here, right exactly where you are. It's generally a good thing because when
you realize that you drove yourself in this direction and you like
where you've gotten to, you can relax a bit, be pleased with
yourself. If you don't like it, you can decide to make a course
correction.

And if you don't like where you are and you don't want to
make a course correction, well, that requires therapy.

But if, like me the morning I moved to Paris, you have absolutely no idea where you are and not a soul who loves you
knows where you are, either, and you feel trapped and more
alone than you have ever felt before and every cell in your body
is shivering with dread and your empty stomach is aching to
throw up you're so frightened, then you know how I felt.

All I knew was that I was, indeed, in Paris. Where in Paris?
I just wasn't sure. The rental agent said he would meet me here
but he was nowhere to be found and, oddly, the streets of Paris
were empty – so empty it seemed that an air raid siren had

warned everyone to go inside and shut the curtains, leaving me here on the street completely isolated and alone.

Perhaps the cab driver dropped me off at the wrong location or, worse, the "rental agent" was a fraud.

I was tired, so tired from the travel and from not sleeping and from being afraid, that I surrendered to my own exhaustion and lied down on top of my luggage right there on the street. Lying on a big blue hockey bag stupidly stuffed with too many clothes, clutching at my purse, I looked up at the winter sky trying not to think about what was happening.

The bitter morning silence pressed in against me.

It was a bit sobering to acknowledge that I had spent my entire life getting exactly right here: cold, hungry, lost, and completely alone in Paris.

∞

My dream of living in Paris never included this growing dread wrapped tightly by slithering fear and self-reproach. It didn't include snow, either. Yes, it was now snowing. Snowing. I'd never seen it snow in Paris but here they came, lots of big, fat, juicy snowflakes spiraling down with a fury from that miserably grey sky.

A blizzard.

I'm not exaggerating. I'm Canadian. I can tell the difference between a snowfall and a blizzard. I tried to breathe normally and it troubled me that I could see my breath, white and fluffy. I was dressed for *chic*, not cold, and I shivered and my teeth clattered and I hugged my thin black coat closer to me.

I was hungry. I was thirsty. I was cold.

Worst of all, I was completely helpless.

∞

There still wasn't a sound, not a soul on the street, not even a pigeon. Maybe the blizzard frightened everybody inside. I listened for the click-click-click of a French woman's high heels stomp by. French women march along the sidewalks in heels in a very unladylike sort of way and you can usually hear the echo of their heels clicking along. But no, not even that today.

Why did you do this? I demanded of myself. Why do you always have to do this? To put yourself out there? To take those stupid risks? See? This time, stretching yourself didn't work, did it? The voice in my head was now shrill. I kept asking myself those 'why' questions but of course I didn't answer. If I actually knew why I did those things, I probably wouldn't be doing them.

The Serpent of Fear slyly began to tighten around my chest like a python and it became difficult for me to breathe.

Well, I thought, at least that scream trapped in my gut won't be able to get out.

Yet another snowflake landed on my nose and melted. I opened my mouth and caught the next one. Ping! Count snowflakes, Maret. Count snowflakes.

So I began to count each snowflake I caught with my tongue.

"Forty-two . . . Ping! Forty-three . . ."

The foundation of my life has been change and uncertainty. I always push myself to the edge without thinking and then just see what happens. It's not always pretty.

"Sixty-seven . . . Ping! Sixty-eight . . ."

The snowflakes relentlessly blossomed out of the sky above Paris, a sky that was a dull, disinterested grey.

I hugged my thin and perfectly useless *chic* coat more tightly to me and looked up at the medieval buildings that towered above, leaning forward into the street and over the narrow sidewalk I was resting on. Their windows looked down on me and it felt like they were almost alive, as though they were watching me. But they'd seen so much in their time, these windows, and they were grey like the sky and just as disinterested.

∞

"Eighty-seven," I said, tongue out. Ping! "Eighty-eight . . . . Eighty-nine . . ."

"*Bonjour, Madame,*" came a cheery voice. "Do you know the code?"

The face of a beautiful African Parisian woman smiled down directly over me. She looked kindly into my face as though it were perfectly normal to see a middle-aged woman lying on a pile of luggage with her mouth open wide, catching snowflakes with her tongue.

I put my tongue back in my mouth.

"*Pardon*?" I asked.

"Do you know the code?"

I sat up and looked around. A cute little yellow postal truck had pulled up beside me and in my complete despair I hadn't noticed. The beautiful African postal agent was standing there, tall and elegant and crisply dressed in a blue postal uniform, her makeup perfect. Even her nails seemed freshly manicured.

She wanted to know the code to the big blue door I was lying in front of.

"*Non, Madame. Desolée,*" I said sadly. In truth, I hadn't actually understood what she'd asked, not at first. At first, when you begin to listen to a foreign language, even when you speak it a bit, you sort of process the words in slow motion and I was in such a glum state that I was certain that whatever she'd just asked me, I couldn't possibly be of help.

"*Merci, au revoir, Madame,*" she smiled and walked briskly toward her truck.

"No! No!" I jumped up from the blue hockey back and ran toward her, frantic. "Don't leave me!" I wailed inside my head but didn't know how to say it in French, so I just kept running toward her.

And that's when I understood that she had asked something about a code, a code for the door. Was that it? The code for the door. In pretty miserable French, I said, "Maybe I do have the code. Maybe I do."

Somewhere.

I remembered that there had been a door code written on the rental agreement. A door code! If it was the right door code, I would know that at the very least, I was at the correct big blue door with the number '8' above it. I ran back toward my backpack and fumbled for the envelope that held the rental agreement.

"*Oui!*" I shouted victoriously. "I have the code!"

I handed the rental agreement to the postal clerk who found the four-digit door code and quickly punched in the numbers on the calculator-like security box at the side of the door and then, *voilà*, just like that, she pushed it open and walked into the pretty courtyard with a stack of mail for this building.

The big blue door quickly slammed shut behind her. Oh, why didn't I follow her in, or at least hold the door ajar? I was so tired, so tired and cold, I wasn't thinking. Just then the door opened and shut again and the very pretty postal lady smiled and thanked me again and wished me a good day and got into her cute little yellow postal truck and suddenly she was gone and I was again alone on this street with my pile of luggage.

But now I had hope and hope, like a good shot of whiskey, warms you right through.

Snow continued to fall but suddenly, knowing that I held the code in my hands, everything seemed all right and just as suddenly, people seemed to come out of nowhere, as if the air raid siren had secretly gone off again, telling everyone they could come out from wherever they'd been hiding. People walked past my heap of mismatched luggage, now topped with a thick layer of snow, wondering who knows what. A sausage-shaped dog with short little legs and a thick layer of snow on its back walked by me looking startled, so surprised that it had to walk along in this white stuff that it forgot to shake the snow off its back.

My brittle fingers worked at the pages of the rental agreement, trying to open to the right page that held the numbers for the code. Just as I began to punch them in, the big blue door flew open.

"Do you know the code?" demanded a short woman with big dangling earrings bobbling just above her shoulders, shoulders hunched forward with her arms were severely crossed in front of her. She was, of course, speaking only in French.

"*Oui, Madame*," I stumbled. "*Sept – Trois – Deux – Neuf.*" Mostly the right numbers but in the wrong order. She didn't budge. "Oh, *pardon*." I looked down at the rental agreement but it slipped from my hands and fell into the heavy snow.

"*Desolée, les numeros sont . . .*" and as I leaned forward to pick up the rental agreement I saw my hands were red from the cold and wet from the now melting snow.

"You're renting from Madame Catellini, aren't you." This was a statement. Her arms were still crossed.

"Yes, but the rental agent, he's not here. I don't know where he is."

"Well you better hope he gets here because Madame Catellini lives in Belgium. Or sometimes in Italy. That's where her daughter lives."

"Do you have a key?" I asked hopefully.

"No." There was no hint of warmth in her voice. "Well," she said after a pause, nodding toward my snowy luggage.

"Bring those things into the courtyard. It's warmer in here." Still no smile. She stepped backward and pushed the door open with her body, arms still crossed – perhaps to keep herself warm, I now realized. Wearing only a thin sweater, she held the door open for me as I lugged the luggage, one by one, into the courtyard.

In a corner of this courtyard, under a balcony and out of reach of the snow, I placed most of my luggage (there was really too much of it) under an awning in the corner.

As I walked back to the woman at the door, I looked up and saw that the window ledges facing into the courtyard still had flowering red geraniums – each flower topped with snow – and the edges of the walls had a greenish tinge from the moss or mold or whatever it was that was growing on the exterior walls of this 17th century building.

"*Merci, Madame*," I said with deep and genuine gratitude. "I'm Maret . . ."

"*Je vous en pris, Madame*," she replied coldly. "I'm Madame Fontaine. The Concierge."

An apartment building's concierge is the cleaning lady, the guardian of the apartment and sometimes its busybody. She didn't look like the busybody type, though, not to me.

"*Enchantée*," I replied and reached out to shake hands.

She smiled and may have mumbled "*enchantée*" but she did it as she walked toward a door set in an alcove next to the big blue door that faced the street. At this spot, in the alcove, was the door to her very little apartment on the ground floor. I could tell she had no plans to invite me in to warm up while I waited for Juan Pablo.

"*Madame*," I said, catching her attention just as she was about to shut her door. She turned and waited. "*Madame*, I'm sorry to bother you. I need to find a telephone. And a coffee. I'm very thirsty."

"Go out this door, turn right, then left. There's a phone there and many cafés," she said. Then she added, "And leave your things where they are. They're safe."

∞

When I stepped outside the big blue door and onto the narrow street where moments ago I'd been trapped with all that luggage, I realized I still really didn't know where I was except that I was, indeed, at the right place. I hadn't gotten my bearings in this part of Paris. It was an area I didn't know at all, part of the medieval Paris that Napoleon III hadn't bothered to tear down to rebuild the *quartier* with wide streets that could hold cannons and lots of soldiers to keep those pesky rebellious Parisians under control (which is why so much of medieval Paris was ripped down and replaced during Napoleon III's time).

Only one street away was *Place des Vosges*, the home of Victor Hugo – writer of *Les Misérables* and *The Hunchback of Notre Dame* – but I didn't actually know at the time that I was so close to *Place des Vosges*. All I knew was that I needed to go out the door, turn right and then left and then, if God had any mercy, I'd find a telephone booth and a warm café.

God had mercy. Even a little more than I'd hoped for. At the corner, before turning left toward the cafés and the telephone booth was a patisserie, its windows fogged up from all that warmth radiating off the fresh baguettes and croissants and other delicious things to eat. I went into the deliciously warm patisserie, got a *pain au chocolat* and ate almost all of it even before getting back out to the sidewalk. The woman behind the counter had noticed my red fingers but simply said, *"Bonjournée, Madame."* I took a moment to swallow and said the same to her, looking back as I walked out the door to admire the pretty, very tiny French pastry shop. Croissants and other buttery breads and Danishes waited patiently on top of the glass counter. Inside the display case were small and large cakes decorated in a way that tells you its *parfum* (its flavor) – a raspberry on top of a raspberry filled cake, dark chocolate sealed all around a chocolate cake, a piece of candied lemon, twisted and placed on top right in the center of a small lemon cake. Behind the counter, tall baskets held bundles of baguettes, standing proudly, all waiting to be welcomed home and eaten for lunch. The shelves around the shop were stocked with marmalades and jams and jars of homemade candies.

As I walked out of the patisserie and turned left as directed by the grumpy concierge, I saw a pay phone a block away. I immediately called Juan Pablo.

No answer.

Deep breath.

Coffee. That's the thing to do right now.

I gulped down two espressos and went back to the pay phone.

Still no answer.

This wasn't how I'd planned to start my life in Paris.

What I had imagined was this: I'd arrive and even before going out for a much-needed strong French coffee, I would pour a deep, hot bath in that big, deliciously deep bathtub I'd seen in the photos on the Internet. I had agreed to this particular apartment only because the tub had looked so perfect and inviting in the photos. As a woman who has lived on 'high alert' most of her life, constantly struggling to earn a living working in technology, working in a man's world starting out when women were absolutely not welcome at all, I've always used a nice, hot bath to come back to myself at the end of a hard day.

To open to my new life in Paris, I'd planned to immerse myself in hot water right up to my nose, then celebrate and sigh away the nearly thirty driven years of working and worrying and wondering if I was being a good mom and doing everything right while still trying to be a Woman and do what I wanted to do, making enough money to buy my family what it needed as well as what it wanted, and as the water drew away the stress of all those decades, I would somehow come back to myself, to the woman who had longed to be in Paris to flow softly through each day, just to be in this city and to read and to write and to take in the spirit that was Paris.

Yes, I wanted to write. The world, in my opinion, needed a book about famous feminists haunting a home in Paris, feminists like Mary Wollstonecraft and Simone de Beauvoir and Olympe de Gouges and even John Stuart Mill. These feminists, and many others, had once made Paris their home, however briefly. The city of Paris had influenced their writing and I wanted to feel the city's influence on my days, my mornings, my nights, and my own writing. I wanted to write about these people, bring them to life, make them feel more human to us in this day and age, bring their visions into the precious landscape of the life we in the West now enjoy, thanks in part to their work. I'd already fully sketched out the book, done the research, and all I needed, I kept telling myself back home was time, just some time, to be in Paris.

I'd planned my first act as *une vrai Parisienne* as bathing because it seemed symbolic. I would celebrate and then wash away the past, a past that had given me too many life lessons as far as I was concerned, and step consciously into the rest of my life. Paris apartments, even many of the chicest places, often only have showers, not baths. It was good fortune that I'd found a place that had both a bath and lots of light. The photos of the apartment had shown there were windows both on the street side and also facing the courtyard and there was a very large bathroom with a very large tub. As an added bonus, I saw that even the bathroom had a window.

Walking through the snow back toward number '8', I stopped in at the patisserie once again and got my second *pain au chocolat*. It was still warm. Maybe the first one had been warm, too, but I was so hungry I hadn't noticed. The center of my being sighed as I bit into the buttery, gooey chocolate pastry. Pigeons trotted along beside me as I walked back to the apartment, nipping gratefully at the flakes of pastry that had slipped and landed on top of the snow.

Finishing off my second *pain au chocolat*, I walked back to that big blue door with the number '8' on it and punched in the security code, the code I'd been holding all along. It felt like a metaphor – don't we each hold the code to our lives in our own hands?

And yet we forget.

The blue door opened. *Voilà!* I said to myself and then looked into the courtyard. Then I felt an imaginary punch to my gut. "Oh my God!" I cried out.

My luggage was gone.

CHAPTER FIVE

Settling In

I banged on the concierge's door. No answer.

I ran into the center of the courtyard and looked around.

There was no luggage. They weren't in the corner where I'd left them and weren't in any other corner, either.

Looking at the empty space where my luggage should be, trying to figure out what to do, where to go and why this was happening to me, I looked again to my left and then to my right. At each side of the courtyard was a narrow, winding staircase leading up into each wing of the building. I didn't know which staircase to take, where the apartment might actually be within this big, old building. I bolted toward the one to my left only because it was about three feet closer and I was in a panic.

Up I raced at full speed, first around one narrow and tightly winding level to the first floor, then around and around again up to the second floor, each heavy thud of my steps echoing throughout the courtyard because none of the windows along the stairway had glass panes.

Then there, right in front of me at the top of the next flight of stairs were three long, elegant blue doors. The one to the left was wide open and I could see my luggage. I was panting, my hand on my heart.

"*Bonjour, Madame Jaks*?" came a warm male voice from inside.

"Thank you for bringing my suitcases," I said, still breathless.

Juan Pablo preferred to speak English, he said, for which I was grateful because speaking in a foreign language is tiring when you're not so very good at it. He spoke English with a tender Spanish accent and had a pleasant, soothing voice, apologizing for not being able to answer his phone since he'd forgotten it at home right after I'd telephoned from the airport. We had to go over a rental agreement, he explained, a new one because it turned out that the company had me sign the wrong agreement. I was now expected to read through four pages of very dense contractual French to understand what my obligations were and what I was agreeing to do. I tried to begin reading and learned that my apartment 'number' was simply: "Building A, 2nd floor, door on the left at top of stairs." No actual apartment number.

"I'm sorry, JP," I said, "But I haven't had any sleep and I can't read this right now."

JP was already late for his next appointment. "Yes, all right. That's fine," he said, still thinking. He handed me two sets of keys. "We will do the inventory and you shall look at the apartment for its condition. *Ça va?*"

Still in my damp coat, we walked around the apartment and made notes of each room's condition and whenever something was less than perfect, JP wrote '*usagée*' (used). JP made very sure that he highlighted everything that he could find that needed repair so that I wouldn't get stuck paying for it at the end of my lease. He even pulled up the very tired Persian rugs to see what the creaky 17th century floors looked like under there and made a note of their condition.

Perhaps it was my imagination, but his big, full lips did turn down just a bit whenever he was forced to speak the landlady's name. JP pointed out that the stove didn't work quite right and, as he tried to get one of the gas elements to light up, he kept wiping grease off his fingers, embarrassed. "Eew, yuck," I thought with a bit of a stomach turn but decided it would just be easier to clean it up later, on my own. What I really wanted was just a good hot bath and a nice long walk to shake off the jet lag and to breathe in the magnificence of Paris, so I kept myself from complaining and continued to pay close attention to the instructions. JP pointed to the cute little fridge that sat under the counter, a fridge almost too tiny for a college dorm room. "It has no freezer," JP apologized, and then went on to describe how to use the tiny little oven that looked more like a microwave.

We finally got around to checking the bathroom. When making arrangements to find an apartment in Paris, I'd told the agency that I had only two requirements: one, a large bathtub and, two, under no circumstances did I want to live in the 3rd *arrondisement*.

The agency immediately offered an apartment in the 3rd *arrondissement*.

The reason I didn't want an apartment in the 3rd *arrondissement* is that it's the gay area of Paris – not that I care that there are gay men there, not at all. It's just, may I point out, I'm hopelessly heterosexual. Now that I was an unmarried woman, it was tough enough not to have sex on a regular basis. It would be even worse when surrounded by The Untouchables –

strikingly handsome, fit men who have no interest whatever in touching a woman.

And let me be clear: I had absolutely no interest in moving to Paris to live as The Invisible among The Untouchables.

Yet with a big, deep bathtub like that? I took the apartment. Living as The Invisible among The Untouchables was the price I'd pay to have that gloriously big bathtub in a bathroom that had its very own window. It looked perfect.

In the picture.

∞

In real life that bathroom was grimy and grey and only the shower worked. The bathtub faucet just dribbled water and there was no way that dribbling would ever actually fill the tub before the water got cold. The sink didn't drain properly and the inside of the toilet bowl was grey with a dark black ring just at the top of the water. Above the toilet and on the wall next to it were two old, wrinkled pieces of paper with warnings in French and English: Put nothing down the toilet except a 'minimal level' of toilet paper – 'no hygienic pads, tampons, makeup removers, condoms, or cotton of any form'. Next to the toilet was a dusty and apparently never used bidet. Quaint, I thought, though I couldn't, at the time, understand why anyone would really use one of these things. The old, tiled floors were filthy and grey and some tiles were missing.

And the window?

It opened to the view of a wall about three feet away, but not directly to a wall. Directly in front of the window, making it impossible to open the thing properly, was a sewage pipe. As if to remind us that it was a sewage pipe, someone two or three stories up flushed at that very moment and the pipe made those gurgling and gushing sounds, so I closed the window.

The shower curtain was shabby and grey at the bottom where mold had gathered over the years, decades, that it had hung there. The towels – neatly folded as you'd expect to see in any hotel -- looked like they'd done their tour of duty back in the Great War and should have long ago been put to rest. Those towels were so thin and ratty they weren't even decent enough to dry a dog with after its bath.

The closet housed more tired linen on shelves that were – I checked with my finger twice – yes, greasy, almost as greasy as the stove, horribly enough. I took a finger to one of the shelves again and showed it to JP. We both grimaced.

"OK, then, we mark this room as '*usagée*'," he said, trying to be cheerful.

"No," I said softly, "We mark this room as unusable."

"Pardon?"

"The bathtub, it doesn't work."

He pointed to the shower. "It works fine."

"I want a bath. Every day."

"Yes, but the faucet for the tub, it doesn't work," he explained innocently, as if I hadn't figured that out when I'd seen that the miserable faucet not only groan and complain as it was handled, but it barely dribble out any water.

"Right. But it's supposed to. You'll arrange to have it fixed before I sign anything, correct?"

"But these are old buildings, with very old plumbing, and we can't fix things like this. This is Paris. It is not like in America."

"Yes, well, the advertisement said it had a bathtub. It's the only reason I took this place."

A volcano of frustration and rage was bubbling just under the surface of my friendly face, a rage fueled by the morning's panic and exhaustion, a hot rage on the verge of erupting and not in a very pretty way.

"So, you'll have the faucet fixed, right?" I said softly, too softly.

"This is how it comes."

I began to snarl, and with each word the volume of my voice increased rather dramatically. "The ad didn't say, 'and here's a photo of the big bathtub that you can just look at as you sit on the filthy toilet in a filthy bathroom in a filthy apartment!" My nostrils were now fully flared. "It said it came with a bathtub, and I expect it to work!"

I stood there in the spacious, disgusting bathroom like a wild dragon in a chic, wet coat.

Silence.

"The faucet should work," I repeated (now in a frighteningly quiet and calm way). "And I won't sign anything until it does." My luggage was here in the apartment, I had the keys, and it was going to be impossible to get this wild dragon out of here without a police escort and handcuffs.

I wanted a bath, and I wanted it two hours ago.

∞

JP scrambled toward the apartment phone and called head office. Then head office got on the phone with me. "Yes," came the casual reply in a thick Australian accent, "But you don't understand. This is Paris. This is how they live here."

"Excuse me," I corrected him, "Don't insult the French. They don't live like pigs. It's not normal to have grime on the shelves in the bathroom…"

"Grime?"

"Sticky, filthy dirt. And they don't have thick black rings inside the toilet bowl and they have bathtubs that you can actually take a bath in. I've traveled through France for years and never have I seen anything like this, not even in a zero star hotel in some god awful hell hole." Then I took an unexpected sigh or maybe it was a gasp, I don't know. I was trying not to collapse into tears. "Please," I pleaded softly. "Please."

"Yes, well, let me speak to JP."

The Australian and the Spaniard talked quickly back and forth in French, JP clearly advocating on my behalf and finally the deal was this: They would send over a plumber at noon and he would see what he could do about the bathtub but they made no promises. Then they'd pay for a cleaning lady for 3 hours – but only 3 hours – and she'd see what she could do about degreasing the bathroom and the kitchen.

JP hurried off to his next appointment while I laid down on the couch in the living room, holding my wet chic coat close to me, shivering, waiting for the plumber. Why keep a wet coat on? Taking it off would have been worse. The French turn their heating systems off when they go out and then back on when they return. There in the apartment, I could still see my breath.

∞

At precisely noon, a cheerful plumber whistled his way up the winding stairs and knocked at my door. He was about 5'

2", in his mid-thirties, and just after saying our "*bonjours*" and shaking hands, he walked straight past me to the bathroom as though he knew the place.

Which he did. Very well.

That was a bad sign but fortunately I didn't understand this at the time.

I sat at the dining room table listening to him whistle and I prayed (quite literally) that he could easily fix the problem.

"All done," he smiled, "and I unplugged your sink, too."

"Thank you."

He pointed to the sign above the toilet and reminded me to be careful with this type of toilet – an electric toilet – and told me not to use the bidet because it had never been hooked up and then wished me a good day. He whistled all the way down the stairs and out to the street, below.

The cleaning lady showed up sleek and elegantly dressed all in black with her own plastic gloves and bucket of cleaning products. She was from Argentina and had moved to Paris with her husband and daughter for a better life.

A better life, cleaning the grunge out of my toilet and tub.

She smiled warmly, rolled up her sleeves, put on her big, yellow cleaning gloves and attacked my bathroom with a vengeance. I returned to the couch still clutching my coat around me and drifted in and out of sleep. I heard Luz the Argentinian cleaning lady pull the closet apart, scrub way at the back of the shelves and pile everything back up neatly. Then I heard her clean the sink, scrub the toilet, the bidet and that big, inviting tub. When she came out of the bathroom, sweating and wiping her brow with the back of her rubber-gloved hand, and asked where the mop was, I asked if she would like some tea.

I always travel with bags of tea and so I dug into the suitcase that I thought might have that box of tea and found it.

As I made the tea, I noticed it was getting dark outside. It was late afternoon, almost dinnertime, and so I turned on the lights in the living room and asked if she might be hungry. "A little," she said shyly. That's when I realized that I had no food in the place, nothing except for the instant maple oatmeal packages I'd brought from Canada, so I dug into the luggage again. I served Luz the tea and put out two bowls of maple oatmeal. I hadn't imagined this, either. No, I hadn't pictured that my first dinner as a *Parisienne* would be sitting with an Argentinian cleaning lady and eating instant oatmeal in the soft light of the early evening. As we chatted and sipped our tea together, I thought, "It feels warm, though. Very warm to speak together about our children and our lives like this, even if we are eating just oatmeal."

Five hours after arriving, Luz was done the bathroom and most of the kitchen. "I have to go, now, I'm sorry," she said.

"It is all I could do with the kitchen."

"But, it's been five hours. . ." I stumbled with my words, trying to figure out how to ask in halting French if she'd be paid for all five, because we both knew that the agency was very clear about only paying for three.

"Yes," she said bashfully, confirming she would only be paid for three hours. "But I couldn't leave you like this," she smiled as she put her coat on. "I'm sorry I couldn't finish the kitchen, but I must go home and cook dinner." It was already 8:00 p.m. Her family was waiting.

I gave her money for the extra two hours. "Thank you, Luz. You've made my first night in Paris perfect."

She smiled shyly and even though I didn't really need a cleaning lady in Paris because I would to be living alone and eating out a lot, I asked if she'd come back each week to clean a bit. She was happy to oblige.

∞

At last, alone in my apartment with a clean bathtub. I took off my winter coat and hung it in the hall closet.

A sigh, then another sigh, one that seemed to be a collective sigh from each cold cell in my body. I filled the tub with hot water, let my tired travel clothes drop to the floor and ahhhh. I lay there and looked around the bathroom. Made a note to buy a toilet paper holder since the bathroom didn't have a toilet paper holder. Odd, I thought. What have people been doing for 50 years? Maybe they used the bidet to hold toilet paper. Who knows. I dried off and made another note to buy new towels.

The very airy bedroom was situated immediately to the right as you walked toward it from the kitchen. As promised in the ad, it faced the courtyard. Directly down under the window were garbage and recycling bins and I thought how happy I'll be when I, too, would be recycling wine bottles in Paris.

My first day was finally over. Finally. Face washed, teeth brushed, at long last warm again, I sat at the edge of the bed, my bed in Paris. I made it. I'd arrived. All was well. I pulled back the sheets and slowly got into bed.

As I rested my head on the pillow, I immediately got a sick feeling in my gut. Oh God, how disgusting.

How truly disgusting.

In the sheets, on the pillow, everywhere around me here on the bed I could smell a man. A man I didn't know. Yes, my gut clenched but my body was so tired it didn't move.

The smell of his sweat oozed up from the pillow. Just beyond the immediate stench of his body odor was the faint smell of what I assumed to be his cologne. This seemed to make him more real for me, the sweaty man. Had anyone ever washed the bed linens? Ever? The only thing that made it vaguely tolerable to lie there and smell this man's body odor was that the guy, whoever he was, had good taste in cologne. But there was no way that I could deal with the sweaty sheet situation right now. There was nothing I could do but fade off to sleep in the company of his smell on my pillow. As I slipped into sleep, I made a note to self: Tomorrow, buy new bedding.

As it was, I slept well despite sleeping with the scent of an invisible man, waking only to the sound of wine bottles crashing into the recycling bins in the courtyard directly below my window.

"Ah," I smiled. "I'm in Paris. I'm really here."

CHAPTER SIX

A Real Aristocrat

At this point I should probably admit that I did have one acquaintance in Paris. To be honest, I'm not sure I could have called him an acquaintance but I can say he was a genuine French Count. We'd met in person for all of five minutes – the amount of time it takes to order and then gulp down an espresso – on my trip to Paris just prior to moving here. Since then, we had stumbled our way through a series of language-challenged emails and telephone conversations.

It's true that during one of his recent emails he had offered to pick me up at the airport and you can be certain that the day I arrived and ended up lying flat on my back catching snowflakes, I deeply regretted not having accepted his offer. Why did I reject his offer? For all the right reasons. I didn't know him except by way of a few emails and telephone calls plus I didn't want to tie the start of my life in Paris to what might be a very bad date. Also, I'd taught my children to never accept a ride from a stranger and he was still a stranger to me.

And a bit strange.

Perhaps I felt he was strange because we had such a huge cultural divide.

I'd met The Count shortly before catching a cab to the airport. After dancing most of the night way with three charming
Swedish bartenders at Johnny Depp's Man Ray Bar near the
Champs-Élysées, I'd woken up that morning very much needing just one more soft and yet strong Parisian coffee – and a
very large pitcher of water. So I nipped over to *Café de L'Esplanade*.

Walking into the café, I vaguely noticed a man sitting with
two poodles – each on its own chair – and saw that he'd noticed
me, but I was in a rush and, besides, he really didn't look like
my type. Short, for one. Older, for another. So I sat in my
usual spot next to the window and waited for the waitress to
notice me which, at *Café de L'Esplanade*, can take forever even
if you're only one of two patrons (well, four if you count the
poodles) in the whole restaurant.

The café is across from *L'Hôpital des Invalides* – a hospital
originally established by the Sun King (Louis XIV) for his war
wounded. The café's interior is lush and white-table-clothed
and brightly serene, and the sun (when it's out) angles its way
directly into the café through the floor-to-ceiling windows that
look out over *Place des Invalides*, a large open green space directly in front of the old hospital grounds. Inside the café, the
chandeliers hang from the ceiling by what look like several
18th century cannons which is perfect because just outside
these large windows – across the street -- are a row of real 18th
century cannons lined up along the military hospital wall, directly in front of the dry moat.

I've always liked this place. According to one food critic,
not only is it overpriced, the waitresses at the *Café de L'Esplanade* consider themselves "just too beautiful to serve a

customer" and generally pretend they don't know English. In a peculiar sort of way, this adds to its charm.

From the *Café de L'Esplanade*, unlike most corner cafés in crowded Paris, the view is wide and open and bright. The view reaches all the way down from the old hospital-turned-French-Army-Museum to the *Place des Invalides* and the leafy park then stretches down to the Seine and meets the magnificent *Pont Alexandre III.* Guarding either end of the *Pont Alexandre III* are gold horses – winged horses – proudly rearing up to claim even the sky. The first time I saw these golden creatures, Paris had been trapped in an all-day fog. A thick mist had enveloped the bridge and you couldn't see the Seine or the road or the bridge, itself. Yet up above us mortals, seeming to leap out of the mist, were these rearing gold-winged horses, strong, proud horses celebrating the triumph that was Napoleon's rampage through Europe.

Just to the right of the café rests the gold dome of Napoleon's Tomb. It seemed fitting that the great general-turned-emperor-turned-captive-turned-hero-to-all-France should have his final rest at this spot where men maimed by his wars received medical treatment and care.

Strange that it had been a king, not Napoleon the self-aggrandizing defender of men's rights, who had thought to care for his soldiers. King Louis XIV, believing that men crippled in war deserved to live out their lives in a measure of dignity, had built the *Hôtel des Invalides* for them. Thanks to King Louis XIV, Napoleon's limbless and broken boys and men were able to live out their lives here, too, when they could no longer march off as soldiers in Napoleon's seemingly endless wars that stretched across Europe and into Russia. Paris owes much of its wealth and beauty and gold-encrusted buildings to Napoleon's widespread and very effective plundering.

This section of the city isn't far from *L'Ecole Militaire* (Military School) and so the area is filled with healthy soldiers, fit and rather handsome in their blue uniforms, short-cropped hair and those cute little French army caps. I liked soldier-watching from this café's large windows. From these windows you can look out and also see tourists studying maps and children trotting off to school and Parisians tromping along or bicycling with baguettes under their arms.

Ironically, it happened to be here near Napoleon's final resting place that I met my first French aristocrat.

∞

As a single, heterosexual woman, I always notice any man sitting alone in a restaurant. Sometimes, if he's handsome, I'll even try to find a table fairly close to the lone gentleman and see if he has a wedding ring. If so, no interest. If not, hmmm . . . On this particular morning, it wasn't the man but those funny little poodles sitting on chairs next to him that had caught my interest. It is said that French women don't get fat and this, from what I've been able to tell, is irritatingly true. But French poodles plump out pretty quickly here. They're spoiled and adored and welcomed in just about all of the cafés and restaurants and stores.

From the corner of my eye, I watched as the two poodles managed to con most of this man's breakfast from him. Then he ordered another basket of croissants and glanced over at me. I smiled, not so much 'at' him but because it seemed those two chubby poodles of his somehow knew that more croissants had

just been ordered. Their wide little backsides wiggled hopefully as they watched the waitress walk away with the empty
basket.

He smiled back and then reached into his pocket and pulled
out a card.

He certainly was well dressed, appeared ever the gentleman,
admittedly a bit short, a wee bit pudgy and not all that handsome, but he sported (and I mean 'sported') a salt and pepper
ponytail, wore a white shirt with those flowing, puffy white
sleeves you see in, yes I'm not joking, in those Three Musketeers movies and he had a twinkle in his eyes and a very nice
smile. He casually walked over to my table by the window
while I was not so elegantly downing my last sip of French coffee. To be honest, I was licking at that bit of sugar that mixes
with the coffee and then gets stuck to the bottom of the cup. He
introduced himself, very softly and very politely, just as I stood
up to get back to the hotel to catch my cab for the airport. He
spoke only in French and said he was Jean Antoine and mumbled his last name.

I said very formally, "Hello, I'm Maret" and went to shake
his hand. Amused, he deftly intercepted my attempt at a hand-
shake and shifted things so that suddenly my palm was face
down and the back of my hand, face up. He held the hand
lightly at the wrist and brought it slowly, determinedly to his
lips, looking over my hand and into my eyes with those bright,
sparkling eyes of his. I suspected he might have been laughing
to himself inside, having a bit of fun with this. In French, he
said softly, "You are a very beautiful woman, *Madame*." Then
he kissed the back of my hand, kept it close to his lips as though
he were about to kiss it again and softly breathed, "*Enchanté*"

(literally, "enchanted"), which is an elegant way of saying, "Nice to meet you."

Well, it was me who was enchanted. Enchanted all over, I'd say. Did that man ever know how to enchant, and he knew that I knew, which always makes it even better. How delicious, I thought later as I looked at his business card. It read, 'Jean Antoine Louis Philippe, *Comte de la Rose*'.

His card said he was a Count.

He was waiting for a client, he'd explained, and had happened to notice what lovely, lovely white skin I had. His eyes shone as he looked down at my one bland white arm and then the other. As he openly admired my ridiculously white skin (I don't like sun bathing which has turned out to be a real blessing because it's kept my skin from aging too quickly), I realized that I'd never actually received a compliment for looking, well, so pasty. He insisted on knowing more about this "charming beauty."

I must stop to make a special note here. In Paris, men fawn all over a woman's "beauty" no matter what she looks like. It's a sort of "nice to meet you" greeting and, in truth, it's considered polite, and the French are nothing if not polite. You'll read this compliment toward me all through this book. Men will say this to women who are perfect strangers on subways, in bookstores and coffee shops, at the market if he catches your eye, anywhere a man meets a woman. So please never think I'm bragging or, actually, all that flattered when I hear this from a perfect stranger in Paris. If you're female and dress somewhat decently, you make an effort with makeup and arrive in Paris, you'll hear this phrase, too. Constantly, even from your waiters and in cheese shops.

I had to leave immediately after that last lick of sugar from the bottom of the cup and so I thanked him for the card, made sure that he saw that I'd put it safely in my purse, apologized for having to go and blurted out in pretty horrible French that I had to catch a plane. Or maybe I said I had to steal a plane. I wasn't sure. The words 'fly' and 'steal' are so similar in French, but I did have to go and tried to say good-bye to the two poodles (the Count had formally introduced us just before I said that I had to go steal my plane), but Bert and Zola's eyes were fixed on the waitress who was now coming back with more croissants.

∞

How is it that life tosses teasers at you just as you have to catch a plane? It's true that I'd not normally be attracted to a short, pudgy, older fellow but I was totally attracted to his elegance, his charm, his mystery.

When a man holds mystery, all things are possible, aren't they?

Alone on the plane with only the mediocre food and equally mediocre movies to amuse me, I played with the possibilities of this funny little poodle owner and me. Even though he was a bit short for my liking, might he be 'the man' for me, this pudgy but charming French aristocrat with the mischievous eyes and the very soft hand-kiss? Maybe we'd fall in love. French men are so confident in their manhood that they make themselves irresistible, so it might be possible, mightn't it? Perhaps he'd introduce me to the Paris that only the French know well and the rest of us hunger for. Maybe I'd suddenly land in the middle of a real Parisian life full of perfect wine and lazy Sunday brunches in the countryside. Just because I might have to lean down a wee bit to kiss him, just because he wasn't technically my 'type' in terms of physique, that wouldn't completely rule him out, would it? No, I'm not a shallow woman. I'm willing to give a short, pudgy Count a chance. *Pourquoi pas*? (Why not?) He could introduce me to so many of Paris' little secrets and those sultry late night summer parties where all the men wear tuxedos (they look so good in tuxedos, don't they?) and everybody drinks champagne and feels the embrace of summer on their skin.

Maybe we would, yes maybe we would fall in love and I'd melt into the fabric of Paris and watch all my dreams (except the part about a tall, dark and handsome man) come true.

On the plane ride home, with nothing else to do, I managed to imagine all sorts of lovely things about him. I could see us together in the south of France, sipping rosé on a balcony looking over the sea and hosting Sunday brunches (he'd have to cook, I don't do that so well) and wandering the streets of Paris, hand-in-hand.

Maybe he was a great lover, I dared to imagine, a great French lover who only has to breathe a few words on my neck in French and I'd open to a whole new level of sensual ecstasy. If he used half as much of his French charm in bed as he used simply kissing the back of my hand and breathing *"Enchanté"* then maybe, just maybe, the Universe had arranged to soften my arrival in Paris.

Or maybe he was married.

∞

When I got back to Toronto, I immediately ran an Internet search on him and, yes, he was a real, live Count. I didn't know much about him other than that, really. Was he married? Living with someone? Did he have children? Was he a 'washed up' Count, someone who had long ago lost the family fortune and just lived a life like the rest of us, or did he travel in marvelous, aristocratic circles that I, personally, have only seen on TV?

It was a blend of both, I learned. He still traveled in exceptionally privileged circles and was always happy to name-drop men he knew at his club but he had made and lost and re-made fortunes over time.

Over several emails and a number of awkward, language-challenged phone calls, I learned that he'd grown up in his family's medieval chateau that of course included a well-respected vineyard. His family's wines were still very good but didn't produce a large enough income so he had to work for a living. He had moved to Paris but found it difficult to keep "the help" back at the chateau – and when he wasn't there his cellars were being depleted of some of his best wines. At the time, he was going through the second of his many divorces and so needed the money. Besides, it was just too far to go for a weekend and he preferred Paris or St. Tropez, so he sold the family castle to a friend of his.

How did it feel to give up the castle that had been in his family for hundreds upon hundreds of years? I didn't ask. For once in my life, I was smart enough not to pry.

Each week, he'd call and we'd struggle through a very brief conversation because we spoke only in French to each other and if it's hard for an English-speaking woman to speak in French while in Paris, it's doubly hard to speak and understand

French on the phone. There are no facial gestures, no hand movements to fill in for the bad (or even missing) vocabulary. Somehow, though, the Count and I did manage to communicate and when it got too confusing on the phone, he'd follow up by emailing immediately.

It was difficult to get a sense of who he really was and what he really wanted in life, what he wanted of me. Yes, he was *un vrai Parisien* but as for the man himself, he was hard to get to know and I think that maybe some of it also had to do with how formally he spoke French. (Counts do this, evidently.) I was told that aristocrats, including Counts, speak in formal French even to their spouses, even when making love! I privately wondered what that was like, if it would make the whole event more sexually charged or just weird.

I learned that he often sailed off the coast of St. Tropez in his yacht with Bert and Zola, those fat little dogs. Though owned by an aristocrat, these were not top of the line, well-bred poodles, just poodles that had had "a hard start to life" he explained. They'd been rescued from a bad home and he felt these two deserved to be plump and primped and pampered. Like just about all dogs in Paris, they were completely in charge. In France, you sense that it is the dogs that walk their humans.

"They keep me on a short leash," he chuckled on the phone. "They are always with me. They sleep with me, too."

He made it clear that he wasn't now married, and I believed him. When a man freely offers his home, work and cell numbers, there isn't a wife or jealous girlfriend around.
Not usually.

∞

Only once when a man gave me all three of his telephone numbers and invited me to lunch did I discover that there was a wife hovering in the background. The man was a Scandinavian diplomat stationed in Toronto. We'd met on the subway. He was lost and I helped him get on the right train, the same one I was taking, and we began to talk. Every European asks a North American their heritage, their family's country of origin. Europeans – unlike the stories we tell ourselves in North America – know very well that our countries and culture of origin influence us, shape us, help make us who we are in both good and sometimes not so good ways.

"Estonian!" he exclaimed when I answered his question. "We Scandinavians love Estonians. They sang the Berlin Wall down, you know. In a matter of speaking, that is."

These days, people don't really remember much about the terrors leading up to the final collapse of the Soviet "Union" or, as the Baltic people call it, the Soviet Occupation. My family had lived those terrors, not just read about them in the papers. Beyond the seething cruelty of the KGB and the madness of Stalin, there was the day-to-day ugliness of living in fear, even in your own home. For example, an Estonian who was found to own an Estonian flag would be sent to Siberia. In defiance, when the Soviets invaded for the 2nd time in World War II, Estonian families secretly held on to their flags, hiding them inside of walls or tucked up high and out of sight in a barn. From one generation to the next, in any given home, only one child – the most trustworthy – would be told of its whereabouts. If an Estonian were to be caught with an Estonian flag, the entire family would be sent to Siberia.

It was also illegal to sing the country's national anthem.

It was Estonians – and their Baltic 'sisters', Latvia and Lithuania – who triggered the fall of the Soviet Empire in the 1980s, three short years after my grandfather who had fought for freedom and had been sent to Siberia, died.

First hundreds, then thousands, then three hundred thousand Estonians sang their national anthem together. When the Soviet police and the KGB threatened jail for the crime of singing and waiving their flags, Estonians laughed. "You don't have enough jail cells, but go ahead." They knew there might be consequences but reclaiming what was rightfully theirs – freedom from decades of Soviet occupation – was more important.

On August 23, 1989, The Baltic Way was formed: Latvians and Lithuanians joined with Estonians to form a human chain of two million people, holding hands across 430 miles, linking their three capitals in a bright and brave moment. It was the biggest human chain in history. Together, they faced Russian tanks and armed soldiers and sang their national anthems and waved their flags – tens of thousands of them, flags that had been hidden by the Baltic people since 1944.

Ole tubli. Live Bravely.

Three months after the Baltic people sang for their freedom, Germans got up the courage to begin to take down the Berlin Wall. This is the moment that history has chosen to remember – the moment the descendants of the Nazis took down a barrier put up by Russian Soviets thanks to their grandfathers' war.

∞

I was happy that this Scandinavian diplomat had given credit where credit was due. Before I could say how proud I was of 'my' Estonian people, he asked for my email and then jumped off at the next subway stop and disappeared into a crowd.

This handsome Scandinavian diplomat emailed me all of his telephone numbers and so I called him and we met for lunch. It turned out that the diplomat was a soccer dad and a married father of three.

Plus, he added, "Long ago my wife told me she was bi-sexual, lucky for me. So my wife and I think it would be very nice if you would join us one evening, any time you'd like."

"Oh, thanks," I said, "But I'm hopelessly heterosexual."

Hopelessly.

He and his wife were very honorable people, he assured me. They were also very discrete. Plus they'd never had an affair on each other and had long ago agreed that they would only have a woman at the same time, together. She wouldn't sneak around behind his back with another woman, and he wouldn't sneak around on her, either.

As we were trying to sort out the bill, the Scandinavian diplomat kept saying that he was perplexed about my "no thanks" response. You're such a "hip" and sexy woman, he kept saying.

"No, really," I said. "You and your wife can do whatever you'd like. It's not my business. But the fact is, I'm only attracted to men."

∞

When my gay friend, Zack, heard about this, he laughed and said, "Oh, Maret. Go on. Try it. Don't be so uptight."

"Hey, Zack," I snapped back. "Why don't you go fuck a woman?"

"Oh, right," he said sheepishly.

If you're attracted to men, you're attracted to men. Of all people, a gay man should know this!

Popular culture seems to be devoted to telling heterosexual women to say yes to just about anything anybody wants of us, whether we want to or not. Sexual Liberation was supposed to be about staying true to yourself, true to your own desires.

Isn't sexual freedom supposed to be the freedom to decide for ourselves what we want? It used to be that girls and women were coerced into claiming that we didn't like sex at all – we just performed our "marital duties" so we could have babies – and now we're publicly coerced through all sorts of weird media gimmicks into basically being someone else's sex toy. If a woman complains about this or even mildly objects, the 'prude' word is whipped out and slapped against her.

'Prude' is an honorable word, in fact. It comes from France a couple of hundred years back, when Paris was building up its prostitution culture by invoking laws that prevented women from safer, more respectable professions. Any woman who used her voice to speak out against prostitution was insulted as a *prudefemme*, the feminine version of *prud'homme*. *Prud'homme* means 'a good man, true' and stems from the word for 'worthy'. Likewise, *prudefemme* used to simply mean being 'a good woman, true'.

Voilà, the word *prudefemme* got twisted into an insult against those of us with good common sense.

Don't be such a 'prude' we women are told if we dare say we don't want to do what somebody else wants us to do for them. Why are we expected to acquiesce to being a sex toy? If it doesn't interest us, it doesn't interest us.

Heterosexual women are the single largest group of people based on sexual orientation and yet we are absolutely not, thank you very much, encouraged to truly express our sexuality – except as bait or as a commodity, something for sale, the Whore. I personally don't want to have sex with a woman. I don't care if other women want to have sex with women and want to add a husband to the mix. If that's what they truly want to do, that's their business. But why expect a heterosexual woman to 'switch over' just to amuse someone else?

At lunch with the Scandinavian man that day, I did coyly point out that since I'm hopelessly heterosexual, I'd be open to the idea of two men but the diplomat wasn't very diplomatic about saying that he would never – under any circumstances – do something like *that*.

CHAPTER SEVEN

Learning the Hard Way

Like the diplomat, The Count had freely offered all his telephone numbers and never mentioned a current wife, although he seemed to have a number of ex-wives. He was vague about children. "I don't see them anymore," was all he'd say.

We emailed back and forth and whenever I took my time replying, he would query whether he had said anything to offend me.

The French are all about *politesse* (courteous formality) and do everything they can to avoid offending, even saying *merci* (thank you) instead of *non* (no) when offered something they don't want. *Merci*, under those circumstances, is "No, thank you" but they're actually saying thank you and you have to understand that it means "no." When they don't want to do something, or disagree, they also don't say "*non*." They say "*desolée*" (sorry). It's a softer letdown that way.

When the Count was sailing in the Riviera, he would always nip into an Internet café whenever he'd pulled his boat into port and send me an email. Occasionally, he'd make arrangements to telephone me on a Sunday morning. I liked the attention, even if I didn't know whether or not he was the man for me. If we spoke too long, one of his poodles would complain in the background. We never got to know each other very well over the phone or through emails. I was struggling in his language and while I suspected that he knew English perfectly well (he had once owned a home in the U.S.), he never broke from French. He enjoyed my accent, he explained. It was very 'charming'.

The problem was, communicating with a highly educated and elegant aristocrat in a complex language meant that there was a considerable amount of room for miscommunication. I used an online translator but discovered that there were some pretty blatant pitfalls in computerized translation services back then. For example, being lazy one morning and not feeling like trying to read French that day, I popped open the online translation service, copied his email into the translation box, pressed "Translate" and read this:

> Good morning my expensive fur-lined sheepskin
> coat...

Whaaaaat? That's getting weird, I thought. Then I decided to read the original text, which read:

> Bon matin, ma chère Canadienne . . .

Good morning, my dear Canadian.

I guess Canadienne is a word that could also mean a fur-lined sheep skin coat in French, and, of course, the word chère (dear) also translates to English as 'expensive'.

When the Count gently started to probe about my sexual preferences, I didn't completely trust how it was being translated, but I also didn't hand the emails over to friends fluent in

French for their interpretation, just in case. I stumbled through these emails on my own, trying not to read too much into them.

A French man does not consider it untoward to ask personal questions about sex. We're all adults, after all. Besides, I learned the hard way that this is a very smart thing to do.

∞

Before getting too familiar with a man, you really should get a few sexually specific facts about him if you can.

When a friend said she wanted to introduce me to someone she'd known since high school, I obviously didn't ask the right questions of him when we met. On the first date, we behaved like polite North Americans and said not a word about sex. Frank was a human rights lawyer who had recently divorced and moved to Toronto.

At the very wrong moment in our getting to know each other more intimately, I learned that he wanted to tie me up, blindfold me, and inflict the "pain that gives you pleasure" because, he explained, it was the only way he could do it. He had four older sisters, he whined (as if that was reason enough for this human rights lawyer's sadism).

You need therapy, I thought to myself, and got dressed.

"I thought you liked it.'"

"Liked what?"

"When I bit you, you know, you just said 'ow' and kept on going."

"I thought you did that by accident," I said, knowing how awkward a first get-together can be, thinking he had nibbled too hard not knowing how sensitive I am and adjusted when I complained. He had done that hard nipping a few times, now that I thought about it. Instead of just being a friendly mistake, it had been an intentional test and I passed, or so he mistakenly thought.

"If you've never tried it, you shouldn't say no." He was now trying to use his courtroom legal skills with me. "The other side of pleasure is pain and you never know, you might like it. I'm very good."

"Frank," I said politely as I put my coat on to leave. "I think that if a man wants to golf, it's probably best to find a woman who enjoys golfing, you know what I mean?

"Yes, of course," he smiled glumly.

Thanks to Frank, I have now learned to speak openly about sexual matters with a potential lover before progressing too far.

Sure, there are some women like to "play", but I don't consider being hurt or hurting others to be very much fun, clothed or unclothed.

And then there are the women who go along with anything a man wants just because, to these women, having freaky weird bad sex is better than not having any sex at all but I personally don't want the 'pain that gives pleasure', ever. I like compounded pleasure, pleasure on pleasure, and I don't need any equipment for this other than the equipment a man naturally carries around with him at all times.

∞

So, when the Count introduced the subject of sexual preferences, I was somewhat appreciative. At least we'd learn a few things about each other before making any decision about getting buck-naked and, besides, there was still an ocean between the two of us. When he wrote to ask if I was bisexual, I sighed (oh how predictable, the French and their *ménage a trois*). This was my chance to learn more about him and his sexual preferences.

No, I replied. I don't make love with women. Only men. And how did he pass the time during the day, and during the night, I inquired. Here's the email I received (and translated online).

> Good morning, my expensive fur-lined sheepskin coat. You asked how I spend my days, and also my nights. Well, as for spending my days, I am enthralled of my job and therefore much of my time is spent at art galleries and miscellaneous shows and such. I make expertise and purchases and sales of art of any styles. I like to go out with friends and to make meetings of every sort and the unexpected. I like to travel also.
>
> The question on sensuality. I like to please the princess with whom I caress and drink of her nectar with my expert mouth.

I'll admit, I slightly swooned, startled and enchanted and curious all at once. I read the French version of the email. Yes, that's what he'd said. Men and their 'princesses'. I suppose that's because boys read fairytales, too.

How funny the French are. More than one French man has referred to his 'expert mouth' in an attempt to convince me of the delights he would make sure I'd enjoy if I would just say yes. Nectar. What a nice word.

I read on.

... and tireless I love accepting her pleasure. Yes, I
think to be sensual is to be attentive to the wishes and
pleasures of my princess. I love making love and all
that shares has two.

I hope that my answers do not shock you and I may
know you and become the one that you search, my
princess. Which concerns your physical appearance,
you are superb.

Jean Antoine, Comte de la Rose

I was sold.

When, how soon, and how often?

Well, not entirely sold. Not really. Entirely curious, though.

The Count's emails were a very pleasant distraction from my daily routine of waking up, going to work, coming back from work, going to sleep.

With my children grown and nobody to come home to at night, the house echoed with loneliness. Since the age of 19, I've had someone at home to look after and now, in my mid-forties, I only had to look after myself. That felt empty, foreign to me. At night, after I'd brushed my teeth and slathered my face with creams, it made me feel a little less lonely to know that when I woke up the next day, there was a good chance I'd have an email from this Parisian man, a man who just might make my life in Paris spectacular. Who knows? With each email, each telephone call, I was hoping to get to know him better but it was difficult. Can you ever really know anyone this way?

In the months leading up to my departure for Paris, I'd been winding down all of my commitments outside of work and had even stopped dating because I just didn't want to get tangled up with someone back home.

Yes, I was just a wee bit suspicious about whether The Count was teasing me or testing me or just being awkwardly open about what I later learned was his favorite pastime. I really didn't know this man and didn't want to move too quickly on any front. When he learned that I would arrive just after Christmas, he not only offered to pick me up at the airport, he also invited me to a New Year's Eve party.

I politely declined both invitations. I wanted the start of my stay in Paris to be on my terms, and my terms alone. Besides, I just didn't want to commit to spending time with a man with whom I may not, in fact, feel comfortable on intimate terms despite his claim to loving 'nectar'.

It turned out to be a very wise decision on my part.

CHAPTER EIGHT

The Ungendered

That first morning living as *une Parisienne*, I managed to control my impulse to call the Count early – he wouldn't be awake, anyway – and took a walk along the small streets of my new neighborhood, drinking in the beauty of the medieval buildings, looking into the pretty windows of all the little shops, seeing the cafés beginning to fill with Parisians and their newspapers and their spoiled rotten dogs. I felt like my whole body, my whole life, was sparkling. It wasn't sunny and it may even have been damp and cold, but I didn't notice the weather. All I could think about was that I soon had a phone call to make, a phone call to a French Count.

The *Café de L'Esplanade* had been good to me, I thought. Not just because of the Count. It was a place where you could be alone and not be lonely, a place that always offered the possibility of meeting someone, someone who had good taste in food and certainly in coffee. It was a place that gave me comfort, a place where a couple of years earlier, I'd gone to lick my wounds.

During that earlier visit, it had been raining – a lot. A cold, rainy day alone in Paris is perfectly miserable, gnaws at your soul. I was bone-cold and wet and cranky and wandering around Paris very much alone and not happy about it. How many movies offer women the fantasy of love in Paris, I'd been thinking, and it's just that. A fantasy. In all the time I'd been back and forth to Paris, I'd not met one lovely man. I'd had a few one-night stands, which amused me at first, but then the whole process grew a bit tiresome. One-night stands are fine once in a while, but I wanted deep conversations, a friendship, laughter. I wanted to share a bottle of good wine and have it mean something, hold memories. I wanted just a taste of some genuine Parisian romance but I began to ruminate in the rain on how pointless it was for me to even imagine I'd ever meet anyone in Paris, ever.

Especially because I was about to have yet another birthday. Paris in the rain. That, too, was made for romance but when you're alone in Paris in the rain, it only intensifies the misery. I wandered here, then wandered there. Half-heartedly looking for *Place de la Contrescarpe*, the pretty little square where Hemingway opened his book on Paris, I took out a map and then it slipped from my hands into a puddle and a car splashed by, pulling my map under its wheels. I gave up and walked back to the hotel.

The rain had managed to seep through my clothes to my skin and when I walked into my hotel room, the 'me' reflected back from the mirror was much worse than the 'me' I had imagined myself to be. My face was white, drawn. My hair? Wet and flat and very, very unflattering in its Scandinavian stringiness. Dull grey semi-circles framed the puffy bags under my eyes. How did that happen? Was that mascara? I went to wipe the grey away.

No, it wasn't mascara. I was just old. Old and tired and nothing – not makeup or cheerful clothes or a smile – could conceal that. It was time to face up to it. I was by now quite well into my forties, about to tip over the edge of mid-40s and you know where that leads.

To fifty.

I washed my face, dried my hair, put fresh makeup on, some jewelry. "Being fifty soon," I said to myself, trying to cheer myself up, "Is good fortune. I mean, growing old is better than the other option: Dead."

But who wants to have to choose between 'old' and 'dead'?

I discovered there's an even worse option than dead: ungendered. Whether we like it or not, women over fifty, especially here in France, regularly hit that third option. We're expected to become 'The Ungendered'. An absolute nothing in sexual terms. Oh, sure, women over fifty dress up and get manicures and have their makeup done but they are sidelined, made invisible in our media and entertainment industries and shoved off into corners of restaurants where The Ungendered either eat together or eat with their poodles. They try to pretend it isn't happening, not to them.

I once did a test on the Internet back in North America. For a week, I listed my age as 44 and I got plenty of online interest. Then I changed my age – nothing else, just my age – to 50 and got virtually no interest except the occasional online 'wink' from men well into their 60s and even 70s.

Changed my age, this time to 49 – just one year under 50 -- and got lots of interest again. What does "Fifty is the new forty" mean, exactly? Does it mean that in previous generations, women were ungendered at 40? Now, with women's 'equality' and excellent hair products that hide the grey, we're ungendered a little later in life?

It's not hard to spot The Ungendered here in Paris. It's just that those of us who are not actually French get so impressed with the beauty of the women over 50 here – how wonderfully well they keep up appearances and stay in style – we miss the look in their eyes. I was once in an ultra-chic restaurant with a group of friends who were traveling with me and there, at this restaurant, was an older woman dining with her poodle. You think I'm kidding? The woman sat at the table next to me with her standard poodle, a white one, sitting at attention on the chair directly across the table from her. It had its own plate and waited patiently until the woman put a piece of food down on the plate. Even then, the poodle didn't snap up the food, not without permission. It waited for the elegant woman to nod and then, *voilà*. The morsel was gone and the poodle was licking its nose. Though beautiful and elegant and poised, I could tell that the woman sitting across from her poodle was terribly lonely. But at least she had the good sense to take herself, and her best friend, out to a really first-rate restaurant.

You also see The Ungendered in cafés and in the shops where these women have their hands all over their husbands' credit cards, buying themselves beautiful things and lots of face creams, trying to make peace with the fact that someone else, someone younger though not necessarily prettier, has her hands all over their husbands.

For a certain type of man, especially in France, beauty isn't half as important as youth.

I was getting old. Who wants to get old? Who wants to watch the skin on your arms bunch up when your fingers pinch at it, showing ridges and arm wrinkles?

Arm wrinkles. Only instead of the wrinkles going inward, like around the sides of the eyes, when you pinch your skin together the arm wrinkles poke outward and scream for something – cream, oil, yogurt, butter, pork fat – anything to soak in and try to plump out a bit. Who'd have thought I'd want to plump up anything? A bit of plumpness in my skin, I thought as I smeared cream all over my arms and legs and feet and face and arms and belly and whatever other part of my body I could reach. Plump up! Gosh darn it! Plump up! Hold onto that estrogen!

On that drizzly grey day in Paris, I confronted my reflection in the mirror. "Maret," I said out loud, "You look like shit and you feel like shit. And . . ." I continued, grief-struck as I wiggled a short skirt up over my brightly colored tights, "It's time to stop wearing short skirts."

But I have such good legs, I inwardly cried out. I like wearing short skirts.

"Nope. Face it. It's time to get rid of all your short skirts." Already mourning the loss of my life in short skirts, I left the hotel for an afternoon walk in the rain, wearing bright tights, good walking shoes (not sneakers, though, thank you very much), a turtleneck to keep warm, a raincoat and . . . a short skirt.

Underneath it all, my skin was slathered with oils and creams.

When my friend Zack turned forty we made a pact with each other: When it was time to stop dressing a certain way, when how we dressed looked too young for our age, when one of us looked 'tragic' as Zack put it, we'd say so.

I now felt tragic. Felt I looked tragic. Each time I looked down and saw how the bright tights looked on my not so bad legs as I walked along, such nice legs even if I was getting older, my short skirt flapping back and forth, I got sadder and more emotionally deflated. When I sat at a table in *Café de L'Esplanade* next to a man who didn't even seem to notice that a woman had arrived, that was it for me. I wanted to crumple up and cry. A man on his own is supposed to notice a woman on her own even just to offer her a smile. Women certainly notice a man on his own, even if he is too young.

I had noticed him. That's why I had picked this table. He continued to read his paper and didn't once look up.

∞

Sitting there, soon to be all of forty-five years old, I felt my life as a woman was over, that I was now expected to just disappear, blend into the wall, stay out of the way, eat in corners where The Ungendered dine.

The 'change of life' for women in their 50s in France isn't only about hormones and the empty nest syndrome. It's also about how they come to view the 'competition'. In the past, when she was younger and less wrinkly, she'd ignore her husband's roving eye. She'd shrug and accept that this was his manly right plus she was young enough to still feel womanly, herself. But when a French woman in her 50s watches as her wrinkled husband notices each and every young female within a 300-foot radius, she often looks desperate or even angry at you, the younger woman.

When they were younger, these same women seemed to enjoy the 'bird watching' that their French men were doing because these women were also birds being watched. When they were young they seemed to forget that, if they're lucky, they'd live to be old birds one day. It's only as they lean dangerously close to falling over the edge of what French men deem to be true womanhood that it hits them, these old birds.

The first time I got a really big glare from an old bird, I was already in my early 40s and had walked into a small restaurant to have dinner, alone. The chain-smoking wrinkled up French guy with his well put-together fifty-something year-old wife craned his neck to look at me, twice. His wife glared at me the whole night. "Odd," I thought, "I've not done anything to deserve that nasty look from you, lady." I was angry with her for that glare but then I saw the panic in her eyes, the simple knowing that she was becoming un-womaned.

Oh, sure. He'll stick around with her, that husband of hers – for the children, for appearances, for the finances – possibly even for the infamous French family Sunday brunches that she pulls together artfully. But there will be a mistress soon, if he hasn't found one already. French men just can't help it, can they? It's expected that he'll get himself a younger lover, even if he, himself, is past his ability to fully satisfy a much younger woman. It's been institutionalized in France and at one time not so long ago, for some government officials, male infidelity was even supported by tax dollars. Maybe it still is, I don't know.

Back in the late 1980s, the President of France kept both a mistress and their daughter in a government-funded apartment (complete with government-funded security) while he and his wife and his other children lived in the Presidential Palace. In North America, we wink and snicker at this and some even like to imagine that it is all O.K. by the wives who suffer, that the French are so 'mature' about their approach to sex and all that.

Ha.

With that deeply Catholic past (and present) and an historic inability to divorce or even to vote (France granted women the vote in the 1945 and likely under pressure from the Americans), what was an aging wife to do but dutifully accept her fate? How many women really want to be put out to pasture?

∞

The fact is, the wives of French officials don't so very dutifully ungender themselves – the government must pay often a price. For politicians in the public eye, it is the wives – not the mistresses – who are expected to attend certain government functions. But wives who have been ungendered don't want to stand around and smile and be polite, give up a night just so that their philandering husbands can keep up appearances. They insist on a bribe.

In the early 1990s, I was told that the French Government had a special fund – yes, paid by the French taxpayer – to pay the wives of men to join them at government events.

A friend of mine in Canada was a young mother and married to a man who was posted to France for one or two years on Canadian government business. They had two young children and she had a well-paid executive position so it was decided that she would stay in Canada and visit him often. At one particularly extravagant and lush official French government event, she arrived in her beautiful gown and was introduced to a number of French officials, a few of whom later asked her husband in a rather uncharacteristically brash way for a French person, "So how much did it cost you to have your wife come?"

My friend's husband was startled at the question. Why would someone ask about her airfare, he wondered.

"About 3,500 francs," he said.

"So cheap? It cost me more than 5,000 francs for my wife to agree to come. Plus a gown," was the reply. Other politicians asked him the same question that night.

Evidently some of these officials' wives who are particularly pissed off at their cheating husbands drive a hard bargain.

The claim that French culture is sophisticated in its wanton flaunting of marriage vows is a bit much. If it was that 'sophisticated', why couldn't all these men just bring their sweetie-pie mistresses to official government events?

Besides, as I've noted before, French women are not O.K. that their men have an almost religious adoration of infidelity, insisting that it's their sacred right as a man to be unfaithful to his wife – especially as she ages. While the older wife might even get herself a lover of her own for a while, French women are just as human as any other group of women and we women generally prefer monogamy. Women don't want our men to stray. It's heart-breaking and it's pretty clear from all of the sexual regulations invented to prevent women from straying that men certainly don't want to find their wives in the arms of some young buck.

As a single, middle-aged woman, I don't lust after young men. I don't pursue them. I do notice them, though, and there in Paris that grey, rainy day at Café de L'Esplanade I kept noticing that the young buck sitting at the table next to me wasn't noticing me at all.

CHAPTER NINE

The Age Thing

I waved to the waitress for my bill. The young man at the table next to me looked up from his paper and smiled at me. "I hope I didn't bother you," he said.

"Pardon?"

"Moving the chair. I needed to stretch my legs."

"No, not at all. That's fine," I smiled as the waitress approached.

He folded the paper and put it on the table. "American?"

"No," I said. "Canadian."

"I'm Canadian, too."

Sure you are, I thought. He had a Middle-Eastern accent with a mix of French and, what, New York? My silence and raised eyebrows seemed to challenge him.

"Yes," he said and pulled out his passport. Evidence. "I studied in Canada, at Queen's. In Kingston."

"Yes, I know where that is," I smiled. I looked at his passport. It was Canadian.

"Then I got my citizenship."

"But you have a New York accent. Sort of."

"Well, then I did law in New York and worked at a law firm there for lots of years. I guess I picked it up."

"And a Middle Eastern accent?"

He laughed. "Can't help it. I'm from Jordan but I left when I was 17. To go to Queen's. In Canada."

"On your own?"

"No, my brother was with me. That's why I went along. He was only 16 and my mother wanted me to make sure he was OK."

Two little boys, really, half a world away from home.

"Family in Canada?"

"No, no family. Other than my brother. He's a doctor now. In Montreal."

"That's nice. We need doctors."

As I got up to go, he said, "Can I buy you another coffee?"

I laughed. It was a laugh of relief, of gratitude. He seemed a bit perplexed by my laugh and smiled shyly, waiting for my answer.

"That would then be my fifth coffee of the day. Thanks, though."

"How about a glass of wine? From a fellow Canadian?"

He was a handsome-ish young man. When he'd stretched his legs earlier, I'd already noticed that he had very nice, long thighs, and it was a comfort to be speaking to someone here in Paris this afternoon and a glass of wine would, I was sure, help to pull me from up from the glum realization that I was now an old woman. Or would it? Would having a drink with a handsome-ish young man just make me feel older? Ah well. Mark Twain once said, "Never refuse to do a kindness unless the act would work great injury to yourself, and never refuse to take a drink – under any circumstances."[ii]

"What part of Canada are you from?" he asked as we sipped our wine, still sitting at separate tables. We were both facing the window, looking out at *Place des Invalides* and occasionally at each other.

"Toronto."

"Oh, well, I don't really know Toronto. I've driven by Toronto a lot, on my way to a small town just west of there."

"Yes?"

"Yes, a small university town. Guelph. Do you know it?"

"Are you kidding me?"

"No," he said. "You know it?"

"I raised my children in Guelph. Lived there for twenty years. We kept our horses at a stable just outside of town. People in Toronto can hardly find Guelph on a map and it's only an hour away from that city. I can't believe I'm sitting here in Paris with someone who knows Guelph." Sitting there with a Jordanian man who holds a Canadian passport, lives in Paris working for a New York law firm and knows the small town of Guelph, Ontario. Population: Just 85,000 when I lived there, though now it's a bit bigger.

"Yeah, it's a nice town. My roommate's family, from university, lived in Guelph. It has a great restaurant/movie theatre place . . ."

"The Bookshelf Café" we both chimed out together.

I laughed. "My daughter's a bartender there. She's probably served you."

"No," said the young man. "I would have remembered her." I looked at him.

"If she's as beautiful as you, I would have remembered her."

∞

So that's how I ended up saying yes to dinner.

It turned out that all his life, Robert only wanted older women. He never dated anyone his own age, he said. Women had to be at least ten years older than he was, preferably even older, to get his attention. It was awkward for him, he said. "Our society just doesn't accept it, but there are lots of us who don't want blather-heads."

"Blather-heads?"

"Young women who go on and on talking about nothing all the time."

When I tried to struggle against the idea of accepting him as my lover – he was so young – it irritated him that I had discounted him just because of his age.

Age.

I understood what he was saying. He was a person. I was a person. As people, we have needs, but . . .

"I'm sorry," I said. "I just . . . can't. No." I regretted that but I had to be responsible. He did look like he would be a lot of fun in bed. He had passion, intelligence, great thighs and, as I looked down at his shoes, big feet.

Robert reduced himself to pleading.

There we were standing under a lamppost in Paris after dinner, its light shining down on us like a spotlight, the damp air around us sparkling a bit because of the way the light hit at the mist. "Please," he said, "My last girlfriend was 19 years older than me and I was much younger then so the age difference would have meant more."

Back in Canada, I have two very handsome single friends who are my age and whenever anyone asks me why neither of them are dating me the answer is simple: I'm too young for them. They only want an older women, fifteen to twenty years older. They had each privately told me about their lifelong predilections because I'd told them that I've enjoyed the company of a younger lover now and again, but never quite as young as Robert.

As 'young' as Robert. He was a lawyer, a professional, a man. Why should I discount a man just because of his age?

I looked at him standing there on the street in front of the restaurant, standing under the lamplight as though we were in some delicious movie together, his eyes sparkling with hope and my ego really needing that sparkle especially on that particularly cold and damp day.

Pourquoi pas?

∞

It was a step back in time for me, a step back to a time when a young man was all fire and steel and confusion. We sat in his living room having wine and chatting, knowing our clothes would soon be on the floor, and I commented on the framed photos around his apartment.

"Yeah, that's all I really have of mine here in Paris. Photos of my family, friends back home."

They were photos, expertly framed, of his doctor-brother, his parents and photos of Jordan.

"Was it hard to leave Jordan?" I asked.

"Not really," he said. "It was hard to leave New York. I really like New York."

And then suddenly our clothes were on the floor and I had Robert, young, rock-hard, vibrant Robert, all over me.

No arm wrinkles on that boy.

Knowing that he was mostly just a boy to me, he worked very hard to prove to me that he was a man. I appreciated this because when we finished our prayers together we were both so tired that the next thing we knew it was morning.

"Why didn't you even notice that I was in the café sitting next to you?" I asked Robert over coffee.

"Are you kidding me? I couldn't stop noticing you. I was trying to be a gentleman but I finally had to move that chair."

"What?"

"To get a better look at your legs. What great legs you have."

"Well, yesterday," I said trying to hold back a few tears at this point. "Yesterday was the day I decided to stop wearing short skirts, so thank you, Robert."

"What? Why?"

"I'm too old. Really I am." Then I laughed lightly, trying to make the weak laugh sound genuine. "So lucky you. Caught me at the very end of my short skirt life."

Robert said nothing to that but when the Mercedes he'd ordered arrived to take me back to my hotel, he leaned forward, brought me close to him and whispered in my ear, "Never, never stop wearing short skirts. Never."

The Lord works in mysterious ways it is said and I felt that meeting Robert – a man who not only preferred older women but liked me in a short skirt and had spent time in the small town where I'd raised my children -- was one of those mysteries, a gift from Life that arrived exactly when I needed to be reminded that I don't have to fall into the trap of what other people think.

So I shall not accept being ungendered and I will wear short skirts if and when I please (well, at least until Zack tells me I'm beginning to look tragic) and when I peer into a mirror and see that I look tired and frazzled and exhausted it's probably because I'm tired and frazzled and exhausted.

I caught my plane later that morning, after having spent the night in the bed of a brilliant and determined young man, tired and exhausted for all the right reasons.

∞

As for Robert, we often 'hooked up' as they say when both of us were in Paris at the same time. He was sometimes out of the country on business but when he was in town at the same time that I was in Paris, we'd have our fun and frolic and, yes, interesting conversations and good wine and laughter. But there was no point in calling him now that I was living in Paris. His law firm had transferred him back to New York several weeks before I'd arrived.

"Bad timing," said Robert one day on the phone a couple of months before my move.

Probably perfect timing, I thought. Robert and I would never be more than just an occasional frolic and frolics become tiresome after a while. For sex to stay fresh and exciting, the man needs to be very skilled and have a certain depth to his being, a depth that comes from time and experience and lots of practice – preferably with the same woman. It's been my experience – and I've confirmed this with other women – that men who had remained in sexually active marriages for a decade or two (and were now single…as I don't date married men) are always better than men who, as the King in The King & I would say, 'flit from flower to flower to flower'. Yes, first and second encounters with a new lover are often breathlessly exciting because everything's new and fresh but a couple who keeps coupling long after the honeymoon really have something going for them and I'm not sure they know how lucky they are!

When I hear a man boast that he's a 'Don Juan' I smirk a bit. Few Don Juans can really make a woman sing past the third date unless they'd already had lots of practice with one and the same woman. A man who has been a thoughtful lover to the same woman for over a decade builds a deep, secret knowing that he may not even be aware of but knows how to put to use. With respect to young Robert, it was probably for the best that he'd be gone once I'd arrived to live in France. The occasional romp with a very fit, firm young man kept things fresh between us. Anything more just wouldn't have worked.

Part Two

CHAPTER TEN

New Year, New Life

And what about my Count? Did he suffer from the Don Juan Syndrome or was there something more to him? It was finally late enough in the morning to call Jean Antoine but in trying to make a telephone call, I ran into technical difficulties. Technical difficulties as in, 'I don't know how to make a phone call in Paris'. In hotels, it's all laid out for you, what buttons you have to press and what you need to do. I couldn't remember how to use a European phone and didn't have a hotel concierge to help me out. It was just me and the phone, a phone like all other European phones that had a strange ring tone, and I couldn't remember which numbers to include when dialing from within Paris versus which ones if you're dialing from outside the city.

After a while, *voilà*. The phone rang and the Count picked up and almost immediately invited me to dinner.

"Tonight?" I asked, a bit startled.

"Yes, if you wish."

"But, but I'm a bit jet-lagged, a bit tired." Dinner in any decent Parisian restaurant starts at 8:00 p.m. at the earliest and, tonight, I'd likely be dead to the world by 9:00 o'clock, which would be 3:00 a.m. "Toronto Time."

"I understand. The first Tuesday in the New Year, then?" he asked. "The best restaurants will only be open then, not before."

"Yes, thank you. That would be very nice."

"Explain again, if you please, why you do not wish to join me for my New Year's party?" he asked.

"Well," I tried to explain, "This is my very first New Year's in Paris and I have a tradition. I use New Year's to build the future."

"Build the future?" I could almost see him smiling, amused, on the other end of the phone.

"Try to plan out what I want to accomplish next year, set my goals. I always go back over the past year and see if I reached my goals."

I struggled trying to say this concept in French and Jean Antoine laughed as if to say, "Yes, yes, it doesn't matter."

∞

On New Year's Eve, alone in my sweet Parisian apartment by the 'fire' that I'd made with a dozen or so fat white candles of different heights and shapes, all clustered together in the now defunct fireplace, I opened my notebook from last New Year's Eve and read the entry: "Next year, live in Paris. Really do it."

The future was wide open, more open than at any other time in my life. Just about anything felt possible, do-able and it seemed all I had to do was imagine what I wanted and then reach for that brass ring as I sailed around this wonderful life. Life is supposed to be a joy ride, isn't it? Maybe that's why

Paris is full of merry-go-rounds. They're everywhere. There's a merry-go-round at the Eiffel Tower, an old one and very pretty, and there's one at the Metro stop, St. Paul, near where I was living. At Christmas, there's always an enormous merry-go-round at *Place de la Concorde* beautifully lit at night and a part of the landscape of Paris during the holidays.

Walking along one afternoon near *Gare du Nord* (a train station) through some back streets, I'd even seen a small merry-go-round just sitting there quietly next to a playground in some nondescript neighborhood. Life feels like a merry-go-round and so often we go around and around and forget to reach for that brass ring because we're holding so hard to the neck of that wooden pony. Somehow, I had managed to let go, not gracefully, I'll admit, but I did finally manage to let go of my normal life and grab Paris.

There alone on New Year's Eve, I sat by the candlelight, my lungs aching with excitement. I had become a *Parisienne*. Yes, I could legally call myself a *Parisienne*, a female living in Paris. But I was a *Parisienne* with nothing much to do.

All that I had on my agenda was dinner with a Count next Tuesday and the rest of the seven months was a huge yawn that would somehow have to be stifled with something to do. I was sure I'd figure it out, but I hadn't really thought that far ahead. Suddenly, my life had gone from working 12-hr days to the silence of sitting in front of a dozen glowing candles on a quiet New Year's Eve in a city where I really didn't know anybody. At the very least I would have to stop being surprised that I'd landed safely inside my dream and start figuring out what next. I sat there in front of the glow of candles with a complete and total lack of to do's ahead of me. No lists to complete, no phone calls to make except to keep in touch with family back home.

No business dinners or after work drinks with clients to rush off to. I had my notes for that book with me and, yes, I planned to write but you can't just sit and write and never speak to someone day in and day out.

Beyond the Count, I'd have to find a way of making friends.

For someone like me, someone who's never had a moment's rest, looking ahead at a full seven months with nothing to do felt like looking down a chasm and not being able to see bottom. It was dizzying. Unlike all of my other sacred New Year's Eve meditations, I sat there unable to push ideas into the future or to build an image of what I wanted. The fact was this: now I had what I wanted but I didn't know what to do with what I wanted. The next 7 months, more than two hundred days, were just empty space.

No matter, I thought as I finished the champagne and blew out the candles. I'll think about that tomorrow.

I went into the bathroom and flossed, brushed my teeth, gargled, used the monster toilet and then put a load of laundry in the washing machine there in that bathroom closet. Even though I would never again put one of those filthy towels against me or ever again sleep in those creepy sheets smelling of a man I didn't know, I wanted them all clean and shoved out of sight to the back of the closet.

With the whirr of the washing machine ready to lull me to sleep, I went to bed on my own fresh, new clean sheets with those puffy new white pillows.

From somewhere in the deepest part of a dream on New Year's Eve, I heard a knock at my door. No, I thought. Not my door. No one knows I'm actually in this specific apartment except Juan Pablo and the cleaning lady. And Pierre the Plumber. I hadn't given the Count my address yet and, even if

I had, I wouldn't have given him the apartment number which as I mentioned was: 'Building A, 2nd floor, door on left'. No, I knew I didn't give him that information.

Knock, knock, knock. More loudly, more insistent this time.

It was 1:15 a.m. I pulled the sheets up over my head as if that would make the knocking stop.

Knock, knock, knock, KNOCK.

I went to the door in my nightgown. "Yes?" I asked nervously, whispering at the door.

A woman said something in French. It came through the door mumbled.

"Excuse me?"

"You speak English? All right, then. You have the washing machine on. It is above our bedroom and I can't sleep."

"Oh, I'm terribly sorry," I said.

As I opened the door to my neighbor she didn't bother to say '*Bonsoir*' like any self-respecting French person but said firmly, "Can you please turn it off?"

"Yes, yes. But . . . I don't know how."

The slender, young French woman standing at the door in her completely unsexy, loose, flannel pajamas, her short hair mussed up, wearing thick black-rimmed glasses and a scowl, marched into my apartment and right past me. "Here. I'll do it."

Like I said, it was 1:15 a.m.

She, like Pierre the Plumber, knew exactly where to go and walked straight into the bathroom, swung open the closet door in there and flicked off the washing machine.

"Your bathroom is directly over our bedroom," she said firmly. "And we hear everything. Everything!" With that last 'everything', she waved an arm in the air. Dramatically. "And the toilet. It wakes us up."

I'll bet it does. It probably wakes up anyone who has a window overlooking the courtyard, come to think of it. That bellowing flush probably echoes out into the 17th century courtyard, swirling around, bouncing off windows and walls, the whole place shaking to the toilet's demand to be heard.

"I'll, I'll try not to flush at night," I offered.

"It's not your fault, I know," she said with not a shred of warmth in her voice. "Someone changed the rooms. This used to be a bedroom. Now it's a bathroom. Where your bedroom is, is where the bathroom was before. I don't know why they did that. Now your bedroom is under Madame Rivolet's bathroom, and our bedroom is under your bathroom. It's 'orrible." Then she stomped out and slammed the door behind her.

And Happy New Year to you, too, I thought.

CHAPTER ELEVEN

Yes, But Who's Counting?

The Count called ahead to say he was five minutes from my apartment and this, I understood, was the cue that I should go downstairs and wait for him by the gate. In Paris, one does not expect one's date to try to find a parking spot and knock on your door, especially in this cramped medieval part of the city where I lived. Finding a parking spot here requires more than just a dollop of good luck. It requires a small prayer and a miracle. As the American writer, Dave Barry, wrote, "Paris has only one vacant parking space, which is currently under heavy police guard in the Louvre museum."[iii]

The Count, I discovered, drove a teeny little Citroën. "Easier to park such a tiny car as this," he explained after we said our shy *bonsoirs*. (Good evening.) In my very high heels, balancing myself with my evening purse and wobbling a bit, I tried to squeeze my way into the car, doing my best not to have to splay my legs as I wiggled through the narrow space of the partly open door (the car was a bit too close to a parked car for the passenger door to open fully). The Count kiss-kissed me on each cheek and then put the car into gear and zipped off before I'd even had a chance to buckle up.

"*Bonsoir*," I said to the two passengers who'd had the courtesy to jump off the front seat and into the back. Bertrand and Zola now had their front paws pressed up against my chair, one breathing on each side of my head as they peered forward, panting, wiggling and waggling and sniffing at me as they struggled to keep their balance whenever the Count suddenly turned a corner.

"Oh," said the Count tenderly, glancing back at his two little darlings. "Don't bother *Madame*. She's much too beautiful tonight."

Remember, French men always, without fail, tell a woman she's beautiful. They also insist on calling her a "young girl", ever a woman. To French men, they're giving you a compliment and no matter how often I said I was a grown woman, they'd balk and correct me. "*Alors, vous êtes une jeune fille.*"

My middle-aged self was dressed in a fairly low-cut but not so revealing black dress with long flowing sleeves that fell open from shoulder to wrist and then elegantly buttoned up at the wrist. This revealed most of my arms and, yes, that white skin he liked so much.

Black on white.

The Count zipped into the courtyard of a group of very old townhouses, waved to the guard at the gate, parked, pulled up the emergency break, looked over at me – his eyes grinning – and repeated, "Much too beautiful."

Holding me by the elbow as he escorted me over the cobblestones and into the restaurant, he leaned slightly into me and said, "Hmmm. You smell very nice this evening, and your skin," he said gently as he softly touched one completely untanned shoulder, "is so beautifully white."

The poodles pranced along beside us, unleashed.

"Thank you," I said and tried to see if I liked his scent as well. A man's scent is what first sends me a shiver when we get up close. Standing in a crowded elevator, men in business suits all around me, oh my. I do my best to keep a poker face but I'm pretty sure that some men catch me taking a whiff of them. I've seen it in their quick glance back at me as we all leave the elevator. Sometimes, they seem pleased. Sometimes, not so much.

As for the Count, I'll admit that he was growing on me. He had style and he was cultured and I knew as we walked under a Paris sky into that Michelin-starred restaurant that I could very easily get used to this for a while. Even if he likely wasn't my 'forever man', this was Paris and grown-ups can have lovers who expect nothing more from each other except good company and a pleasant frolic now and then.

The restaurant was in a regal townhouse in the 1st *arrondissement*, walking distance from the *Place de la Concorde*, the city's major Metro hub and the place where revolutionaries guillotined aristocrats and, by the way, thousands of commoners, too. Prior to the revolutionaries guillotining thousands of people here, the nobility used the same spot to sit around and watch mostly rather poor criminals receive their court-ordered punishment: being dismembered alive.

Although he actually opposed the death penalty, Dr. Guillotin felt that if the state had to murder people then it should be done somewhat humanely and so he proposed the idea for the contraption that bears his name (though someone else invented it). For decades, the guillotine was felt to be a far more 'humane' method of execution. Compared to being dismembered alive in front of a crowd of rich people, I'd agree.

The restaurant doubled as an exhibit space for an auction house. It was packed with centuries-old art crowding all the walls and every room was stuffed with richly carved antiques, glistening silver trays and tea and coffee sets and big, thick candleholders, all available for the right price. I later learned that this restaurant's website advertises by saying that it's "where collectible objects, paintings, sculptures and music flirt with each other . . ." and, indeed, everything here felt sensuous, flirtatious. The lighting was romantic – a blend of candlelight and a glow from several chandeliers hanging sensuously low overhead. These were over-the-top, ornate crystal chandeliers that looked more like they belonged in a castle than in a restaurant, even a very nice one.

The Count explained that the only reason these chandeliers were not in their own castles was because they, too, were for sale.

The *maître d'* walked up, smiled as he took a bit of a bow, and then smoothly took my coat off. As the Count's coat was removed by one of the restaurant staff, this somewhat portly but very elegant 'gentleman', my date, openly admired my body without saying a word. His eyes were bright, hopeful. He saw me watching him and he smiled in that rascally sort of way that I had come not only to expect, but to like. He was playful.

I smiled back.

The Count nodded to the *maître d'* and then put a hand behind my back to guide me toward the table. His hand felt experienced and gentle and very interested in knowing more – in the Biblical sense of 'knowing'. You can feel so much in the simple touch of a skilled man's hands. We were then seated at an antique table set with real crystal and silverware that was actually silver. I tried not to act impressed, tried to act like this was normal for me. We had been seated at a table for four, not two, because Zola and Bertrand each needed their own chair. Both of them hopped up to the same chair next to the Count and then curled up together, obviously well practiced at dining out.

How civilized to allow dogs to join us here, I thought.

When the host returned, he gave us menus that were really more like novellas and offered to get us an aperitif.

"Champagne," said the Count and turned to me. "A bottle?"

"Oh, no, that's too much. Just a glass for me."

"Two glasses," he said and opened the novella to read pages and pages of what the chef was able to offer us.

"This is too complicated," I said as I flipped through this small book of dinner options. "I don't understand."

"Would you like a menu in English?" he asked.

"No. Not English. I can read French. But there are too many choices."

"Yes," he smiled, still reading. "That's what I like about this restaurant. And each choice is a superb offering."

Then he smiled at me, looked me in the eyes and softly licked his lips.

∞

The waiter came back with our champagne. Another waiter brought a small menu with today's specials written on them.

I indicated that I'd have the special, the tasting menu of seven courses. Jean Antoine agreed it was a good choice and ordered a different seven-course meal.

I watched Jean Antoine as he put his reading glasses on to study the wine list. He asked what I would prefer but we both knew that he knew best.

"Shall we have a bottle from my estate?" he asked.

"With pleasure," I said, then wondered . . . I thought he'd sold his estate.

"They carry my wine here which is another reason I like this restaurant. I don't bother to keep an extensive cellar anymore, but did keep some acreage after I sold the château and we still make our wine. It's rather good."

My, it was very good. "This is drinkable art, Jean Antoine. Magnificent." The Count could tell how much my palate understood and appreciated his wine. He smiled as he looked fondly at *la robe* (translation: the 'dress', which is the color, texture, depth) of his wine and took another sip.

Jean Antoine and I made a lot of pleasant small talk, easier to do in a foreign language when you're face-to-face rather than on the phone. He did a lot of art dealing and enjoyed working with those aristocrats who hadn't yet sold their castles. Many of these castles, he said, are really rather cold and damp and the art should be properly stored, not left to rot in those musty old buildings. His eyes brightened as he spoke of his work.

"Did you study art when you were young?"

"Oh, no," he dismissed. "It's just a really easy way to make a lot of money. And I'm good at it. I don't have to work hard, like you do. That's all."

He asked me how the duck he'd ordered for me was. It was quite fine, I noted and then offered, "Would you like a taste?" and immediately felt embarrassed. Do you offer a Count food from your plate? Probably not.

"Very kind of you, no thank you. I like duck, though. Very much. Every autumn I go to a large farm in the south, the *Périgord* region, you know it?"

Yes, the *Périgord* region where all they serve is duck and you see ducks everywhere peeking out from every field. All the postcards have ducks on them, and once, in the restored medieval village of Sarlat with its soft yellow buildings lining the narrow streets (where all of the telephone wires are buried so that you get a real feel of ancient times except when someone hauls out a cell phone), I ordered just a simple salad. I couldn't bear the thought of eating any more duck.

Turns out even ordering a salad in Sarlat won't protect you from getting duck, a huge mound of it on top of lettuce with a few bits of cucumber. My stomach churns just thinking about how much duck I was forced to swallow when visiting the *Périgord* region in the south of France.

But duck in a fine Parisian restaurant, once in a while, will taste like nothing you can make at home unless your name is Julia Childs.

The Count continued. "Yes, well, for many years, every autumn, I go to this farm with others, for the weekend. We make our *foie gras*, eat duck for breakfast, lunch and dinner. Because this farm processes duck, packages it and sends it to Paris – so much duck! – at night we are able to enjoy '*Demoiselle*'. Delicious. Marvellous. Have you ever had it?" I shook my head. "Oh, you really must. You don't know it? Well, you see, they take the carcasses of the ducks, after they've removed most of the meat, and they rub herbs and salt all over the bones and then they grill the bones, with the herbs and the bits of meat that remain. It's heavenly. Divine."

"What did you say it was called?" I asked.

He smiled that smile of his. "*Demoiselle*. 'Young Lady'. Do you know why we call this marvelous dish 'Young Lady'?" He licked his lips slowly, remembering the past fondly or the future hopefully, I'm not sure. Looking straight and knowingly into my eyes, he said softly, "Because every French man knows that meat is sweeter, more delicate, next to the bone, so we call this delectable dish 'Young Lady'. Apropos, don't you agree?" Our eyes locked. I swallowed. I blinked. It gave me a bit of a pleasant shiver, the way he whispered, "Simply divine, delicious." He sat back with his wine glass, still smiling at me, and then took a long, slow sip of the wine as if he were washing those deliciously divine memories down with this sip, and then he licked his lips again.

There was a slight pause in the conversation.

"I think we're speaking very well in French, don't you?" asked Jean Antoine as they took away the third of seven courses.

"Yes," I lied. Actually, he was speaking well and I could understand him, but I fumbled with the vocabulary and usually he was forced to cock one ear toward me, straining to understand. When he got it, he'd sit back and nod.

"You have such a sweet little accent when you speak French," he said.

There was still this fact that we didn't know anything about each other, really. We were both divorced, we were both within each other's age range, Jean Antoine clearly liked my look and I started to relax and enjoy his company, his warm eyes and that sly smile of his. I wasn't really sure what he wanted of me, exactly. Climbing into bed with me, well, that was pretty clear but beyond that, I didn't know. We had spent months emailing and occasionally speaking by phone but I still didn't know if he was planning to get serious with me or not. I was pretty sure he wasn't the right man for me but, I pondered, maybe he's the right man for right now.

"So Jean Antoine," I said, "What are you looking for?"

"My princess," he said softly. He rested his fork on the plate, his eyes shining warmly at me. "I'm looking for my princess."

"I'm not a princess," I teased.

"Yes, you're a princess. You're so elegant and beautiful. You're a princess, yes you are."

"No," I said coyly. "I'm not a princess. I'm the Queen."

My date looked at me without knowing what to say.

"*Desolée, mais je ne suise pas une princesse*," I repeated in a teasing sort of way and again said I was The Queen. ("*Je suise La Reine.*")

"Ahh." Jean Antoine sat up straight, leaned toward me a bit and was now very, very interested. "The Queen?" A pause as he thought about this and then a knowing smile. "So you're a Dominatrix."

"No," I spurted, trying not to spit out the wine. "I'm, you know, not a Dominatrix, just too old to be a princess and, well, at work I'm the boss of things. I'm the Queen."

"The Dominatrix," he restated, a bit puzzled.

Zola and Bertrand looked up from where they were sleeping as I coughed. I tried to clear both my throat and my nose of the expensive wine. For a moment, the two poodles looked a bit worried.

I'm the Queen. I run multimillion dollar projects and command attention during big presentations to executives of big banks. I didn't think The Count would understand this, really, since his world of art and galleries and wandering through creaky old castles looking for treasures wouldn't really touch my world of banking technology and project status meetings.

I shook my head and repeated, "No, no. Not that."

He slouched a bit. "Oh, well. I'm the Dominator, anyway."

∞

Nonchalant is a good word that works quite well in both languages and I tried to act it as we continued our dinner. Now that we had touched on sexual preferences, he wanted to continue in this line of chatter.

"So, yes. Your fantasies," he probed. "Tell me of your fantasies."

"I don't have any," I blurted out (not true).

"Hmm." He didn't believe me. "How many lovers have you had?"

"That's not a polite question," I said, feeling that I was being cornered.

The Count had plenty of table manners but at this moment he was absolutely not behaving in a very gentlemanly way.

"How many lovers?"

"I never tell. That's my secret."

He waited. I kept quiet. "My princess," he said, "You're in Paris. There's no shame in having lovers. You know this."

It's not shame, I thought. It's just not your business.

The Count looked at me, peering over his wine glass as he took a slow, long sip. He then put his glass on the table and waited. He wanted the answer and he would wait until I'd counted them all if that's what it took.

"O.K.," I sighed. "More than 10, less than 100."

He thought a moment and smiled at me as though I were a child. "I've had more than 1,000, less than 2,000. Yes, about that."

About that? You mean he couldn't narrow it down to a tighter range, like within the 500's or something? What about, more than 1,000, less than 1,500 or perhaps between 1,500 and 2,000?

More nonchalance required on my part. I took a sip of the wine and thought, 'Well, we're in for some kind of night' and tried to think of something to say to the 'plus or minus a thousand' estimate.

The wine went slowly down my throat. The silence between us was awkward in a different way now. At least, for me it was. Without thinking, I spoke in English. "So, Jean Antoine, how did you manage that? I mean, that's a lot of lovers. A lot."

Jean Antoine continued in French which is when I knew he perfectly well understood English. "Oh, I enjoy the clubs, you see. We have many in France. My wives were always jealous. You're not the jealous type, I can see that. No, but my wives didn't understand. Not far from here is my favorite club. I could take you later, if you'd like."

How did this happen, I wondered. How did we get from "looking for my princess" to "let's go to a sex club and do it with complete strangers in front of other complete strangers?" I sighed quietly, smiled politely and said, "No, thank you" and then kept eating.

Shamelessly, he continued. "So your fantasies," he probed. "You certainly must have fantasies you would like to enjoy. Tell me one of them."

"I don't have any fantasies," I defended.

"Surely you do," he scoffed and laughed at me as he raised his glass to his lips.

"I've lived them all. I've lived all my fantasies."

He peered at me over the top of his wine glass wondering whether he had misjudged me. Was I the worldly lover he had expected or was I the goody-two-shoes who needed 'awakening'.

"Really, Jean Antoine," I said, "I've done everything I wanted to do and now I'm just looking for the right man for the rest of my life."

"Have you had two men?"

I didn't answer, so he took it for a yes.

"African lovers?"

"I've had an African lover, yes," I blurted out defensively. This lover was a highly educated, sophisticated man who spoke three languages and just happened to be from Africa. We weren't lovers because I was 'having' an African man. He was my lover because we liked each other. He happened to be African – actually born in Africa, educated in Europe and living in Canada.

Jean Antoine was as calm as I was jangled. He sat back in his chair, having lost interest in the food on his plate and said, "Well, I love to offer my woman two men, especially African men."

"Pardon?" I mistakenly asked. Oh, silly me.

"I just love to see black skin on white, don't you?"

"I don't know." The fact is, the nights with my African lover were quiet in a powerfully silent sort of way. He'd told me that "Africans don't speak when we make love" but he was really over-generalizing and I knew it. What was true, though, was this lovely African man from the Ivory Coast who of course spoke English with a French accent didn't speak when making his woman sing in the silence we shared. I would slip in and out of the pleasure and notice that his dark hands looked so beautiful on my very white skin, especially in the moonlight.

"It's so magnificent, black skin on white. It's really magnificent . . . Three men? Have you had three men?"

"Not at . . ."

"Three men at the same time. Oh, well, I could give you that." He leaned back comfortably in his chair. "With me, you can have anything you'd like." Then he leaned forward again and held my hand and looked into my eyes. "You can have anything, anything at all. Your eyes are so blue, my princess."

"Queen."

"Yes, yes. Queen. Your eyes are so blue, my Queen. And your skin," he sighed, "is so white. Yes, there is a club not far from here and it is a place I could introduce you to. It's the most elegant one in all of Paris. You would like it, *Princesse*."

"No, I'm not a princess." Then I broke into English. "And I need to find the washroom."

"Washroom?"

"*Les toilettes*."

He directed me upstairs. Zola, the female dog, followed me as if she, too, needed to freshen up. What? Did The Count train this poodle to trot off with his date to the ladies' room? Zola bounced along ahead of me as poodles are known to do, especially fat little happy poodles. Looking into the full-length mirror, I began to laugh. Zola stood beside me and looked into the mirror and then up at me, her head to one side. I laughed and laughed and laughed and kept watching myself as though my reflection in the mirror was someone else and we were sharing a joke. I finally forced myself to stop laughing and wiped away the tears that had smudged my mascara. Zola barked her approval. She'd had enough of the bathroom by now and wanted to get back to the table.

I straightened out my dress, tried to close up the long slits in the sleeves that exposed my terribly white skin (it didn't work), fixed my mascara, took a deep breath, and headed back.

When we arrived at the table, Jean Antoine stood up like a gentleman, waited until I sat down, and then he continued. There was no stopping him. I'd hate to be a short-on-cash aristocrat trying to bargain with him over a piece of art.

"You just need to feel comfortable with the man, that's all. I'm sure you'd do fine in the clubs."

Blondes would always do fine in French clubs. Indeed-e-o.

"You can always trust me. I would take care of you. It would be my pleasure to have you join me."

Yes, it would. It would certainly be his pleasure.

Now, most people only know about these sorts of clubs based on what Hollywood or French films choose to divulge. Occasionally, one gets a bit of titillating information in the newspaper about one of these clubs and because there are dozens of such clubs in Paris, sprinkled everywhere including in cozy family neighborhoods, people like to imagine that this shows how Paris is so 'hip' and sexually 'mature'. After all, these are places where married people come to exchange partners.

But it's not really quite so 'cool'. It's just based on the same tired, old Virgin/Whore storyline and it's all about men trading women.

The price to get into any swingers' club in Paris is a female ass. This means that any woman gets in for free. And for her, the drinks are free, too. Lots of drinks. Lots and lots of them. Getting young women really drunk is, quite frankly, the objective. And plenty of women oblige without really understanding what they're getting into. I mean, not even prostitutes long to offer oral sex in a place where other people stand around and watch, even hoping to get in on the action.

A man, on the other hand, needs to pay a hefty price for any drink he consumes (the very high cost of a man's drink covers the huge quantities of alcohol consumed by the women at the club) and, to get into the club, he needs to bring along a female ass and cough up money for a ticket, too. Why? Well, someone huffed at me once (as if I didn't understand the human condition in this oh so liberal Western world), "Because otherwise there would be 98 men and only 2 women in there. Who wants that?"

Perhaps all of the women who really didn't want to go to a sex club but end up there anyway, drunk and helpless. Some women want to go, yes, but there are plenty of other women who get teased and cajoled, called a prude, and are even threatened until finally their resolve breaks down. Otherwise, there probably really would only be 2 women in there on any given night.

Yes, a man must pay by offering up both "his" woman and some money. A woman is always completely welcome to walk into one of those places alone and, if she were completely clueless, she'd go. They aren't very safe places for women. Not even the "nice", more upscale ones. The Count made sure I understood that these places could be rather dangerous for a woman on her own and he would certainly protect me in there. He knew his way around, being a frequent customer and all that, so he'd look after me. Not to worry.

Such a gentleman.

∞

I continued my complete look of disinterest and said softly, "No, Jean Antoine. No thank you."

He reached across the table and took my hand. "You can trust me, Maret." I didn't budge. Almost didn't breathe. Without skipping a beat, he then said. "Or we could go to the Loire together. I'd like to take you to the Loire region, maybe in February. It's very beautiful there. So many beautiful castles."

Any clubs? I wondered.

"And you know, I like to caress and cuddle, too," he said flirtatiously. French men bat their eyelashes when they flirt. It's true. A French man, when he's trying to convince a woman of something, will bat his eyes at you while he holds and strokes your hand.

"Oh, well," I said without committing to anything. "I'm very tired. Thank you so much for dinner."

We had our espressos, and he paid the bill and drove me to my apartment. I knew for a fact that I didn't want to put myself in a vulnerable position with a man who considers himself the Dominator and it was a shame, too, because outside of the sex clubs, I'm sure his life in Paris would have fascinated me. His circle of friends and business acquaintances, the names he'd dropped who were regulars at the sex club, were impressive but not intriguing enough for me to want to meet up with any one of these famous French men in a naked condition who might be hoping I'd jump into a cage or something.

The Count must have been praying as he drove me home because a miracle occurred: right there next to my apartment, there on the narrow, winding streets in this medieval part of Paris, was a parking spot.

Oh dear. The moment where the man hopes to be invited into the woman's apartment.

As Jean Antoine and the poodles walked me to the door of the building where I lived, he slowed his walk and said softly without looking at me, "Erections aren't so important for you, are they?"

Are you crazy? I thought. Why bother being a heterosexual woman if erections aren't important? But I didn't say anything. The Count continued. "You see, for me, erections aren't always so important. That's why I offer them to my lover at the club." He stopped for a moment and looked at me. "I have diabetes and it is very difficult for, well, you understand." We continued walking.

Ooh la la la la la la. (That's, right, it's "*Ooh, la la la la la la*" if you're saying it in French, you say 'la' six times). The horrible side effects of diabetes. What a cruel nightmare to live in a man's body when diabetes has robbed you of erections. Oh, poor Jean Antoine.

"Thank you for an interesting evening, Jean Antoine," I said as we reached the big blue door to the courtyard where I lived. Before pressing the code to enter, I turned and kissed him on each side of his face. He stood there, hoping for more.

I couldn't.

"May I call you again?" he asked.

"Yes," I said, not knowing what else to say.

He took my yes as an invitation to kiss me and he kissed me gently, one hand on my face, holding me softly. He smelled fresh and warm and masculine and a bit like the espresso we'd just had.

"Good night, Jean Antoine," I whispered and turned to enter the code to the gate.

∞

Jean Antoine did call me two or three times after that, encouraging me to join him for a week in the Loire Valley to see the castles and enjoy some nice meals and spend a few days and nights together but I was non-committal. I really just didn't know what to do. I couldn't flat out say no, because a part of me still really wanted to get to know (fully clothed, that is) this very odd man and his exotic, castle-trotting life in Paris with all those famous people he'd named, but I couldn't say yes, either. So I finally just said "*peut-être*" (perhaps) and this seemed to startle him. He never called again.

It was only much later that I learned I'd said a terrible thing by saying *peut-être* to him. A straight translation of *peut-être* simply means "perhaps" but in French male-female etiquette, when a woman says *peut-être* to a man's offer of a date, she's actually saying "there's no f'ing way I'd ever go out with you." As I've explained, the French don't like to be rude and just say no. In French, there are all sorts of code words for no and gradations of "no" and, sadly, I'd used the strongest possible term with The Count by just saying "perhaps".

I've really always had a very hard time remembering how to say "no" in French without actually using the French word for "no" (*non*). When a beggar or your teenager asks for money, you say *desolée* (sorry). You say *peut-être* to a man if you never want to see him again and *merci* when you don't want a second cup of coffee.

It gets a bit confusing.

True, I liked The Count's poodles and his style and he was very kind, really. And I liked his soft kiss. I just didn't want to spend a whole week in the Loire Valley where he would no doubt continue to encourage me to have sex in public places with perfect strangers just so that he could buy me the erection(s) that he himself was unable to offer so that later in the night, he'd get a kiss and a cuddle from me as his mind replayed over and over again the events of the night – in black and white.

Merci.

Oops.

I meant *peut-être.*

Wait. I meant *desolée.*

CHAPTER TWELVE

Learning French, Sort Of

"Perhaps French classes?" I said to myself one day as I wandered over to *Ile St. Louis* to do my morning yoga. French
classes would at least get me some human contact and maybe
even a bit of a social life. Sure, they wouldn't be French people
I'd be meeting but at least they'd be people and at least I'd have
something to do during the week. As it was, I hadn't yet managed to sit down to start writing that book about famous
feminists but I told myself I had to settle in a bit, get familiar
with my neighborhood, do a bit more research. I could take
French classes in the afternoon and write in the morning and, I
enjoyed imagining, use the nights in Paris with a lover, if I ever
managed to find one.

The next session of French classes at the *Alliance Française*
across town would start up at the end of the month so I noted
the date in my completely empty calendar. Whether or not I
learned anything in class didn't matter much to me. It would at
least give me a purpose, a place to go during the day. Plus, it
would be exhilarating to have a daily walk through the medieval part of Paris, over the Seine to *Ile St. Louis*, behind the
Notre Dame Cathedral, past the Sorbonne, down the streets of

the Latin District and through the Luxembourg Gardens. These parts of Paris hadn't changed much since Hemingway meandered along these little streets and boulevards except now there were shops selling cell phones and all of the buildings had indoor plumbing.

It was the middle of January and I would wake up feeling stressed about the lack of a social life so I tried not to think about it. Occasionally, I'd meet a man in a café who'd flirt with me and I'd soon learn that he was so free with his flirts because he was married, already taken. These men always made a point to say they liked my *petit accent* because it was *mignon* (cute) and when I declined their invitation to a frolic, they'd look down their noses at me as though I were a child and say, "You Americans, you are such prudes."

Sitting at a table next to a flirtatious married man, I'd always look like I was considering what he had said (so that I'd keep him focused) and then I'd say, "A prude? No. I'm just a woman who deserves a lot more than part of another woman's man. I deserve at least one whole man to myself." My eyes would brighten and I'd add, "Or maybe even two!"

They didn't like that answer, one woman having two men for herself. The strength of my smile made it clear that they were to leave me alone. A very stern, very polite smile means *peut-être*.

Walking along and stopping at cafés and even having married men flirt with me were pleasant distractions in Paris and of course I managed to enjoy myself for several days like this but on each of those days I'd feel all those lonely months stretch out ahead of me and ask myself, over and over again, what on earth I was to do.

Nothing to do, no rhythm to my days.

There I was in a sweet little apartment, alone. In a beautiful city, yes. But alone. I ate my breakfast alone. I took walks along the Seine alone. I went to the Sunday morning market alone and bought my fresh eggs and chanterelle mushrooms and *crème fraîche* alone and then made myself an omelet and ate my dinner alone in front of the fireplace full of candles. I drank glasses of wine alone, sometimes at a café and sometimes back at the apartment. I did my best to keep my spirits up, smiled politely and sometimes hopefully at a handsome man, with no luck. They always seemed to be married or completely disinterested.

Not wanting to burden my daughters back in Canada, I'd telephone them and say how much 'fun' I was having. They were happy for me, they said.

But it's not so much fun, really, when you wake up and the only person you're going to talk to that day is the waitress, Francine, at the café on the corner near *Place des Vosges*.

"*Bonjour, Madame, un café et un croissant avec la confiture?*" [Good morning, ma'am. A coffee and a croissant with jam?]

"*Oui, s'il vous plaît.*" [Yes, please.]

And then, "*Merci, bonjournée.*" [Thank you, have a nice day.]

Voilà. The sum total of my daily conversations, aside from those married men who approached me.

Where were all the handsome and single French men? OK, with French men you can't expect tall, dark, and handsome because they're generally awfully short but you can expect a handsome single one once in a while, can't you?

Nothing. Nobody.

I needed to find a date for God's sakes.

To people who have been married for a long time, dating looks like fun. In the movies, the whole dating process – from being asked out on a date to figuring out what to wear and then to actually having something to say to someone you don't really know – appears so seamless, so natural.

It's not.

Especially not when you've got quite a lot of your life piled up behind you. By middle age, you're pretty much "baked" as I like to say. You know what you like, what you don't like, you pretty much know who you are. That makes it a bit harder to find the right piece of the puzzle, unlike when you're young and supple and a bit more foolish.

As for finding some sensual company, I did manage to find some pleasure with a man in Paris and also encountered several frighteningly weird fellows who were interested in me, fellows for whom I had no interest at all. How did I do this?

With a little help from the Internet.

Of course, who wouldn't prefer to meet a man in Paris the way you see it done in the movies – at a small café or in a museum while you're standing there admiring a piece of art as a stranger, a man who will soon be your lover, is standing there admiring you? Nobody thinks of going to Paris, logging on to a website and working your way through profile after profile like it was a job or a research project or something. It's a bit tiresome to even think about it, I know, but enough time had been wasted worrying my way through what to do with myself now that I was actually here in Paris "living the dream" pretty much isolated and certainly without a social life.

I had to get on with things, didn't I?

∞

I opened myself a bottle of champagne to take the sting off the cold hard facts of having to manhunt here in France using a computer and walked the bottle back to the wee little fridge.

The floorboards of this 17th century apartment needed tightening or something because in the silence of a quiet night, each time I walked across the living room to the small refrigerator in the kitchen to get myself a refill on this glass of champagne, the floorboards squeak-squeak-squeaked. After a few glasses of champagne and all that squeak-squeak-squeaking there was a loud knock at my door.

"You are stomping all over the floor," claimed the Neighbor Below, the one who had 'welcomed' me to the neighborhood by banging on my door after 1:00 a.m. to tell me about the bathroom noises she didn't like hearing. She stood there with her hands on her hips, disgusted. "It would be making you a good neighbor if you walk more quietly. I can't concentrate."

"Please," I smiled (the champagne made me do it) and opened the door wide. "Come in and show me how to walk quietly on old, squeaky floors."

She hesitated.

"The floors are old and they squeak," I said flatly. "That's what happens in an old apartment. What, these are three hundred year old floors, right? No, I think the floors are four hundred years old."

I very much wanted to add, "And, look, lady, you're only 30 and you squeak and squawk non-stop, so give the floors a break."

In other words: For God's sake, leave me alone you freak.

Luckily, I hadn't had enough champagne to say that.

"They make so much noise," she stated sternly. "You must inform Madame Catellini that she is to fix the floors."

I shrugged. The French, they shrug as a form of communicating any number of things and the shrug is done in all sorts of different ways. I chose the "I'm just not going to bother with anything you say" sort of shrug, a shrug done politely but firmly, with the head cocked a bit to one side, shoulders up and held there a moment, and then shoulders down, all the while appearing like you're about to say something and then don't, can't be bothered. I managed to pull off this very French shrug without having yet attended my first French class.

I told her good night and closed the door and I really felt like squeaking my way over to the bathroom and flushing the toilet 'just because'. Up to this point, in deference to her need to sleep and because the monster toilet was right over her bedroom, I had kindly taken to not flushing the toilet after 10 pm and to taking baths before then, too. Sometimes in the middle of the night I'd sit on the toilet and try not to tinkle too loudly, adjusting the aim so that the urine hit the porcelain and not splash directly into the water. It's water hitting water that makes the tinkling sound. It wasn't at all pleasant to be put in the position of thinking about a couple lying in their bed directly under your toilet who, through no fault of your own, were forced to listen to the sound of your bodily fluids being released.

As it was, given the placement of my own bedroom beneath Madame Lambert's bathroom, I personally woke up each morning to the sound of her bathroom noises, starting with the tinkle.

Madame Lambert was a cheery old French lady, squat and grey-haired, always smiling and openly delighted that her fifty-year-old son had never married. That way, she could make him his Sunday brunches and keep him all to herself. Sometimes, even during the week she'd trudge up the stairs after the market with a skinless, dead rabbit, its wild-eyed head hanging limply over the side of her basket. "I'm going to my son's house tonight," she'd say brightly, "to make him dinner." I don't think it's quite right that a mother wants her son all to herself, but there you have it. This woman seemed to suffocate her son and he seemed to like being suffocated. Well, he ate like he liked it because he was a little butterball and since he wasn't much taller than his mother, who wasn't tall at all, he was verging on being completely round, a meatball that waddled.

I guess Madame Lambert didn't drink too much in the evenings, or else it was the fact that I am a heavy sleeper, or perhaps all of us here in this old apartment building with the haphazardly placed bathrooms had developed the same peculiar peeing etiquette of aiming for the porcelain, because I never once heard Madame Lambert's middle-of-the-night tinkle and absolutely never heard a midnight flush.

I squeaked along back to the dining room table to continue my online search through the men's profiles but just as I got to the table, realized I'd not gotten that glass filled up because the neighbor's knock at the door had interrupted me. Squeaked along back to the kitchen then squeaked straight over to the table on the other side of the apartment where my computer was sitting on the coffee table by the fireplace. I could only imagine the rage boiling up in the blood of that grumpy young neighbor below as she heard me do all of this, probably imagining I was squeaking all over the floors on purpose just to bother her. This was something I'd not yet started to do.

∞

There was still half a bottle of champagne left and so there'd be plenty more squeaking tonight. I just wouldn't answer the door the next time she stomped up the stairs. It seemed to encourage her when I opened the door, seemed to help her build her growing sense of misplaced righteousness. No, tonight, here by the warm glow of the candles in the fireplace, tonight I wrote out my profile in two languages and waited to see what would happen. As I mentioned earlier, I stayed online only long enough to be queried by two different men about my preference for penis size. Did I like, as one man put it, a 'big penis' or, as the other fellow asked, did I like a 'boy with big sex?'

Gee.

I had imagined a little more romance from the men in Paris. It's not that I have anything against penis talk but there's a time and a place for it. Now that I was actually living here, my first date with a French man had been The Count, a man who wanted to lure me to sex clubs to 'do it' with African men.

My next contact with a potential lover was with these two yahoos who'd instantly responded to my online dating profile.

What was happening here? I wondered.

But maybe I didn't want to know.

It was late, well past toilet-flushing time and so I decided to save the rest of the champagne for tomorrow. Had to wake early to get to my very first French class. Time for bed.

First, a squeak over to the bathroom. Then a very delicate tinkle. Brush my teeth, wash my face. Then a squeak over to the bedroom.

I climbed under the covers, rubbed my face into the fresh pillow – wearing a champagne smile, that relaxed, 'oh gosh everything's so perfectly all right with the world' sort of glow, mumbling *bien sûr* – and slept straight through the night, waking the next morning to the sound of Madame Lambert upstairs, directly above my bed, tinkling into her toilet.

I doubt I would have so cheerfully and hopefully hopped out of bed that morning had I known what French men had been writing to me about all night.

∞

That morning's email 'in basket' of my Internet dating account was full of hope: emails and invitations from men asking me to read their profiles, men who wanted to connect with me, get intimate. A couple of years earlier, when an old German friend of mine, Heinrich, and I took a summer walk along the sea together in the South of France, he asked me what I missed most about marriage. I said flatly, "Sex." We both laughed and continued to walk along the boardwalk next to the sea, eating our lavender ice creams.

But the truth was that my flippant answer about just missing married sex wasn't true. It was one of the things I missed about marriage, certainly that. Married sex, when you're married to a good lover, that is, is oh so much better than dating sex.

Truthfully, married sex can't even be compared to dating sex. It's like comparing fresh oranges and canned oranges. Both are oranges. The fresh ones are better.

You see, at the end of the day – within reason, of course – it's not so much about the size of anything except the size of your husband's heart. When he is open, alive, present, giving, alert and loves the very depth of your soul, those moments of bliss and serenity, the knowledge that just for this moment, for now, all is right with the world, you're safe, and you're seen and you're loved and desired and not alone but together facing the world and all that it offers and takes away from us, that's when married sex is best.

"No, actually, it's not what I miss most," I confessed. "It's what I miss a lot but not what I miss most."

He walked along the *Promenade des Anglais*, a walkway next to the Mediterranean Sea in the city of Nice, licking his ice cream waiting for my answer.

"The small intimacies. Making the bed together. Grocery shopping. Sitting with a cup of coffee, reading the newspaper in silence . . . Waking up on a Sunday morning and not being alone. You know, just having someone to talk to when all the world is quietly cozied up together in their homes."

You wake up and the whole world's sleeping or sleeping together and it's too early to call anyone and you're alone. Completely by yourself in a sea of people you know are out there somewhere, being together.

Heinrich nodded. "Yes, Johnny Cash has a song about Sunday mornings, how lonely they are."

My German friend and I walked along the boardwalk in the dark by the even darker sea watching couples walk past us, couples in love and couples in like and couples like us who were just having good company.

If you're wondering why this man and I never made it beyond a solid friendship, it's simple: he was nearly my father's age, a severe chain-smoker (3 packs a day), drank way too much rosé each and every day starting at noon, always had two lovers on the go so that he could be entertained by jealous rages and intrigues, and was still very much in love with his ex-wife

who had left him a quarter of a century ago because he had stupidly decided to behave like a French man and take a mistress.

While a terrible husband, I'm sure, and a faithless lover, the
fact is that Heinrich was always a very good friend to me. We
made each other laugh.

∞

On that first morning of emails from strangers in Paris, it
was of course not just sex I was after. I was looking to enjoy
Sunday mornings with shared sensual prayers, to find that man,
the one I've been looking for and hoped was looking for me, to
start building those small intimacies, to share moments that
softly open your soul to another. I got up that morning fully
immersed in this deep hope and sat down next to my computer
with a bowl of maple oatmeal (from packages I'd brought from
Canada) and read through the emails that French men had sent
overnight.

It turned out that the intimacy I was being offered here in
Paris was just the silly sort, theatrical. More invitations to sex
clubs. More emails about the size of a man's penis (don't get
me wrong, that interests me, but first I need to know if he's
smart enough not to put that kind of information in an email).
One man wrote that he hoped I would tie him up and let him
worship my feet. Another wrote very politely saying that he'd
like to hurt me, if that's what I wanted. I assumed he wanted
to hurt me while either one or both of us was naked, but I didn't
pursue the question. I just replied, "*Desolée*" and deleted his
email without even bothering to look at his profile.

A while back, I had a date with an educated and very suc-
cessful man who was all charm and elegance over dinner and

then, during the 'foreplay' (if one could call it that) he became really rough, violent. He threw me on the couch, kissed me hard (forcing his face so fiercely against my lips that it made my teeth hurt), began to rough me up a bit and even growled. I began to laugh.

"What?" he said innocently, almost like a little boy, sitting up on the couch, his face all gentle and tender as before.

"This is funny," I said, not the least bit aroused either from sexual excitement or fear.

"You're not turned on?" He was disappointed, hurt.

"No."

"Not even a little bit?"

"Nope."

The night ended abruptly. He was embarrassed and so he should have been. To wrap yourself around a woman and be so out of touch that you can't tell whether she's even the teensiest little bit interested in brutish frolic is ridiculous. The whole point of connecting physically is to connect at all levels and there is more to a connection than just skin on skin. Anyway, when getting up close and personal, you should at the very least be able to tell if the other person is bored stiff or not.

Some of the emails I looked through before going to my first French class were actually pleasant, polite. After reading one from a fairly handsome fellow, I clicked to read his profile and, *voilà*. More weirdness.

> Single guy with strong foot fetish is looking for a girl
> that will [sic] like to have her feet caressed, massaged
> and taken care of. I love girl's feet but I also love to
> go to the movies, traveling, nice dinners, music and
> good companie [sic] perhaps developing to a good

and stable relationship. I like feet, but I want commitment, too. I will wash your feet with passion, but I will
also kiss your mouth with love. Wanna give it a try?

Nope.

In his email to me, this guy hadn't even bothered to mention his foot fetish but right there in his profile for all the world to see along with his photo was an advertisement about his special need regarding feet. *Merci.* On to the next profile.

Ladies: Ever wanted to Dominate a man? Even for
just an hour or so? Someone to do your bidding, fulfill
your every fantasy, respond unquestioningly to your
every wish or whim? Be bathed, massaged, waited on
hand and foot, vent your anger, indulge your sadistic
side, have your chores done, be worshiped the way
you deserve! I'm your man. Awaiting your command.
– Umbriel.

Um, no thank you, Umbriel. First, I don't think about all the ironing and the dishes and sex in the same breath and, second, I'm not a sadist. Or, I wasn't at that time. Only much later did I learn that I do actually have a wee bit of a sadistic side – but the guy deserved it.

There were several invitations from married men to join them at 'couples hammams' (sauna, showers, public bathing with other couples) and some genuinely tragic emails from men who probably wrote to every female who ever signed onto this site and who probably never once got a positive reply or perhaps any reply at all. Everyone deserves love, even these sorry men, but I wasn't going to offer myself up to any of the tragic ones.

Then there was an email written entirely in French so I popped it into the online translator.

> With regard to your chip [profile], I wish with a real want, to know you. Your face sniffs charm and softness which every normally constituted man would like to have in his sides. Your expression of face lets appear the woman, all at once, volunteer and audacious whom they would like to accompany while having keeping a side child whom they would like to protect. Leave me this chance and you will be able to judge by yourself if it deserves the detour because I have the impression definitely to miss something big. You belong to the women that perfume its flowers. To read you, Salvatore.

Pardon? "Your face sniffs charm?"

The limitations of online translators.

Poor Salvatore, a man who said on his profile that he wrote in both French and Italian but not in English, was probably saying something quite poetic in that email of his but the reason I said "*Desolée*" had nothing to do with what he'd written. We could have stumbled along together in French, most likely. No, the reason I said no thanks was because he was a smoker.

∞

It was time to start my day, anyway. My days in Paris began to develop a certain rhythm. I would have coffee at my neighborhood café and then take a walk to the Seine and do thirty minutes of yoga on *Ile St. Louis* down by the lone chestnut tree that faces the Louvre. Over time, that chestnut tree and I became friends. I would greet it each morning and wonder why it was almost always just the two of us out there in the morning, that chestnut tree and me. Fourteen million people lived in Paris, and yet here I was – alone with a chestnut tree that had the best river view in the city. Mornings by the Seine always had a deep stillness, a calling inward. Then I'd walk back to the apartment, sit down and do my French homework, putter around with the Internet dating emails and then it was time to go to class. It became a routine for me to reply "*Desolée*" and move on to the next email.

Sometimes, yes, I got a date. It usually went like this:

"Nice to meet you, you're so beautiful." (Oh so predictably French.)

"Thank you."

"Do you want to go to a sex club?"

"No thank you."

Occasionally, I'd meet an elegant man like Etienne, a very handsome and very creative man. There are lots of photos on Internet dating sites, whether in France or North America, that make me cringe. Why would a man imagine that a profile photo taken while standing in front of the bathroom mirror (oh, gee, so arousing to see you and your toilet) or looking fairly dumb in bad lighting with his webcam shots taken in the basement would be a 'lure'?

Etienne was different. His photo had him sitting in a lush park, or perhaps in someone's private garden, in a huge plush velvet art deco chair, grinning and holding up a glass of red wine, looking straight into the camera. Dangling at a slight angle just in front of him was an enormous gold frame taken from some 17th or 18th century painting and there he was, sitting in that chair right in the middle of the empty frame with a great big smile and his wavy dark hair falling down over one eye. His by-line: "Life is a work of art."

How true, I thought.

Better yet, neither his profile nor his email said anything at all about sucking my toes or taking me to a spanking contest or wanting to get naked with me while a whole lot of strangers watched.

∞

Etienne and I met and had a pleasant conversation over coffee (he was absolutely as handsome in real life as in his photo) and he said he'd take me to lunch the next day but never called.

Then there was Philippe, the CEO of a software company who asked me to meet him at the upscale hotel, Hotel Costes. The guards (hotel guards are also known as doormen) were dressed in what looked like Armani suits and sunglasses, even at night. They were tall, impressive-looking hotel guards with big feet. I couldn't help but notice.

Philippe's profile had said simply, in both English and French:

> Single man looking for single woman for a beautiful
> love story without an end.

This man met me at the hotel bar, bought me two glasses of champagne, and then when our drinks were done said he'd take me to dinner – I just had to wait for him to get his car. He never came back. He called while I was waiting at the front next to the handsome doormen who were bored and listening in to my call with Philippe. He said his car had been robbed. Sure. When I suggested that I come to meet him while we waited for the police, he said, "Oh, a policeman is right here, just here at the store buying cigarettes. This is good luck for me."

"Just one policeman?"

When he answered "yes, just one," I got in a cab and went home. Policemen in Paris always come in threes. They shop in threes, too. Even in those tiny little police cars, you always see three big guys packed in, generally fairly cheerful and sipping cans of soda and chatting away. It's about police safety, to always have three. Better management and control of the suspect to have two dealing with the potentially dangerous fellow and one standing back, ready to smack a head or pull out a gun.

Shortly after I arrived back at the apartment, Philippe called me again. "I'm afraid that the police officer expects I will have two hours of paperwork. It is best that you go home and . . ."

"Philippe," I said softly as I poured myself a glass of wine, still wearing my coat and hat, "I already am home."

Oops. Caught. Oh. The boy was caught and we both knew it. I took my first sip and waited for what he'd lie about next. "Oh, home? You're home already? I . . . I have . . . oh, well, I'm very sorry we did not have dinner but I will call tomorrow. We can go out again."

We both knew he was lying but for some reason, French men think we women like to be lied to rather than to be told the truth.

"That would be nice, Philippe, *peut-être!*"

I don't think I actually said the sentence correctly, from a French language perspective, but at least the last thing Philippe heard from me was *peut-être*.

Look, I don't expect every man to fall for me but the fact is, I'd gotten myself back into pretty good shape for a woman of my age and I'm clean and intelligent and friendly enough. It's not out of the realm of imagination to expect that at some point I'd get a second date. But no. There was always the promised invitation and then the invisible brush off.

Just because it was invisible, silent, cowardly, didn't mean it didn't hurt. I kept trying to stay positive, keep a cheery disposition about it all and remain polite, civil.

True, back in Canada there had been some unusual situations, too, but here in France it was such a consistent and relentlessly insulting barrage of brush offs. It scraped away at my dignity each time but I kept on trying. Surely to God there had to be someone, just one man, here in France who would offer to take me on a second date. It had become exhausting, all these first dates. Never getting to a second date or a reasonable kiss, let alone a bit of French 'action', was a mystery.

What was happening? Why?

Was it something I said, or kept saying, that frightened all these French men? So far on this great adventure of mine, every man I'd met on French soil wanted me to go to a sex club or wanted nothing at all to do with me.

That was a pretty sobering thought so I tried not to think about it.

CHAPTER THIRTEEN

Serendipities

It was strange that I was having so much trouble meeting a man. Over the years, I've actually met lots of men in Paris, sometimes three at a time. Meeting a man in Paris was always interesting for me because they can be from anywhere in the world but there's one thing for sure: if he's a foreigner who's chosen to be in Paris, he's got good taste. Writing that book and sharing time with a man with good taste was one of the reasons I really wanted to live here for a while. I felt justified in believing that, darn it, if I'd gone to all this trouble to live here, I should at least be able to find a man to enjoy, if not to love. Why on earth was it now proving so hard?

The weekend I'd originally met the Count had been during a visit just prior to moving here when I was trying to make all the necessary arrangements in person. For a foreigner to actually live in Paris for longer than three months, you can expect to do one of two things: just sneak in (fairly easily, as the hundreds of thousands of undocumented migrants currently enjoying free health care and public education at the expense of French citizens will tell you) or apply for a visa and be tortured with rounds of paperwork, potentially bizarre questions, and then just sneak in anyway.

The French love paperwork spiced with just a touch of what feels like sadism because any time you need to do anything official, there are forms to fill out but before you can fill out these particular forms you need to get copies of other forms that aren't yet printed but in the meantime you can complete this form here to get a copy of the as-yet-unprinted forms and, when you do, you will need to cough up more evidence of who you are and what you want. And then the bureaucrats always smile with a bit of a wicked grin as they ask you, the foreigner who wouldn't have a clue that this question was coming next, "Do you have a gas bill?"

It seems that this question is always the punch line to whatever administrivia you must accomplish in France. Someone who had lived here a while back had warned me about this before but I didn't believe it. Really. A gas bill.

But it was true.

In advance of my move to France, I thought I'd get myself a bank account in Paris so I walked into a French bank with my Canadian passport, a letter of introduction from my own bank and a certified check in euros. You'd think they'd be happy to see money walking in the door. But no. The bank official frowned, peered down through her bifocals and lifted up the letter of introduction, looking at it on both sides while occasionally peering suspiciously at the check sitting on her desk. I sat across the desk from her and waited. She slowly examined the certified check, first the front, then the back. She stroked the top of the check and said, "Yes. I see." Then the wicked grin and a smile. "Do you have a gas bill?"

"My gas bill?"

"Yes."

"But, why my gas bill?"

"*Madame*, to prove that you reside here in France."

"But I don't live here yet," I said. "I'm just trying to get things organized for when I arrive."

"Yes, I see." She pretended to think about this a moment but I'm sure she'd been through this round with plenty of naïve foreigners. She probably kept a count and compared her stats on a weekly basis with other banking friends over a petit café. She looked up at me and said decidedly, "I'll need your gas bill from your home in Canada, then."

"My gas bill from Toronto? Why would I carry that around with me?" I asked.

She shrugged in the way that only French bureaucrats – and bankers – in total control of your fate can shrug. "To open an account, we need a gas bill. That's how it is here in France."

Think, think, think. I put my hand to my head. "I could get someone to fax a copy of my gas bill," I said hopefully, trying to figure out whom I might get to rummage around my town-house back home to search for one, and where on earth I might suggest they look.

"I'm afraid we need an original gas bill. You understand." She smiled, pushing the certified check toward me as if it might be infected. "These are our rules." Now we both just went from an afternoon with an overload of paperwork ahead of us to an afternoon having nothing to do at all. How lovely for her. She smiled sweetly, again in the way that only French bureaucrats – and bankers – in total control of your fate can do. "Please feel very welcome, to make another appointment when you have your gas bill. *Bonjournée, Madame*."

With that, I was dismissed.

Fat chance I'd be coming back to this bank, I thought as I returned her smile and thanked her and dutifully replied *"Bon-journée."*

This peculiarity regarding the need to walk around France with your gas bill perplexes other Europeans as well. I knew a Swiss man who had lived in Paris for several months without a telephone because he couldn't cough up a gas bill. This was before everyone everywhere had at least one mobile phone and to get a telephone line, you needed (and still need) a gas bill. He was renting a few rooms in a large home and it was his landlord who actually paid the gas and that landlord wouldn't offer up an original copy of one of his precious gas bills to help out.

The trouble it took to open a simple bank account (I actually never did manage to get myself a French bank account and just relied on bank machines for cash and my North American credit cards) made me dread what lay up ahead for me in applying for a French visa. If opening a bank account or getting a telephone line was really that difficult, how much more wildly tiresome and administratively ridiculous would applying for a visa to live in France be? And what if I applied and after all that hassle they said no? I mean, to just sneak in without applying is one thing. I could claim ignorance. But to be turned down at the French consulate and then just sneak in, anyway ... that would put a cloud over the time I planned to live in Paris. Every day I'd be worried that someone would ask me for my papers and I'd be *sans papiers* like those who now live in France and chose to skip the French paperwork.

Only unlike all of the other immigrants who had chosen to ignore French law, I would be *sans papiers* with an official French "note to file" indicating that I'd actually applied to live in France but that France had said no and I had come, anyway. That would be worse than just being *sans papiers*.

So I decided to go with 'option 1' (sneak in).

∞

I left the bank with the politely unhelpful bank manager feeling more than a wee bit irritated. I'd have to redeposit this certified check back into my Canadian bank account. I'd already paid a foreign currency fee to change the money to euros. Now I'd have to keep this check safe for the rest of the weekend and when I got home, I'd have to pay a fee to get it back to dollars. But, I said to myself as I walked along in the shade down the chestnut tree-lined *Rue de la Motte-Piquet*, was it really worth it to be irritated? At this moment? Today I was in Paris, on a very short 4-day weekend vacation and there was no need to dwell on bank accounts and gas bills and worries over illegally entering France later in the year. That could all be fretted over when I was back home getting myself ready to become an illegal immigrant.

For now, I decided to console myself with a drink at The Ritz, alone. During that trip, my young lover, Robert, was in India working on a merger-acquisition. At this point, I was here for only 4 days and wasn't particularly interested in meeting anyone. As I walked through Paris toward The Ritz, I felt a sudden urge to drink a Serendipity and smoke a cigar. Smoking a cigar wasn't the unusual part. I liked them. But my palate could sense the perfection of a cigar matched with a Serendipity.

A Serendipity is an all-season drink with a refreshing, happy feel to it at the first sip. Colin Field, the bartender at The Ritz, invented it. Known as the World's Number One Bartender, he speaks four languages and knows not only how to mix a perfect drink but also how to size up a patron at the bar. I've watched him in action. He knows just how to amuse a lonely person (sometimes me) and engage her in conversation or get her talking to another person alone at the bar, and he knows exactly when to leave you alone to your cigar and your drink and your private thoughts.

The World's Number One Bartender works at the Bar Hemingway, a bar situated right at the back of The Ritz. It's a tiny bar that pays homage to the writer with photos of Hemingway everywhere you look, first as a young man and then as a mustached middle-aged good ol' boy smiling in all his manly success (hunting, fishing, changing wives, writing) and then as a weary, older, somewhat pudgy fellow looking like he's grown full of regrets.

This bar drags you back in time with its rich mahogany walls and dim lights and small tables nudged close together. Sometimes, Colin turns on the old turntable and 33s scratch out tunes that Hemingway had probably once listened to right here, puffing on a cigar, no doubt, and drinking, drinking, drinking.

Hemingway had boasted that when Americans were liberating Paris after World War I, he was busy 'liberating' this little bar at The Ritz. He had written of his early years in Paris in *A Moveable Feast*, published after his death. Writing as an old man, remembering back to his time in this city as a young writer and young husband, the book paid homage to both the love of the wife he'd abandoned and to the city that never abandoned him.

When at the bar with The World's Number One Bartender, I always order a cocktail, never a glass of wine or a beer. You have to order something for The World's Number One Bartender to do other than unscrew the top off a beer bottle or pop a cork. When Colin asks what I want, I always say, "You're the artist" and let him come up with something for me.

That's how I encountered the Serendipity.

"It's just a bit of champagne, a splash of Calvados, apple juice, some mint – crushed – and ice," said Colin as he swirled the mixture together and then gently placed an orchid into the glass before putting it down on the bar in front of me.

"Don't you think it's a bit dangerous, Colin," I asked, "to put flowers in the women's drinks?" I placed the orchid down next to the other orchid. "I mean, now every man in this bar knows exactly how many drinks I've had tonight."

Colin raised his eyebrows. "Ah," he said. "This is true." Then he raised only one eyebrow, leaned over the bar toward me and whispered, "But it's not really such a bad idea, helping a lady keep count with flowers, is it?"

The two women to my right (a mother-daughter team from Denmark, blond and beautiful as the Danish are known to be) probed Colin about his upcoming vacation. The mother already had three flowers – roses – sitting next to her drink plus there was still a rose in her nearly empty glass.

"Oh, it's not a vacation really," he said as he prepped drinks for them, pricking the base of thorn-less roses with a toothpick and putting one each on the side of their glasses. "I'm going to Normandy. Work-related."

Normandy is where Calvados comes from, brandy made from apples, a drink which I prefer to the cider that the region also makes.

I finished off my Serendipity with my nose in the air, sucking at the mint-spiced ice at the bottom of the glass (bad habit), looked at the two orchids on the bar in front of me and wisely ordered a glass of sparkling water to pace myself. Just then, to my left, three men walked up and stood closely together beside me in a spot that would actually fit only one man comfortably. I turned my back to them. I didn't want any friendly chatter, not tonight.

They were speaking not French, not German…but really, I couldn't tell what. Normally, I'm pretty good at guessing.

Colin glided down the bar toward these three men and asked them, in French, what they'd like to drink. Colin couldn't understand their really bad French, and despite the fact he speaks four languages, it was clear that whatever these three were muttering amongst themselves wasn't one of them. I turned slightly to watch.

Two of the men finally looked hopefully toward the one who apparently thought he could speak French. The poor man fumbled with French a bit more and then gave up. "Do you speak . . . English?" he asked Colin hopefully.

"Why, yes," Colin the British bartender smiled. "What may I bring you?"

The three men huddled quickly and then placed their orders through the one who spoke English. He spoke in rather complicated terms about each of the three drinks, each different. Colin confirmed the order, gave a slight nod, and breezed off.

When the men got their drinks, they held their glasses up to each other like the Three Musketeers would do with their swords and said, "*Skol!*"

I turned to face them directly. "Ah, so you're Swedish," I said warmly.

∞

Now, before you start imagining what these three Swedes looked like, picture this: Two are in their late thirties, early forties. One is short and plump and jolly. The second one is tall and very, very skinny with spiky hair. The third one is very young, very, very short (up to my nose) and is wearing a cheap black suit and a silly smile that he never took off. When I looked down at his feet, I saw that for whatever reason he was wearing bright white shoes that were really too big for him and way too white, a terribly ridiculous and stark contrast to his black suit.

And they were all brunettes. No brooding blonds in sight.

"Yes," smiled the tall one. He was the leader of the pack, the one who had tried to speak French earlier. "We're Swedish."

"Well," I held out my hand. "I'm Estonian." Then, knowing that only a Swede would understand what I was about to say, and understand the absolute truth of it, I added, "And my family forever thanks the People of Sweden for sending us those boats."

"You're welcome," laughed the plump jolly one.

I shook each of their hands, the tall one translated what I'd just said to the very short young one who brightened when he looked at me and shook my hand, smiling, nodding as if to say "you're welcome."

Long before IKEA and its Swedish ways invaded most of the world, my family – and tens of thousands of other Estonians -- already had a strong relationship with this country going back centuries. Sweden, like so many other countries, once occupied Estonia but unlike the Germans and the Russians who treated the People of the Land as farm animals, the Swedes were nice occupiers. In the 1700s, they built Estonia a university and even gave them a day of rest each week – Sunday, of course, which was never a religious day for Estonians. Thors Day (now known as Thursday) had been the religious day of the week but, no matter, Estonians appreciated their one day free of the back-breaking work they endured. Estonians still refer to this occupation as "The Good Old Swedish Times."

When the Soviets invaded Estonia in 1944 and my grand-mother and mother made their escape, it was the Swedes and the Finns who tried to help. At this point, in just this particular war alone, the 1944 invasion was the third invasion Estonia had suffered in four years. The first WWII invasion had been as a result of the Soviet-Nazi Molotov-Ribbentrop Pact that the So-viets signed on August 23, 1939. The deal was this: Russia could keep the Baltics and part of Poland if they stayed out of the war the Nazis were about to unleash in Europe. This agree-ment basically gave Hitler the green light to march into Poland a week later, on September 1. He believed he had placated the Great Bear into sitting on its thumbs while the Nazis marched their way through Europe and the Soviets marched their way into the Baltics in 1940. Thousands of Estonians, Lithuanians, and Latvians who had spoken out against previous Russian oc-cupations were quickly 'disappeared'.

In 1941, Hitler invaded the Baltics 1941 and kicked the So-viet occupiers out of the three small Baltic countries, replacing the occupiers with Germans.

Both of those occupations were brutal but there was an im-portant difference between the levels of cruelty that the Estonians endured. As one man explained to me, "The Ger-mans, they'd kill the man they were after. The Russians, they'd make the man watch as they killed his wife and children in front of him and then they wouldn't even have the decency to kill him, too. They wanted him to live with the memory of that."

Russians also sent tens of thousands of Estonians on cattle cars to Siberian concentration work camps. The conditions were so horrific, half of them are still buried there.

As World War II was coming to a close, the Soviets again laid claim to Baltic war booty. The Soviet army moved in at The Front and tens of thousands of Estonians, including a small part of my family, were able to escape only because of the Swedes. It was my grandfather who insisted his wife and daughter get out of the country in 1944. He knew what had happened in 1940 during the first Soviet invasion and knew they had to get out.

"Come with us," my grandmother had begged as my grandfather helped her and then his little girl, my mother, up onto the horse-drawn carriage that would take them to the sea. "Please."

My grandfather stayed to fight at The Front, to hold the Russians back for as long as possible.

The Swedish men who volunteered to man the boats to rescue Estonians knew that some of the Swedish sailors would never return. The Baltic Sea was full of Russian submarines and the Baltic sky full of Russian aircraft fully armed and scanning for boats filled with families too far from shore.

Many of these families and some of the Swedish crews ended their journey at the bottom of the sea, including a medical boat with the sick and injured. Few outside the Baltic States remember any of this, but my family would never forget.

∞

These memories flooded back to me there at The Ritz. What a wild juxtaposition of reality, I thought. Here at The Ritz in the most expensive part of Paris enjoying severely overpriced drinks, living well beyond comfortably, remembering that my grandfather, a man who had known privilege and wealth, had managed to survive the three invasions during the horrors of World War II and then spent years and years in the bitter cold Siberian concentration camps watching so many others die.

I quietly thanked my grandfather's spirit, took a sip of my drink, and then let out a deep sigh to push away my grief and sorrow for his noble, horrifically hard life.

"So what brings you to Paris?" I asked the three Swedes.

"We're here for the bartending competition in Normandy," said the tall one.

"Oh, you're bartenders? Well, you know that Colin, here, is the Number One Bartender in the World."

The three Swedish bartenders looked down the bar and beamed at Colin, smiling widely, gazing even. Olaf the plump and jolly one sighed, "We know . . ."

Of course they would know, I realized. They were all bartenders. It was their business to know these things.

It turned out that these Swedes had won National Awards (Swedish National Awards, that is) for their designer drinks and they were now on their way for the really big competition. The tall, skinny Swede was The Coach. Really. He called himself a coach and, in all seriousness, leaned toward me, pointed to the young one who was still wearing his silly smile and said, "He's a genius." The young one, he explained, had invented such a great drink that he was expected to win some sort of award in Normandy.

"But," said The Coach leaning toward me and whispering, "We don't expect to win first place. The French, they always win first place. But we're hoping for second. I don't tell him that, of course," and he nodded toward the young one. Turns out the young one was just 19 years old.

"Colin!" I called out over the delicate din in this tiny bar.

I introduced the three now very shy bartenders to Colin. "Normandy?" said Colin. "You're going to Normandy tomorrow? Well so am I. For the competition?" The Swedes nodded in unison. "I'm going as well," Colin continued. "I'll be one of the judges."

They continued talking about the competition, the various drinks they'd made from Colin's book of cocktail recipes and these Swedes never stopped glowing. I offered to take their picture together.

As we finished up with the photo shoot, Colin apologized and said he had to get back to work. "But gentlemen," he said as he took the time to properly shake each man's hand in a meaningful way, "I shall see you tomorrow in Normandy, and tomorrow night you shall dine at my table."

Now that was elegant.

∞

The three Swedish bartenders seemed to suddenly get taller and I'm sure that if I'd looked down at their feet, I would have seen they were floating a few inches above the carpet. While I merely walked, my new Swedish friends glided down the long and sparkling hallway and out of The Ritz. "Thank you, Maret," they each kept saying as they dreamed of Normandy and dining with the Number One Bartender in the World. What stories they would be able to bring back home. What serendipity!

"We would never have had the chance to speak with Colin like this if it weren't for you."

Yes you would have, I thought, but kept it to myself. Colin is a great bartender, and as a great bartender, he would have gotten the three of them talking and in no time figured out that these fellows were here for the competition in Normandy. He's not the World's Number One Bartender for nothing!

I did make one mistake that night, though. Even though I had to catch my flight home the next day (the day I met The Count at breakfast), I took 'the boys' as I'd begun to call them, to Johnny Depp's Man Ray Club, a club that cost far too much money for these struggling artists. That wasn't the mistake. I just casually paid their way in, turned to them and said, "Hey, consider this as an Estonian thank you to the Swedes for those boats, for the incredible Swedish courage and generosity back then that helped my family," and they completely understood and accepted the gesture. I paid for their expensive drinks even though they genuinely tried to object. That wasn't the mistake, either.

Together, instead of saying *Skol* we said, "To Sweden!" Over and over again.

That was fun and the beginning of the mistake.

They were, indeed, artists in their trade and they each ordered different cocktails and kept insisting that I try them and I kept complying.

"Try this, Maret," said The Coach. "It's the drink that first inspired me to try to make an even better drink. I'm still trying, mind you, but he's got the gift," and he again nodded toward the young smiling one whom we'd by now just openly called

The Genius and I never did get his name. This young man never said a word all night, not even in Swedish, except to utter the name of the drink that he was about to enter in the competition: Summertime. Now that was smart. Name a drink Summertime in Sweden and how many Swedes on a cold, dark night will pipe up at a bar and say, "Give me Summertime." While he didn't speak to me or anyone else except to utter "Summertime," he did very well in the universal language of offering his glass so that I could try a bit of this and a bit of that.

Each time I would take a sip or two of each Swede's drink and nod and smile and say, "Oh yes, very nice." Of course, we danced and laughed and hugged because by now, with so much alcohol racing through our veins, we were all in love with each other.

Then very suddenly I had to leave. I'd mixed sips of who knows how many cocktails and they were sloshing around in my belly and lighting up all the veins in my body, and not in a good way. My brain went wobbly all of a sudden and I was afraid that if I didn't leave, leave right then and find a pitcher of cold water and a cab, I would have to shimmy along the walls just to get out of the club and I wasn't sure I'd be able to find my way back to my hotel in that state.

The boys were disappointed but I explained they were a dangerous bunch and that I'd really had too much to drink in just too many small and inappropriately mixed quantities and that I had to get back to my hotel and, yes, I had to go back immediately. Right now.

As I lay in bed the next morning, feeling like the alcohol was burning in my bones, I gave myself another rule to live by: Never, never, never go drinking with three Swedish bartenders."

This is a good rule to remember.

∞

The post-script to this story is two-fold. One, the Genius did, indeed, win second place as his coach had predicted (France won first place at a contest in France – *quel surprise!*) and, two, Estonia, after finally freeing itself of generations of merciless Soviet occupation, was welcomed into the European Union.

It was 2004. For the Estonians and the other Baltic states, the Second World War had finally ended.

It meant I didn't have to sneak into France, after all. You see, my mother is considered by the Republic of Estonia to be an 'Estonian in Exile' and all of her future generations are considered 'Estonians in Exile', including me. All I had to do was fill out a one-page (one page!) form and prove I was my mother's child. I didn't even have to cough up a gas bill.

"Your passport will be ready in the new year," said Ellen, the woman from the Consulate of Estonia in Toronto.

"Oh, but I'll be living in Paris by then," I said. "Can you mail it to me?"

"No, we're not to mail passports. It's against Estonian law. But," she offered with a broad smile, "you can pick it up at our Embassy in Paris."

Now that was serendipity!

CHAPTER FOURTEEN

Husbands and So On

Soon after arriving in Paris, I had called the Estonian Embassy but there was still no passport for me, not yet. It didn't really matter. I had the legal right to live and even work in Europe now and here I was.

As for my French classes, all the students were about my children's ages. There were generally two reasons they were trying to learn French: one, they had fallen in love with someone in Paris or, two, for their job. I was the only one taking French because I had nothing much to do.

I woke each morning, had my croissant and *un petit café*, did yoga by the Seine and walked back to the apartment to do my French homework and a bit of tortured writing on my book. It was horrible. I didn't know how to write but I knew how to read and I could tell the story was lifeless. Sure, I was writing about dead feminists and the irony wasn't lost on me. Without fail, the moment I'd get stuck on the writing part or feel hopelessly demoralized, I'd jump back into the online ads, searching. One morning, I found this one which piqued my interest:

Do you ask a lot of questions?   Do you like to crit-
icize the media, haircuts, and bad personal ads?
Are you beautiful without make up? And enjoy living
in the moment? Single male looking for some-
thing..........great!   I like: holidays, The Sun, Louis
the 14th, fresh fruit, and strange places. If you grew
up in Europe, bonus points.

I wasn't raised in Europe but once my Estonian passport
came in, I would soon be a 'real' European.

I can't tell you if there was anything wrong with the fellow
who wrote the above profile. His picture looked O.K., and he
was tall enough and didn't smoke. No idea what he was like –
other than I could tell he was rude because he even didn't
bother to reply to my email, not even to say *desolée*. I would
even have preferred a *peut-être* to being completely ignored.

The world of Internet dating is a lesson in building inner
fortitude. I felt so hurt when a man ignored me online, wondering what I'd said in the email that might have offended him,
why he didn't like my profile or my photo. It was always worse
when the guy wrote back and forth with you, invited you to
coffee or something, and then pressed the 'radio silence' button. Wham. Done, and not even a "thank you, Ma'am."

Where were all the handsome, single French men?

I ached for an excuse to put on my date clothes and wear
some high heels.

∞

When I was forty-two, I had become single again. At that
point, I had somehow managed to build a good business in the

technology field, had zipped through three marriages and had gained sixty pounds. I would wake up every day, take the train to the city, come home and try not to think about it.

And eat.

Except for the lack of a man and my floppy belly, what did I have to complain about? I had a home. I now had two wonderful children. I had some money in the bank. I had good friends. What else did a woman need?

Sex.

Male tenderness.

Breath on skin.

There's a lot to be said for knowing where your regular supply of relief is coming from and, once you're no longer married, it's not so clear cut any more. By now, sneaking up onto nearly 200 pounds, I didn't have the confidence to flirt. I'd also had the wind knocked out of me from that third marriage.

Well, it's not quite true that I 'zipped' through three marriages. My second marriage, to a man named Mel, had lasted fifteen years. The loss of that marriage meant I'd lost a friend.

My best friend ever.

Yes, we loved each other, we were such good friends, but somehow, no matter how hard we had tried in our marriage, we brought out the worst in each other. I was intense, focused. He was laid back, forgetful. I became more demanding and openly hostile. As the years wore on, he became more surreptitiously hostile and seemed to love forgetting things, like our wedding anniversary for one. It doesn't take a skilled psychiatrist to know that when anger is buried, unspoken, it bubbles up, oozes out in ways that the secretly angry one doesn't have to own, pulling the life force out of a relationship. It was never clear to me why he was so passive-aggressive until the day I told him I had fallen in love with another man.

You see, Mel loved me, yes. I know he did. But he didn't romance me. Not once in our fifteen years of marriage did my husband say "You look beautiful" or ask me out on a date. In some ways, I can't blame him. To pull myself up and out of the nightmare that had been my life as a single teenaged mother, a time when North America had widespread restrictions against working women and especially working mothers – with laws and customs still insisting that a woman either sentence herself to the pink collar ghetto (i.e., be a secretary and perpetually broke) or get married – I had become, as one man noted with some amusement, "a force to be reckoned with." This 'force' was fueled by the terror of not being able to fulfill that promise to my baby. That unrelenting drive kept me focused on winning in the workplace against all odds. Back then, if you walked into the office where I worked and saw a woman who wasn't a secretary, she was the coffee lady or the cleaning lady ... or me, the only female consultant in the company at that time.

I'd taken one computer course and somehow actually managed to become a consultant (a 'junior consultant', but still...) and was working with executives of big banks. The odds had been wildly against me, a single mother with a high school degree.

Yes, I started out as a secretary but early on my brain had latched onto computers and I could tell there was money in that line of business which meant that if I worked like a mad dog, I really could buy my daughter that promised horse one day. Mel and I had met at the same time that I started working as a junior consultant and I had to make my mark in a world where everyone still kept expecting me to pour the coffee and take dictation. In those days, not so very long ago, women like me not only had to work hard for a living but we had to constantly fight ourselves out of boxes that people were trying to lock us up in. We also had to fight for legal changes left, right, and center.

It was exhausting!

To think of it now, it's almost unbelievable that back in the early 1980s, stalking and terrorizing a woman was still legal and 'domestic' violence wasn't taken seriously by the police. Family Law didn't recognize that a woman had a right to half of the family assets and as a result, divorced women were often sentenced to a life of poverty. The house was usually in the man's name, after all. She had to right to it. Women were expected to have a man bring home the bacon and if she didn't have one, that was her tough luck. In the 1970s, companies excluded women from being part of the pension plan because they'd be expected to find a husband before they ever got to the age of retirement.

Going to the office then, for a young woman in a suit, was hell. I was the only woman in a domain reserved for men and so I grew tough and sharp and fierce, able to negotiate deals and get the job done when none of the men in the office believed that a woman could or should be working except in jobs that couldn't possibly support her. Yes, it was exhilarating for me to be able to keep that promise to my little girl and give her a home and piano lessons and even a horse but working like that was also life-changing in ways that I hadn't expected.

With all that stress and nervous energy, always needing to be on edge, constantly having to defend my right to earn a decent living and be treated as an equal at the office (and anywhere else, for that matter), it's no wonder I gained a shield of sixty pounds.

I was still human, still a woman. I needed candlelight and someone to say he found me beautiful, even if it wasn't true. When I was finally able to put words to this and shyly mentioned it to Mel, he fobbed me off. "You're a beautiful woman. You know that."

But with sixty extra pounds and after two children and so many stretch marks that my tummy looked liked it was covered in Egyptian hieroglyphics, I didn't actually know that. No. I needed someone to whisper it to me, even if it wasn't really true.

∞

So when André, a French man from Québec (the *ooh la la la la la la!* French province in Canada), began to circle my life and tell me how my smile brightened a room and that he'd never seen such beautiful eyes and how he wanted me, oh how he wanted this sexy woman with the extra sixty sexy pounds, I fell for it. Not immediately, no. I had to figure things out. I was married. I'd been faithful. I'd made promises at the altar and I'm nothing if not a woman of my word.

Finally, I understood what had to be done. It was time to leave the marriage. When I told Mel, straight out, that I'd fallen in love with another man, he asked, "Why are you telling me this?"

"Because," I hesitated, "because, I don't want to be unfaithful. Because I love you and I promised that I would be faithful and if we don't get divorced, if I don't leave, I'm going to be unfaithful. I need to leave our marriage."

Mel's face went white.

"You mean," he thought about it a moment and then turned to me. "You mean, you haven't had an affair, ever?"

"No. Never."

He seemed more upset to learn that I'd been completely faithful all those years than the fact that I now wanted to leave the marriage for another man.

"Maret," he said slowly. "I thought . . . I thought you did. I thought you'd been having affairs."

So there it was. The bullet straight through the heart of the marriage. He had tried and convicted me, sentencing me to a marriage infected with an unspoken anger, never accusing me directly or even just asking whether there was someone else or not. Yes, I stayed out late at night and a few times even had to suddenly stay over in the city, wear the same clothes to work the next day. The answer why was very simple: I was working. Project delays, crises. I traveled to other cities and stayed in hotels and, yes, sat in hotel bars and spoke with mostly men because there were almost no women in business back then and certainly even fewer women who were traveling. Business travelers do that, sit around and talk to each other at airports and hotel bars. It's lonely traveling for work. While it's true that they also talk each other into going to bed together a bit too often, I didn't do that. I never did.

I was working, working hard, always afraid not to have enough money, hour upon hour, working my life – and my marriage – away.

By the time Mel was happily married to someone else, I was already finished with my third marriage, the one to André. Not a proud moment.

Two days after marrying André I realized I'd made a horrible mistake. Caught in yet another lie, he yelled at me, called me names, and I kept weeping, "But, I'm your bride. Your bride." Our out of town guests were still visiting and I had to keep trying to cool my burning eyes and refresh my makeup when we went to have lunch with friends and family.

"Tired, eh?" asked someone who saw my bloodshot eyes. "Yes," I tried to smile. Tired. Very tired. Tired of being a foolish woman and believing a man would love me the way I needed to be loved. Kindly. Fully. Sensually. Romantically. Deliciously. For who I am.

I suppose I'd married André because I needed to justify why I'd left Mel. I'd left Mel just because a French Canadian man called me beautiful and I fell for it. I could tell myself and anyone else who would listen that the end of my marriage to Mel was all about the power of romantic love with André. I didn't just give up with Mel, I just couldn't resist a French man. No, I wanted the end of my marriage to Mel to have 'been right' and it could only have been the completely right thing if André and I were 'meant to be', I convinced myself. We were 'right' together. I even briefly referred to us as soul mates. Who can say no to a soul mate?

Ha. Had I been wiser and less worried about the story I was telling myself, I would have been able to understand the reason André could never tell me why he loved me. Why did I keep asking, he wanted to know. He married me, after all. That's what I wanted, wasn't it?

Obviously something inside me, some small little niggle, knew. What I suspected but couldn't, wouldn't, put words to was that he didn't actually love me. He loved how I made him feel. He ignored everything I needed to feel safe inside love.

For whatever reason we had a brilliant amount of chemistry between us and it remained, despite the sorrowful marriage, right
up until the day I snapped out of it.

I don't read romance novels. I'm not a woman with crazy,
unrealistic dreams. It's just that I . . . I . . . it didn't matter. We
got married, he began to say even more awful things and then I
sobbed every day for seven weeks and, seven weeks to the day
that we'd married, I woke up and decided, "That's it!"

Yes, embarrassingly, I was now about to beat my own record of a very brief marriage – no longer would I feel ashamed
and have to admit to a six-month teenaged marriage. No, I
thought as I sobbed on the beach while we were on vacation
with our younger children (from our previous marriages), I'd
have to admit that I'd been married for only seven weeks. And
really, I should have left after two days. I knew on the second
day after the wedding that our marriage was doomed but spent
the next seven weeks arguing with myself about what had to be
done.

So, really, it was a two-day marriage. I rarely ever say that
out loud.

It was my own stupid fault. He had been unfaithful to me
even before we were married and refused to say he was sorry
for putting a knife through my soul and I married him anyway.

Why do women, intelligent women, do that?

Well, for sex and for something else. If you look at the situation in which girls were raised not so long ago (and still are,
in some cases in the West and certainly almost everywhere
else), we were treated differently than our brothers. I think
women constantly seek tender acceptance in the arms of a man
because we feel it will somehow validate us, confirm our wor-
thiness. Although there are some people in these so-called

post-feminist days that can't seem to accept the truth, the fact is we have all been born into a world and into homes that openly value males more than females. Although the West has thankfully worked hard to try to free itself of this, the roots of sexism – like racism – are deep and tangled up in so many facets of life that it will take us more than a couple of decades to undo.

Unlike racism, where the whole family shares the same skin tone and do their best to resist society's racist views of them[iv], sexism penetrates family values and the psyches of little girls and boys in an insidious way right in the home, right where you are supposed to feel safe and loved and valued. In my progressive family, for example, where my brothers also had to do the dishes and the girls also had to mow the lawn way back in the 1970s, all of the family's excess cash and absolutely every weekend were devoted to the boys' hockey games (very Canadian). There was no money or time left over for what the girls wanted to do, like take skating lessons or ride horses or do something other than sit around in smelly cold rinks and watch their brothers play hockey.

This kind of thing sends an unspoken message, a very loud and clear one. Girls grow up understanding that boys have more value – both culturally and in the home – and when this gets all mixed up with genuine parental love, it does things to you, makes you ache to find somebody, somewhere, to love the fact that you're who you are, a girl.

So it's not so strange that so many women focus on finding love from a man.

∞

When I married André, I ached for the warmth of his accepting arms, curled up together in the stillness of the night, and he gave me that. I was still sixty pounds overweight and couldn't imagine anybody else would want me. So that was probably another reason I pushed forward into that marriage.

But seven weeks to the day was absolutely it for me. I'd made my decision. Done. Our blended family included our children so I'd be affecting all of us, not just two people, by stepping out of this marriage. All of our children – young and older – were at our wedding and seemed to be happy for us. But, no. I couldn't do it. I had to get out. On that beach vacation with our two youngest children (from separate marriages), I cried constantly, always hiding my face in the towel when the children were around and if they questioned me, I'd complain about sand in my eyes or make up a story about cheap mascara. When we got back from vacation, I'd tell him, I had decided. Yes, I would tell him then.

By now, we'd been married for seven weeks and it was six weeks and five days too long. Just had to wait one more day, I told myself. We'd be home the next day.

When we did get home, there were 26 voice mails for us. They all seemed to be for him, one after another person speaking in rapid-fire French, breathless, frightened. I handed the phone over to my new husband and said, "Someone wants to speak with you pretty badly." Then I began walking up the stairs to go and have a bath.

That's when I heard the wail. A man screaming out, the man I loved and had married was screaming out from somewhere so primal I'd never even heard a human sound like that before.

"What?" I yelled back and ran down the stairs. "What's happened?"

André, phone still in hand, looked at me wild-eyed and sobbed,

"My daughter is dead. My daughter! My daughter is dead!"

Your daughter is dead. He had heard this from a voice mail.

His only daughter, a feisty young woman who had graduated from university and was living on her own, had taken a dive into the wrong end of a pool. Snapped her neck. It had happened the day before, on the very day I'd decided to leave her father, but we were on vacation and no one had been able to reach us to tell us directly.

We loaded up the car and as we took the five-hour drive to where she had once lived and was now about to be buried, I sat there next to my husband listening to him babble, for it was only babbling and sobbing he was able to do. "Maret," I thought, "You're a lot of things. But you're not a cruel woman. And it would be cruel to leave him right now. Nothing's going to change. You know that. But you're giving this man two years. Two years. Then you can leave."

I stayed for three. I loved him, which is why I stayed. Did I love all of him? No, I didn't love his nasty streak and I didn't love his inability to tell the truth when it suited him to lie.

But I loved the way he made people laugh, I loved the way he cared about children, I loved his way of being politically engaged, I loved the way he held me in the night when I needed comfort. I loved the man I was married to, but then the hopeless isolation of living inside a marriage like ours grew more terrifyingly lonely than the thought of living the rest of my life completely alone.

CHAPTER FIFTEEN

Farewell to Fat and All That

After that third marriage, I remember lying in bed staring at the ceiling and saying to myself, "Maret, you're fat. And in two years, you're going to be two years older. Forty-four. There's nothing you can do about that. But you can make a decision today. You can be forty-four and fatter." That horrified me. "Or you can be forty-four and the same weight." Same horror. "Or you can be forty-four and thinner. Which will it be?"

That's the moment I gave myself a two-year goal and set out a plan and began to walk for an hour every day and drink gallons of water and meticulously watch what I ate. Sometimes, I wasn't really so meticulous and I'd eat too much and gain a couple of pounds. But, darn it, I had made a decision that morning – a decision, not a hope – when I had glumly stared up at the ceiling from my bed. It had been a decision, a promise to myself, a promise to a future that I wanted to live *slenderly!* With that, I'd forgive myself and get on track again.

With my target of being 'forty-four and thinner', I would lose those newly found pounds and then a few more. Well along on my month-by-month trudge towards 'forty-four and thinner' (I'd already lost 30 pounds by then and was pretty proud of myself), my daughters invited themselves for dinner. Of course, they'd bring the dinner. It had always been my job to work hard and earn money and it had been my second husband's job to cook and this delicious skill, happily for me, he'd passed along to the girls. For dinners, I was only tasked with finding the right bottle of wine or opening a bottle of champagne. That, I could do.

I took a bottle of champagne from the fridge and put it in my silver champagne bucket, tarnished not from neglect but because I liked it that way. Champagne had become a symbol to me, confirmation that you can live your life any way you'd like to live it. The times when I'd have to hold up a glass of gingerale in a toast and say, "One day, this will be champagne!" were over, yes, but it didn't mean that there weren't other struggles lurking there in life. This life of ours, we have to figure it out mostly on our own and what better way to figure it out than with champagne? This old, tarnished champagne bucket had been one of two gifts I'd kept from my first nightmarishly short little marriage. The other gift was Kaia, my eldest daughter.

Anneli was the gift from my second marriage. And my third marriage? What? Oh, yes, from my third marriage I got a poodle. I got a poodle and a great life lesson. Don't even listen to what a man says before marrying him. Read his soul.

I reached down to give little Pidou the Poodle a pat on the head. Pidou looked up, hoping for a scratch behind the ear.

It had become a family custom to always keep a bottle of champagne in the fridge for emergency celebration purposes. The girls were coming over tonight. That was reason enough to celebrate.

I heard Kaia's car pull up and two doors slam shut. "Hi, Mom!" They whisked their casseroles or whatever they had in those pots right past me and Pidou, straight into the kitchen.

"Hi, Pidou," said Kaia in acknowledgement.

"Yeah, hi Ugly," said Anneli. Anneli was still in high school but staying at her dad's that week.

I walked the icy bucket of champagne out to the porch wondering what these two were up to while my girls got the glasses. As the cork pressed against my hand, threatening to pop open, I turned to my daughters and said, "Quick! Make a wish!" I had long ago told them, and anyone else who cared to know, that a bottle of champagne holds enough wishes for everyone. Both girls closed their eyes. I wonder what they're wishing, I thought. I really do. My wish is always the same. As the cork popped out, I timed my wish just right: May my daughters be well loved by at least one good man.

Each, of course.

I poured champagne into the glasses and asked, "Do we have an emergency celebration tonight?" We all knew the routine. The first toast always had to be a toast to something wonderful . . . or to the hoped-for silver lining in an otherwise bad situation . . . but to something. It was family custom.

∞

Years earlier, when Kaia had managed to screw up the courage to tell me that she'd quit school, dumped her boyfriend and was running off to Mexico for three months with a pastry chef, I had managed to open a bottle of champagne and somehow find something to celebrate.

"Here's to new beginnings," I'd said to Kaia back then.

Kaia looked at me, ready to cry. Grateful, so grateful she was that I had not confronted her choices, judging her, scolding her. It was no longer my job to do that. She was a woman now. Both of us understood – as we took that first sip to new beginnings – that this was the first time I was honoring her, woman to woman. All a mother wants is for her daughter to be happy and how does any mother know, really know, whether or not her girl will be happy roaming through Mexico with a pastry chef? The stories of some of the happiest, most accomplished people I know didn't go in a straight line. As one now prominent lawyer said to me after she told me how she'd taken all the 'wrong' turns in life – dropped out of school, married the wrong man, took to the bottle – "I took the scenic route."

That night back then, when Kaia and I toasted to her "new beginnings", I thought, "Geesh, my daughter's literally taking the scenic route."

∞

But tonight, what? What did my girls want? Yes, I was glad that my daughters had made me dinner and, yes, I was glad we were sharing champagne and spending time together. But they were up to something, weren't they?

I turned to Anneli. "It was you two who decided you absolutely had to have dinner with me tonight. So you make the toast. What's so good about today?"

"I think . . ." Anneli looked at her sister, then hesitated. "Um . . ."

Kaia leaned forward a bit awkwardly and held her glass up. "To new beginnings."

"New beginnings? Did someone quit school?"

"No, Mom," said Anneli. "It's just that . . ." Again, she looked over to her sister.

"Mom," said Kaia. Then paused. "Well . . ." She looked at Anneli.

"What?" I asked looking at one daughter then the other. Pregnant? Was one of them pregnant?

"It's just that, well. . ." Kaia sat up straight. "We've come to a decision."

"A decision?"

Anneli nodded.

"We've decided that it's time for you to start dating."

Anneli nodded again.

Kaia seemed to be looking for words. "It's not right," said Kaia. "You've been divorced now for over a year and you haven't gone on one date. Not even one. You have to get out more."

"I go out," I said defensively.

"Where?" asked Anneli.

"Work, you know. I'm out there. Men see me. And I'm tired by the end of the week with all that commuting and after what I went though with He Who Shall Not Be Named, I like being home alone on Saturday night. With Pidou."

"You do?" asked Anneli.

"That's not the point, Mom. The point is you're still young . . ."

"Right," said Anneli, though as a teenager looking at a mother in her 40s, she didn't seem convinced.

"And you should get out, go dancing. Have a life."

"Well," I said. "I would go on a date but no one ever asks me."

Kaia put her glass of champagne on the table and adjusted her seat cushion. She then put both hands on the table as if she didn't know what to do with them. "Mom," said Kaia softly. "You don't give a man a chance. No way in, no way for him to ask. You're a woman who projects that she needs nothing. I mean, you don't show a point of vulnerability. A man needs that. He needs to see it."

"If a man can't take me as I am, I don't want him."

"It's not that. You're wonderful. We know that. You're our mom." Again, Anneli nodded, this time with a bit more conviction. "Inside, you're soft and all squishy. We know that. We do. But how's a man going to know what to do if you don't, I don't know, lighten up or something?"

I gulped back my glass of champagne as if it were a shot of scotch and then poured myself another.

Both girls waited.

"OK, girls. OK."

∞

They'd been talking about me behind my back. Sure, moms expect that. But we don't expect our daughters to talk about us behind our backs like this, trying to help their poor old mother 'get a life', as they'd say on a less helpful day.

They were right, of course. It wasn't just that I'd been divorced for well over a year. They had seen me suffer through that third marriage, suffer in a way that no one but my own children had seen up close, and then I remained curled up at home with my poodle each and every weekend, afraid. Afraid to go out on a date with a man, afraid to even look a man in the eye in case he asked me out for what, a cup of coffee even.

Look what a mess I'd made of my life – three husbands by the time I was forty-two. The horrible thing is, that never goes away. Once you have an ex-husband, he's an ex-husband for life. I have three ex-husbands and there isn't a pill I can take to make this fact ever go away. I am a woman with three ex-husbands and always will be.

Imagine how inspiring that sounds to a potential suitor.

One of the unthinking things that people do after you've managed to screw up a third marriage is ask: Do you ever want to get married again? I used to say, "Oh, no. I couldn't bear to fill out the passport application" and of course they'd ask why and I'd explain, "Because there's only room to note three marriages and I really don't want to have to write 'see next page'."

That wasn't the truth, of course. The truth was that I wanted to be married. Why else would I keep getting married over and over again? Clearly, I'm the marrying kind and I wanted to be married right just once in my life. Just once. Just right. But I was no longer sure it could happen.

Not for me.

Mothers owe their children happiness, their own included. Mothers as martyrs just raise more martyrs and the world has enough of those. No, I've always felt I owed my children the vision of what it is like to be an adult embracing life, a woman who knows how to "Live! Live! Live!" That was one of the driving forces that helped me start to lose all that weight. The thought that kept me from eating all those peanut butter and jelly sandwiches (my terrible weakness) was this: I wanted my girls to know that a woman remains womanly and sensual and fully alive until, well, until the day she dies. Giving my girls a fat old mom who'd given up on her womanhood was wrong, just plain wrong. Aren't we supposed to be examples to our children? But I realized that night as I sat with them sipping champagne that I'd given them a not-so-fat older woman who had, in a way, not just given up on her womanhood, but on life.

My heart had been pummeled then shredded into little tiny pieces and there wasn't a spot left that hadn't been bruised, painful to the touch. I let it happen, I know, but the problem was that at this point I didn't know how to not let it happen again. It became easy, comfy even, to let the weeks go by, one by one and then a whole year of them.

I looked at my daughters sipping on their champagne and felt like a fraud. Long before I could actually afford champagne, I had started collecting cheap champagne glasses I'd find at garage sales or in secondhand shops, started collecting these flutes and imagining they held my hopes for my future, yet here I was with lots of champagne glasses and plenty of champagne in the house, feeling hopeless. I had taught my girls to face life head-on and celebrate even the sorrows it throws our way because in those dark moments there is always something to build upon, something to learn from, a way to make our lives even just a little bit better.

Kaia had come back from that whacky trip through Mexico without the pastry chef at her side – she'd left him there – and she got herself focused. She went back to school, a different one, and found her niche in the world. She was happy with herself now. She had made her own new beginning.

As for me, my transition from the shock of my third marriage was simply to curdle into a sour and nervous woman. Sure, I wanted a man in my bed but not in my heart. At this stage, it didn't really matter either way – I had neither a man in my bed nor a man in my heart and I didn't know how to find one.

Something had to change.

∞

"Just go online," said a woman at the office.

The Internet.

What a delightfully easy way to get a date, even if one has to go through dozens of cups of coffee on the way to find the right match.

First, I studied the profiles, including those of 'the competition' – other women's profiles in my age range. Then I thought about where on this particular site I wanted to be: Just Dating, Relationship or 'Intimate Encounters'. That last one was a bit euphemistic. The gay site on this same service said bluntly, 'Sex'.

I was now a middle-aged mom who hadn't dated in over twenty years. How does a mom with two grown daughters date, I wondered. How does a middle-aged mom get dressed for a date? At that time, I didn't feel ready for a full-blown relationship and couldn't imagine picking a man off of a computer screen to get 'intimate' with and so the 'just dating' option seemed like the right fit for me.

On the emotional side of things after all that heartache I'd manage to steer my life right into, I needed to go slow. You'd think men would have liked that about me, the fact that I didn't want to jump right into a relationship but was, instead, rather hungry for sex. No, the fact is that some people – men and women alike – are so desperately lonely that they want to bond with anyone who sort of seems reasonable. I knew one apparently pleasant man at a client site whose wife of twenty-five years had left him and within a year he had lost thirty-five pounds, became more outgoing and was living with a woman he'd met at church. "How wonderful to be in love again," I congratulated.

"Oh, I'm not in love," he said glumly. "It just beats the alternative."

"What alternative?"

"Living alone."

"Does she know that?" I had to ask.

"Know what?"

"That you don't love her?"

He shrugged.

I was lonely, yes, but not so lonely that I would just shove a guy into my home and make him 'play house' with me so that I had someone to look at in the morning at while eating my Cheerios.

∞

Living there in Paris and experiencing those early days of social isolation, I thought back to the many coffee and dinner dates I'd managed to land from the Internet back home. One good thing about having done a lot of online dating back in Canada was that I no longer hyperventilated before meeting a fellow for coffee. On my very first date after my daughters had had that chat with me, I'd gotten myself so worked up that I couldn't breathe properly. Kaia kept saying, "You'll be fine, Mom, you'll be fine."

"No, no," I said, softly hitting my hand against my chest (and my heart, although that part was subconscious), "I can't breathe. I can't breathe. I think I need to call the guy and cancel."

Kaia gave me a paper bag to blow into and I stood there, breathing in and out of that stupid paper bag. Feeling so embarrassed, I vowed to figure out what was terrifying me so I went up to the bathroom – with the paper bag still on my face – closed the door, put the toilet lid down and sat there on the toilet. "What the hell is going on, Maret?" I demanded of myself.

I was afraid.

Afraid of what? I couldn't put words to it, exactly. But I was very good at berating myself. There I sat, figuratively wagging a finger back at myself, saying, "What do you know about love? Look what a mess you've made of your life. What the hell do you know about love?"

"It's only a coffee for God's sake!" I thought. "It's just coffee."

I did manage to show up for the coffee date and appear normal even though I knew quite well that I'd slipped off the deep end earlier that day and my daughter had witnessed it. Oh well, who else but family has the fun of seeing you at your worst?

My dates back in North America were interesting but no one held my attention for very long because I had my sights set on Paris. That city was waiting for me to join her even for just a while. Nothing was going to prevent me from living there, becoming a *Parisienne*. Hemingway's love for Paris had transferred to my own heart long ago and I wanted to focus on that, on getting to Paris, on embracing the dreams that had gotten me through so many difficult nights all on my own with a crying baby who deserved more from life than I was able to give her at the time.

Both daughters were now doing very well and soon, Anneli would be at college. It was time. My time.

Some plans had to be adjusted at the last minute. I'd always planned to bring along my little poodle, Pidou, but it turned out she suddenly developed a severe allergy to rabies shots and this meant I couldn't take her to another country. A family friend agreed to look after her then went and spoiled her rotten and asked to keep her forever. I reluctantly agreed that she could keep my little Pidou because in every photo my friend sent of the two of them together, I swear that poodle was smiling.

CHAPTER SIXTEEN

When Two Spirits Meet

I'm sure I'm not going to get many replies but I'm only looking for one genuine person. There must be more to life than the spinning hamster wheel. Let's make an effort and go out to enjoy London and Paris and each other. Tall professional chap, mature, clean-shaven, intelligent seeks soul mate if that's possible. Arts and culture appreciated.

Sounds nice, doesn't it?

From what I could tell, it was probably a British fellow living in Paris who'd written it. I have nothing against British fellows, especially if they live in Paris, and I particularly like 'mature, clean shaven, intelligent' men if they aren't too, too 'mature'. I especially like men who like the arts and culture.

What was my problem with this profile? Why did I say *desolée* to the fellow?

What would you say if you saw that his byline was this:

Keen to date a lady with long nipples.

Then there was this fellow:

I am a man seeking a woman who loves to wear white socks, thin, perhaps knee-highs.

I want to have an elaborate play with her feet in white socks. I enjoy their scent and taste. Talk on the phone and I will lay on the floor massaging, kissing and sucking your toes. If you like, give you a massage all over.

No nudity required, NO INTERCOURSE (unless agreed upon later).

Alas! I don't wear thin white socks.

Waking up and checking my online dating in-basket in Paris had stopped being fun.

∞

Then one morning I woke to discover an elegantly written, very pleasant email from quite possibly a very pleasant man named Norbert (it was written in sophisticated French, too complicated for the online translator so I couldn't make much sense of it but I knew enough French to tell it was very well-written).

Norbert. In French, it's pronounced *Nor-bare* but is that a name you can call out in the middle of an orgasm? "Oh Norbert! Norbert!!!!" Not really. But I am certainly not shallow enough to flip off a *Desolée* email just because his name would sound funny during sex. Besides, that would be getting out ahead of the game. There were enough things to slog through on the dating front before worrying about whether I could say his name out loud at a delicate moment.

A friend of mine once told me that, to avoid calling out the wrong name during sex, all you had to do was shout, "Oh Baby!" That did the trick for her, she said.

"Really?" I asked. "Why not just make it a habit of remembering who you're in bed with?"

And who could forget the name Norbert?

As for his photo, well, to say he wasn't particularly handsome is being extremely polite, so I'll leave it at that. He was tall and this is unusual for France unless you're a German living here. Norbert said he was 6' 3" and his photo showed that he had a *mélange* of blond and grey hair, a big funny nose and his head seemed too narrow and tiny for that big body of his. Maybe it's just a bad photo, I thought.

Before reading his profile, I read his by-line, that one-liner at the top of the age / weight / location / marriage status summary, and when I read it, something inside me softened. My own by-line was 'The shortest distance between two people is laughter' – a very slight variation on something I once heard Victor Borge say on TV.

Norbert's byline was: 'When two spirits meet'.

That was enough for me to say "yes" even without being able to read his profile which as I said was written in complex, highly sophisticated French. I didn't really understand it, all those verb tenses.

Later that night we began a pleasant online dialogue. I asked him to write in what I called 'baby French', asked him to use only simple verb tenses like past, present, future. Norbert complied as best he could, said he was a composer and writer (oh, aren't we all writers and artists here in Paris, I thought, but later learned it was true). At present, he was out of town on a bit of a vacation and would be back the following week. He enjoyed spending time in Luxembourg Gardens, he said. Would I like to join him there later next week?

Bien sûr [certainly!] I wrote quite happily.

∞

To try to fight the croissant calories I enjoyed most mornings, I had taken to walking across Paris and then through Luxembourg Gardens each and every weekday on my way to and from French classes. Sure, I thought, it would be great to meet Norbert in Luxembourg Gardens on my way to class. How perfect was that?

Life was getting easier on me it seemed, especially because the next morning the apartment phone rang. Ever since I'd said *peut-être* to the Count, the apartment phone never rang, not even once. On very rare occasions, my European cell phone rang but that was usually just to arrange for drinks with young people from the French school. Friends back home never, ever called me. They just wrote emails.

People in North America seem to imagine that the Atlantic is a huge brick wall, unbreachable, telephone-wise. What would it cost? Four, five dollars? They never called. I even gave my daughters special calling cards which would cost a penny a minute but for whatever reason, calling overseas was not part of their routine even though when I lived back home, they called me all the time.

"Did I wake you up?"

"No, no," I said, not recognizing the voice. "I've been awake since 5:30."

"Oh, right, you like to be the early bird, catching worms and all that."

An accent. In Paris, that's to be expected, but this voice had a New Yorkish tinge to it.

"Robert?" I asked. "Is this Robert?"

"Yes." He seemed pleased that I recognized his voice.

"How are you liking New York?" I asked.

"I'm in Paris."

"What? The transfer fell through?"

"No, I'm on a stop-over on my way back to New York. From India. Had some paperwork here and thought I'd over-night it. Thought maybe we could get together or something."

"Sure, when?"

"How about now?" he asked boldly.

That was his style. And I liked that. I also liked the idea that on this sunny morning I could push aside my French home-work and frolic with a very fit, very firm, very fine young man.

Yes, I did have a few short skirts with me and I put one on and shoved a half bottle of champagne in the fridge. Why not? *Pourquoi pas*! And thank you very much!

It was cold outside on this wintry day and yet the sun shone brightly through the courtyard in through my bedroom window and splashed onto the bed, a bed that was presently neatly made and tidy but soon would look all tangled up and messy, in a happy way.

"Here's to a pleasant surprise," I said to Robert as we made a toast.

"Only pleasant?" he teased as he looked down toward the bulge in his pants. That's what I like about young men, always at the ready.

"Here's to a *mighty, big* and pleasant surprise," I laughed.

So all morning it was like that, mighty and big and pleasant. As for the pleasant surprise, it was that he couldn't seem to get enough.

"This doesn't usually happen," he said.

"Pardon?"

"Twice. I usually can't do it twice. In a row like that."

"Well, you know what they say," I laughed as I poured the rest of the champagne. "If it happens once, it's a miracle. If it happens twice, get ready for the third time."

"No," he said, a bit shocked. "I don't have the energy. Just don't."

I laughed.

"Don't worry, you're safe," I said and patted him on the cheek like a little boy. See? That's what I mean. If Robert stayed around too long, I'd get all motherly on him.

"I have to leave for class soon," I said as I got up to get ready. "It's all your fault that I didn't do my homework. What will I tell the teacher?"

"The truth," said Robert. "Why not? This is Paris."

"I'm glad I emailed you my telephone number."

"Yeah, good thing," said Robert. "I wasn't sure all the paperwork would be ready in time so I didn't call earlier but, *voilà*, everything was sorted out yesterday and my flight back to New York is scheduled for tonight and my bags are packed and I thought, '*Pourquoi pas?*'

∞

Pourquoi pas usually goes along with a little French shrug. It's a particular type of shrug that goes with *pourquoi pas*, one that tries to mask excitement or surrender, giving in. I once caught myself saying that (only inside my head, thank God) to a 92-year-old man.

It was a Sunday and sunny that day near the *Champs-Élysées*. Children were playing in a park full of chestnut trees that were in their last stages of blooming, some of the petals of their flowers already fallen. A few old women and one old man and I were sitting in the shade on various park benches, each of us alone. The old man over there in his hat and his Sunday suit and tie, wearing his good shoes, all buffed and shiny, was feeding the birds and seemed very lonely on that park bench. I looked away for a moment and he was suddenly sitting at the edge of my bench. He started talking brightly and shifted closer and closer until he was pressed up against me and holding both my hands in his two big hands. He had a tight grip, too.

It all happened so fast and while I wanted to pull my hands away, I knew he was harmless and this simple act of kindness – of letting this old man hold my hands in his – was really not such a hardship for me. As a child, I used to volunteer at seniors' homes and I know how hard it is for old people not to be touched and I thought that allowing this little bit of human comfort for a funny old man wearing a suit and a hat and holding my hands on a park bench in Paris was harmless enough.

"Do you tango?" asked the old man.

"No, I don't."

"I could teach you the tango," he offered hopefully.

"No, thank you."

"You're such a beautiful woman," he said (as all French men say to all women the first chance they get) and then, peering down at my bit of cleavage, he added, "And so young, too."

I tried not to laugh.

"Had I known that I would meet such a beautiful woman from Canada, I would have learned English. Before the War, everyone learned German, not English." He couldn't seem to stop talking, so hungry was he for contact. "My wife died two years ago," he continued, "but she was very sick that last year and I haven't had sex for three years. We always had sex. Always. It's been hard for me these past three years," he said.

I understood how he felt, but not really why he was telling me all this. I switched the subject and we made some small talk but then he got back to the subject of me, a woman sitting on a park bench in Paris. Yes, I had been married before. No, I'm not married now. I have two children, both girls. Yes, I'm alone in Paris. He cut to the chase, took my hands to his chest and pleaded, "Will you be my mistress?"

It was an almost cartoon-like moment, a moment where you can only laugh out loud but I didn't laugh because it wouldn't have been right to laugh at a man like this. He was desperately lonely and there's nothing, absolutely nothing, funny about that.

"*Desolée*," I replied. "I can't do that."

"Why not?" He seemed surprised.

"Because . . . I don't even know your name."

"It's Maurice," he said as if now my answer would have to be *bien sûr*.

I shook my head. "There are other women here," I said, looking toward the old ladies sitting on the park benches.

"I tried," he said dismissively, waving a hand their way. "They don't want sex."

"Then why not a prostitute?"

"Oh," said Maurice, visibly insulted. He put one hand to his heart while keeping a tight hold on my two hands with the other one. He must have once been a farmer or something, his hands were big and strong. He took a big breath and sighed out, "That's not romantic! Not at all!"

That's right, Maurice, I thought. Prostitution is awful, a disgrace to any society that claims it honors human rights. When someone like me tries to speak up against it, we're silenced with the tiresome statement "prostitution is the oldest profession in the world." Hah.

Prostitution isn't the oldest profession in the world.

Motherhood is.

In the 18th and 19th centuries, a third of the prostitutes in Paris (and 50% in London) were former maids.[v] Typically, a maid would "get herself" pregnant (very often by the master of the house or by one of his sons), get fired (generally by the lady of the house) and then was completely unable to earn a living any other way than prostitution. In France back then, it was illegal for an unmarried woman to name the father of the child – convenient, eh?

Those tiresome claims that since prostitution's been around forever, we've just got to accept it, legalize it, get some taxes off the backs (or, more accurately, the mouths) of mostly very young women fresh out of childhood just exposes an ugly truth about a culture that still has not embraced women's equality. Even now, in the 21st century, slavery still exists and that's been around for thousands of years, should we accept that, too? Robbers have been robbing for quite a while, should we accept that? War has been a relentless part of human history, should we cheer it on? Anybody who claims that a person should have a "right" to sell their mouths and other orifices to men needs to ask themselves this: Do they want this "right" extended to their daughter? Their mother? Their son?

Anyway, no matter which way you slice it, prostitution is not a victimless crime. It's just that the victims – the women, both the prostitute and the woman at home whose lover is betraying her – are almost always silent in their suffering.[vi vii]

So Maurice was spot on when he looked disgusted at my suggestion – a suggestion I didn't support at all, obviously. I was just trying to figure out a way to make Maurice let go of my hands.

Maurice was genuine in his aching search for sex and I felt for him. Men become ungendered at an older age than we women but it hurts just the same.

"I have a large apartment in the 18th *arrondissement*," he said hopefully, "and a country house. A nice one." He waited for me to say "Okey dokey, then" but I didn't. "And I won't live much longer, you know that."

His pleading was making me sad, so deep and painful was his loneliness, his longing. As his big hands held tight to mine – for a moment, just for a moment – I thought, *Pourquoi pas*?

No!

I stood up and gently said *Desolée* and that I was late for a lunch and I was really sorry and hoped he'd find someone soon, someone special.

When Maurice stood up to say goodbye, I saw that he came only up to my shoulders. His strong hands had made him feel so much taller to me. He took one hand and kissed the back of it gently. "I am in this park every Sunday all summer, except when I'm at my country home in August," he said. "Please consider it."

Of course, I never once considered it and don't know where the heck that *pourquoi pas* had come from inside me.

It's much easier to say *pourqoi pas* – and totally mean it – to a younger man, as I'd told Robert that first night we met.

As I walked over the bridge across the Seine on my way to French class, I thought about Robert, about his young skin and his bright eyes and the rock-hard loveliness of his manhood, and hoped that the next time we saw each other it would only be for a drink because at last, at last, I would be involved with someone or maybe even completely in love -- and so would he.

We both knew it would never be with each other.

∞

At French class that afternoon, the Nicaraguan-Italian kept trying to get my attention. I didn't know her name because the teacher, Pascal, only called us by our nationalities. When Pascal (called Pascal-the-Rascal because he was always flirting with the young female students) had asked me my nationality, I'd said, "Canadian."

"No," he said. "What are you really."

"*Canadienne*?" I said again.

"No," he insisted. "Everyone in Canada is from somewhere else except the Indians. What are you, really?"

"*Je suise Estonienne*," I said and for the first time in my life, understood how incredibly true that was. All these years, I've carried my ancestors in my bones, in the marrow of my soul. Their history is my history. My future is their future. Our job on this earth is to honor our ancestors by living as best we can with at least a drop of gratitude in our hearts. We owe that to them.

The Nicaraguan-Italian, whose name I learned was Istmania because until that day I only knew her as "*L'italienne*", was a beautiful woman in her early thirties, her hair down to her waist and her eyes always shining, her smile very white. She and The Bulgarian, a very pleasant but lost-looking woman in her late 20s, came over to me after class.

"Something's happened," said Istmania. The Bulgarian smiled. She didn't know any English.

"What happened?"

"To you. Something's different."

Istmania turned to The Bulgarian and said to her in French, "She looks different today, no?"

I looked down at my clothes. No, I'd worn this outfit before and remembered that The Bulgarian had complimented me on my fabulous black boots with the big buckles up the side.

In honor of Robert, today I was wearing a short skirt, but I'd worn this very same short skirt with these buckle up boots before.

"Nothing's different," I insisted.

"Your face, something. Something happened to you today."

I laughed. Yes, something had happened.

So I confessed. "I had sex."

Both young women put their hands up to their mouths and giggled brightly.

"Twice," I added, holding up two fingers.

Then we all giggled.

"I knew it," said Istmania. "I knew something was different about you. You glow!"

Glow. Yes, I glowed. I could feel it. I'd found some relief and when that happens, everything's softer about life, about me, my voice, my movements, my view on what tomorrow might bring.

Everything was going fine, just fine.

CHAPTER SEVENTEEN

The Blue, Black, and White

A few days later, the apartment phone rang. Twice in one week!

"Tere, proua Jaks. Helistan Eesti konsulaadist. Meil on Teie pass."

"Pardon?" Then I recognized the language. Estonian. "Do you speak English?"

"Yes, of course. This is the Estonian Embassy. Your passport is ready. You can pick it up any time at our embassy."

Our embassy. Ours.

When I went to pick up my Estonian passport, it was snowing in Paris. Again. Well, that's appropriate, I thought. After all, Estonia is buried in snow for large parts of the year. Even its flag pays homage to it, so I tromped along the fluffy white streets and chose to imagine this was somehow a small celebration to what not long ago had been the impossible – and the impossibility had nothing to do with my young self, hoping to live in Paris one day. It had to do with the fallout of war.

∞

When I was growing up, there was no such place as Estonia except in the minds of the old people. It no longer existed on a map. The Cold War was in full throttle. With the Soviet Union's illegal occupation, the rest of the world had given up on Estonia, left her for dead. Raised by refugees from a place that no longer existed, I grew up hearing the stories, seeing the faces of the people who sat in our kitchen drinking coffee, speaking softly of a sister, a mother, a lover "back home", someone we all knew they'd never see again. As a child, this land of my ancestors felt in some ways to be a mythical place even though I knew that my own grandfather was still locked away there, trapped inside a nightmare behind The Iron Curtain.

My grandfather's unwilling absence became a presence in our home. He was alive but unseen, unheard. Both my mother and my grandfather wrote of seeing each other again, one day. But my mother couldn't go to Estonia (the Soviets might keep her if she did) and he couldn't get out. The Soviets permitted my grandfather to use the telephone and speak with his only daughter only once in his life, when she was thirty-four years old. By then, my mother had forgotten most of her Estonian and my grandfather was so excited to hear his daughter's voice that he used his allotted five minutes speaking very quickly, trying to fit everything he wanted to say – rather, everything he was able to say while the Soviet sitting next to him formally listened in to the conversation – into the only time they'd ever hear each other's voices. To this day, my mother doesn't really know what he'd said but hopefully he never knew that.

His letters carried a layer of sorrow though he tried to be pleasant, hopeful, and sometimes the Soviets would let a Christmas package get through to us. One year, when I was eight or nine years old, my grandfather sent the family one juniper beer mug. It had a wooden lid and when we opened the lid we saw that the mug was stuffed with chocolates wrapped in tinfoil. My mother put it under the tree and wouldn't let us touch those chocolates. We could sniff them, yes, so I would open the lid, put the mug up to my nose and smell the earthy mix of chocolate and juniper and think of my grandfather. Each year, she put the juniper beer mug back out by the Christmas tree and each year I would put the beer mug up to my nose and float for a moment in thoughts of chocolates and my faraway grandfather. Many years later, my mother said, "O.K., go on. You can have a chocolate."

I was an adult by then but when I reached for a chocolate from the juniper mug, I became a little girl who was about to eat a candy from her faraway grandfather. The moment I touched the tinfoil wrapping, poof. The chocolate was powder and the tinfoil collapsed in on itself.

Of course, the chocolate would have turned to powder. Had I been thinking, I would have known that but, to me and to that little girl inside of me, the chocolate had always been proof that I really did have a grandfather locked away in a place that nobody else except other Estonians-in-Exile seemed to know about. There were no books you could find about this country and few photographs to prove it existed. The Soviets had erased our story from the map and did their best to erase my ancestors from history.

In defiance of reality, every Estonian-in-Exile I ever knew had at least one Estonian flag on the wall. The Blue (for the Estonian Sky), Black (for its Earth) and White (for its Snow) represented hope. One Exile living by the highway even painted his garage the colors of the flag and it was only other Estonians-in-Exile driving by who could understand the coded message in those three colors. "We have a land," the colors of the Estonian flag claimed, "a land that belongs to us and to our ancestors and to our future generations."

But I didn't believe it. How could I? It had become a dead flag and it upset me to see it.

For the first five years of my life, during the height of the Cold War, my family had lived with my grandmother and her second husband. Even though I don't speak the language, as a child I could understand what the old people were talking about. Later, after we'd moved away to the U.S. and my family would visit my grandmother's house for Christmas or *Jaanipäev* (Summer Solstice), my brother and I would sit around eating pickles and eavesdrop on the grownups.

"What are they saying?" my younger brother would whisper.

"They're talking about freeing Estonia, what they're going to do when Estonia is free." I chomped on a pickle and added, "Silly old people."

It hurt too much to listen to them dream stupidly. I was still young but old enough to know that the Soviet Union had a chokehold on half of Europe. It had managed to slice across families, scar us forever, and I knew there were too many people living like my grandfather, people who were alive as well as dead. Trapped.

∞

That snowy afternoon in Paris, walking into the Embassy of Estonia and seeing the Blue, Black and White – no longer just a coded message on a garage door but the actual flag of The Republic of Estonia – something snapped inside my heart, unlocked itself. It was the family dream that I'd pushed away, buried, did my best to ignore. As I grew older, as I grew to feel the sheer horror of what was really happening to all our families under Soviet rule, thinking about the dream of the "silly old people" hurt too much. To live with those who had been ripped away by war and forced to live a lifetime never seeing those they loved – for no good reason at all – and then be expected to fill my heart with an empty hope that it would all change one day, that was something I couldn't carry.

Back in the 60s and 70s, it was nonsense talk to imagine a free Estonia. We were all in the grip of the Cold War with terrible threats of the Russians lobbing nuclear bombs at us here in the West. Estonia was gone forever. Nothing could change that. Nothing.

Yet here she was. I was standing at the Estonian embassy in Paris under her flag, a living flag that represented a place on a map, represented the strength of a people, my people, who had somehow in the face of the KGB, and so many other Soviet atrocities, managed to keep their song alive.

I was standing in a building that was governed by The Republic of Estonia and here was her flag hanging proudly, claiming her right to be embraced by Europe, claiming her right to be. Tears exploded in my chest, burned, and when I couldn't contain all that emotion, I began to cry. It caught me off guard.

Ole tubli, live bravely, the Estonians say. Dream bravely, too. The "silly old people" had dreamed Estonia back to life.

Here in Paris I was, by some glorious miracle, standing in the future that my grandparents and so many others had been determined to claim. At this moment, I understood that I was here at the embassy to recover what was rightfully mine: my heritage.

We Estonians are known to call upon our Ancestors and so I called to the spirits of my grandmother, the refugee whose bones rest in the soil of Canada, and of my grandfather, a survivor of the Soviet concentration camps in Siberia whose bones now rest at home in Estonia. Together, we stood in our Embassy under the Blue, Black and White and we went up to the counter and I asked for my passport.

"Estonians in Paris meet the first Tuesday of the month at a café in the 6th," said the receptionist after handing me the passport. It was a non-event for her, handing me the document. This is what she did for a living.

I signed for the passport and made a note of the café.

"*Äitah*" (thank you), I said and walked into the snowy white of Paris.

Getting my passport, a passport acknowledging that I was European just like the 5,000 years of my ancestors before me, was no longer about having the chance to live in Paris and avoiding French paperwork.

It was about remembering who I was.

Part Three

CHAPTER EIGHTEEN

Queens, Bees, and Other Things

Ah, yes, everything was going well. I had my Estonian passport and thus the legal right to live and work in Europe. Not that I could actually work in Paris. I didn't speak French well enough. But I was taking classes and meeting up with people from class for a glass of wine and sometimes dinner and now that I had a date arranged with Norbert, the man whose online by-line was "When two spirits meet," maybe he'd help me improve my French and give me a reason to stay in Paris longer than I'd planned.

What I hadn't realized as I floated along with a smile on my way to meet Norbert was that after meeting him I would have to immediately, quick as a bunny as fast as I could, rush home and quit the Internet dating site.

For good.

I just couldn't take it anymore.

We had agreed to meet at the Duck Pond which is behind the *Senat* (French for 'Senate', which is where the French federal politicians meet) at Luxembourg Gardens. It's not a pond so much as a big, round, aboveground pool with ducks floating around in it and a duck house in the middle. Given the amount of *foie gras* (fatty duck liver) that the French eat, it's always surprised me to see how lovingly they treat the captive ducks here at the park. Ducks on farms are force-fed until their livers get enormous (and probably very painful) and then slaughtered by the millions each year. But here, in the pond at Luxembourg Gardens, the ducks swim and preen in the sun and have little baby ducks and when it gets too cold or too hot, they take shelter in the cute and well-maintained duck house paid for by the French taxpayers. In a semi-circle around the duck pond, like so many serene sentinels, are statues of elegant women in long dresses.

As I waited at the duck pond for Norbert, I tried to not to appear too eager and kept a lookout for a tall, funny looking sort of man whom I knew very little about. Well, I knew nothing about him, actually, other than he sent elegantly written emails that I partly understood.

Then my cell phone rang.

"Are you the blonde or the brunette?"

It was Norbert. He hadn't even said *"Bonjour."*

"The blond," I said.

What, he'd forgotten? Or had he gotten me mixed up with some other woman (or women) he'd scheduled for later today? The Internet offers people up like items on a shopping list, after all. I shouldn't have been surprised. Lots of people who use the Internet to find love tend to think that the right one is behind the next click. Then the next click. Then the next.

"Oh, I see you," he said and hung up.

There in the distance was a tall man with a little head. Must be Norbert, I thought without feeling the least bit inspired. I could see from where I was sitting a number of fairly contented looking guards and police officers and a few military men sprinkled here and there. There were probably undercover cops all around us, too – this being the parliament buildings for the government of France. No matter who Norbert was and what his intentions might be, I was in safe territory.

Right there, directly in front of me now was Norbert, big and tall and blocking the sun from my eyes. He was balding a bit and what was left of his hair was cut short, a brush cut, and it stuck straight up. I don't remember whether his ears stuck out (they probably did) because it was hard not to focus on that huge, slightly bent, bulbous, almost clown-like nose of his. And, let's see. His profile said he was 56 – a lie. He was at least 65, maybe a fit 70. It was hard to tell much more about him from the way his parka hung from his body, loosely, and long at the wrists.

Yes, curiosity always gets me. I pretended not to notice that BIG FAT LIE about his age and the fact that he looked like something you'd see in a cartoon. I gracefully shook his hand and we exchanged our *enchantés*.

Norbert was a 'man of the people', in his opinion, a writer and composer who lived in the same loft once used by a very famous sculptor I'd never heard of but obviously should have had I been properly educated. The now dead famous sculptor had lived there in the 1930s but since I hadn't even heard of that artist, I missed the opportunity to be impressed. Did I know much about these gardens? he asked and of course the answer was "no" even though I walked through this beautiful place every day on my way to French classes. Well, he knew all about these gardens, he said, and very much enjoyed walking them, soaking in the culture, the history. Did I want a tour?

I had more than an hour to go before class. Even though I knew that I absolutely wouldn't under any terms or conditions be hopping into bed with this fellow, I wanted to understand what made him tick. I like to try to understand people, know who they are. He was a man who loved France, the people, its history, ideas, and he enjoyed very much showing people what he knew and so began to give me a contained art history lesson -- contained to the art in the gardens -- pointing things out as we walked along, things I'd never noticed before and certainly never understood the significance of, like that semi-circle of statues around the duck pond.

"These statutes are of French queens," said Norbert, "women traded by their families for money and power. Poor things. And off in corners of the park," Norbert pointed in the direction, "you will find statues of literary men, writers, thinkers. Oh, can you read this? What does this say?"

Norbert pointed to a small sign just behind a short barrier that protected the grass from human feet.

"Something about stay off the grass," I guessed.

"Yes, but why?"

I wasn't going to hazard a guess. In French parks, it's usually forbidden to step on the grass. Period. Here in Luxembourg Gardens, the good thing was that people were occasionally allowed to park themselves on certain patches of grass but it wasn't always the same patch of grass because the gardeners kept moving the 'no stepping' signs around to give the previously legally stepped upon grass a 'rest'. I've seen police officers vigorously chase people off the 'resting grass', people who had been right there the day before doing the same things were now technically doing illegal things like yoga or picnicking or just sitting there – on the grass! Never mind that yesterday it was perfectly legal. The sign was moved and today it wasn't.

"I can't read that word, '*abeil*......'."

"Bees," said Norbert.

I laughed.

"Bees! Is this what the French government has been reduced to? Scaring tourists off the grass with fake bee warnings? Well, they should write it in English if they want us to understand the message."

"Look around," said Norbert, knowing the secret.

"I don't see any bees."

"Don't you?"

"It's March, for gosh sakes. Where are the bees?" I scanned the grass again, grass that looked lush and inviting and was completely bee-free. It almost made me want to take off my boots and step on it but I knew that would alert the police or maybe even a secret agent. You could never tell where they were here in this park. You know, in Paris, you can drink alcohol from a bottle in public, have wild, drunken parties by the Seine with so much booze that the empties spill out of two entire garbage bins, but don't – under any circumstances – stand on park grass when a sign says not to.

Norbert looked a bit to our right. My eyes followed. Ahh. Beehives. Lots of them, too. "Wow," I said, "The French are pretty serious about keeping people off the grass, aren't they? They've outsourced the job to bees."

We were actually warming up to one another as people. Norbert was now explaining something about the Medici Fountain, an impressive rectangular pool marked by a set of statues depicting the jealous (older) Greek god, Polyphemus, looking over the young lovers, Acis and Galatea. In Greek mythology, the older man kills the younger lover. Triangles, triangles. The French just love triangles. Anyway, for some unknown reason, from within the center of this pool of water another statue rises up – a very pink, breathtakingly enormous nose. Just a big nose. Who knows why.

And who knows precisely why Norbert used this spot and this particular moment to turn to me and warmly ask, "What are you looking for, Maret?"

"I'm looking for the man who fits well with my life," I replied, hoping that he would very much understood that an old guy with a clown nose wouldn't fit with my life at all.

"You know, so many women say they are looking for 'the man of my life' or 'the man of my dreams'. We are only men. There are no dream men, except in dreams."

"It's no fun sleeping only with a dream. I need a real man."

"Yes." He thought a moment. "You are. I can see that."

"It's difficult to find the right man," I said feeling the pebbles under my shoes, listening to them crunch along. "I'm not looking for a man to cover my loneliness."

∞

So we kept walking and talking and he kept teaching me new French words, explaining that the French have different words for, say, 'one-night-stand' (a good *cou*) and a lover, with no commitment, and a boyfriend (*mec*, he's a good *mec*, or she's a good *blonde*, girlfriend) and then, when older people don't really want to live together but want to make sort of a friendly commitment, they use the same word we do: *companion*.

But what I find so odd about the French language is that they don't differentiate between love and like and the variations in between. It's just love. Always love. That way it can mean everything, or nothing. And the word *embrasser* (to kiss, to hug, or to fuck) and *rendezvous* – a date or a business meeting or a dentist appointment or meeting up at the bus stop or an entire afternoon of lovemaking.

It is said that a language builds up around what is important to that culture and the more words to describe a thing, the more important that thing is to them. For example, the Inuit in Canada's far north have around forty words for 'snow'. Snow is important when you must survive most of the year in the middle of it. Strangely, though, the French language seems to challenge this view that the more words for something, the more important it is. In French, there is no word for 'home' (just 'house'), there are many, many words for 'shit' (specifying whether it was produced by a pigeon, cow, human, who knows what else) and only one word for all levels of affection.

"*J'avais un rendezvous avec une femme. Je l'aimais beaucoup. Nous nous avons embracé après dejeuner.*"

O.K., the man said either: "I had a date with a woman. I love her a lot. After lunch, we had sex." Or, he said, "I had a business appointment with a woman. I like her a lot. After lunch, we hugged (a light hug, a way to say good-bye)."

Or, given the current state of Google Translate at this moment, it could mean this: "I had a date with a woman. I loved him very much. We went up in flames after lunch."

Went up in flames after lunch.

Plus if a term is gender neutral, according to Google Translate, default to male.

What does the word 'love' really mean when it can mean everything or nothing at all?

"It's a wonderful language, French," said Norbert. I nodded in agreement, still wondering about the vast number of words for shit vs. the one French word for love. "So, Maret, how many lovers have you had?"

"Norbert. That's not a gentlemanly question."

"True," he said, "but I'm not a gentleman." He grinned. Little did I know how true that was.

I used my standard line. "More than 10, less than 100."

"How much less?"

"I don't know." I looked him in the eye.

"You can tell me these things. It doesn't matter," he said softly.

"I don't know," I admitted.

"You don't, do you? That's refreshing. Do you know how many women . . . There . . ." He nodded toward two attractive-looking women. "Look at these two."

We glanced over at the two French women who stomped their way (as only French women can do -- stomp along in high heels with their short, quick, hard steps and still look elegant) quickly through the Gardens. Each woman was fit, one was downright French-woman-thin, and both were well groomed, perfectly coiffed and had their makeup done just right. They were, to a North American eye, impressive looking.

"Those two, they probably haven't had sex in five years."

"Whaaat?" I said. "That's sad. They're so beautiful."

"Oh, no, it's not so sad, really. They don't want it. Not really." He wandered along for a bit. "You know, here I am, meeting so many women, women your age and, well, how am I supposed to relate to them? I mean, they've probably been married, what, 20 years . . ." Sort of like me, I thought. ". . . had one, maybe two but very briefly, lovers since their husbands left and then they get into bed with me and, pfff."

Well, not like me, I thought.

"They don't know how to make love. For them, it's just… You know, something to do once a week to keep the man, oh, I don't know." He sighed. "Look," he said, "You're a woman of the world. You know about things." He waited for me to nod. I nodded. "So, imagine me trying to make love to someone like this. Me, a man who has had more than 5,000 lovers."

"Five thousand lovers?" I laughed out loud from the shock of it and then I looked at him and we laughed together and walked slowly as I tried to regain my composure. When the laughter had finally calmed down to a friendly chuckle, I covered my smile with my hand and tried to talk. "Norbert. Five thousand lovers? Five *thousand*!" I started to laugh again. I couldn't help it.

"Yes, about that." He thought, calculating something I guess and said again, "Yes. About that. Maybe a bit more."

"Well, no wonder, then. You and these women are from the same generation but had two completely different upbringings. I mean, the poor women you're meeting up with were raised being told, flat out, that there should only be one man in her life and not to worry about how good he was in bed because the Catholic Church said God had decided it was only about getting her pregnant, nothing more."

While Norbert was a boy struggling with existential issues, reading poetry and encouraged like so many men in France to lay claim to his manhood by having sex with a prostitute or the neighborhood 'whore' (by the way, another French word for 'shit' also doubles as the word for 'whore' – impressive, isn't it?), French women of his generation were being told that sex was wrong, bad, sinful, a punishment for what Eve did way back when. And out of this soup of sin and shame came a very perverse sexual 'revolution' that Norbert and so many others in the West jumped right into, a revolution claiming, among other things, that public displays of female nudity are empowering while at the same time any man who shows his 'junk' in public will be charged with a criminal offense.

"Yes, different worlds," he sighed. "I never wanted that world. Do you know Murger?" he asked, changing the subject. "No? He was a poet, wrote the story that the opera, *La Bohème*, is based on, but no one remembers him. I came to Paris because of Murger. In my 12-year-old mind, living in a boring village with so many boring people all around me, I decided, 'When I grow up, I'm going to go to Paris and meet Murger' but of course, he was dead, or nearly already dead, by that time."

"OK, so, you get to Paris and decide that since your hero's dead, you'll drown your sorrows in 5,000 lovers?"

"No. I became a doctor."

I waited.

"A psychiatrist. Yes. It's hard to be a good psychiatrist if you really care about helping people. Very hard." Another sigh. "I worked with schizophrenics, the impossible cases. It was a madhouse, that hospital. Yes, it was. One day, I just left. Walked out the door and didn't go back. Couldn't, really. I was 30. Thirty years old. A doctor who couldn't doctor. It was too hard, those poor souls. What was I to do?"

It was hard to tell if Norbert could that he'd probably had a complete breakdown or something.

Another sigh from Norbert. "And so, you see, I was a doctor with no job so I started to work in clubs as a piano player. That's what I did. I played piano by night, but work didn't start until, what, 8:00 p.m. The club was just next to the National Library, so I started to do research in the library during the day, like a second job. I would get to the library at 1:00 p.m., every day, and at 5 minutes to 8:00 p.m., collect my notes and books and run into the club and start playing. It was good, too, because I got free meals every night."

It was very unnatural for me to keep my mouth shut but I did. I wanted to hear this man's story. At first, it had just been idle curiosity for me with nothing else to do before French class. But now I understood that he needed to tell his full story. To someone.

CHAPTER NINETEEN

The Stallion

"Here," said Norbert, pulling out his wallet. From it, he pulled out a yellowed, frayed at the edges photo of a young, handsome man with a beard and long dark blond hair. "I don't know why I keep it, this silly photo," and he handed it to me so that I could look at it more closely.

"You're very handsome in that photo," I said, knowing that this was what I was expected to say. It was true, though. He had been handsome. Long ago.

"Yes, hair on a man helps what I call 'the handsome factor' along, don't you think?"

"Depends where the hair is," I said.

He chuckled and took a long look at the photo before putting it back in his wallet. "True enough. . . So, you see, I was this young man working at a club – did I tell you it was a Swingers' Club? You know, Swingers' Clubs, where people come for having sex with each other."

"And with the piano player, too?"

"Not at first but then one night, well, they needed a stallion." He grinned. "And I obliged."

A weird image of Norbert playing the piano while "stallion-ing" at the same time flashed in my head. If sex was a sin at home, wasn't it a bigger sin at a club? Surely it must have been illegal or even against French union rules to have an employee hired to play the piano also be expected to offer up erections for hire. I mean, in France everything's unionized and each worker is classified to do a certain job and is never, ever to cross over into another type of work outside his or her job title.

And if things like walking on tired grass is completely ille-gal in France, what about stallioning?

Mouth shut, nearly zipped up for God's sakes because I just had to hear more.

"It was good. It was fun, and I was usually set up as the Dominator." A chill ran through me. "You know, the harmless S&M stuff, really. Although, every club says that. The Swing-ers, they'll say, 'Well, at least we're not into S&M and those who practice S&M will say, 'Well, we don't do the really bad stuff. The really bad stuff, that's done at this other club. And you go to that other club and they'll say, 'Yes, well, we're a bit rough here, but they're really terrible over there . . . and so on." A long moment of silence. "I've seen some really bad stuff. Really bad." More silence. Then softly, he said, "I never want to see anything like that again." He was somewhere else, now, seeing in his mind's eye whatever it was that had troubled him and I'm glad he didn't speak up and offer me that horrible im-age in conversation. Norbert took a breath to shake it off. "But what I did, it wasn't so bad really. Not really."

Yes, he fell into "Category #1 - The Cheerful, Friendly, Just Out for a Bit of Pain and Torture Fun S&M." I looked to see whether he caught the irony of what he had just said. He hadn't.

I finally spoke, wanting to distance myself and find a way out of the conversation. "I know some people who like this, you know, S&M and clubs and all that. It's really their business, I guess. But it's not really something I go for. I just don't understand the attraction. I prefer to get pleasure from pleasure, not pleasure from pain."

"But it's almost mystical." He was now glowing, smiling, his thoughts back in a torture chamber somewhere. "The really, almost magical, almost mystical qualities. You know," he turned to me and stopped walking, speaking slowly for me to really understand him, or try. "Some of these women had husbands who couldn't do much with them anymore, you know what I mean. It's normal, after a certain age, for the man to, well, have a hard time with certain matters and so these men brought their wives to me, their young wives. Very often it was the older man who had married a really, really beautiful young wife but couldn't please her. He'd be rich, though. I was really well known by this time, and, well, we'd punish them. They'd be all dressed up for punishment, these women. They wanted it. And the women who were crazy, I mean not the really crazy ones, just a bit crazy, they bring you to a different place. They bring you to an almost spiritual high . . ."

It's not politically correct to say this, I know, but I'm quite certain that we should never inflict bodily harm on each other for fun – especially during sex. Sure, there are some people who can only do it that way but it should be a private matter, not a whole industry devoted to encouraging people to get pleasure from hurting other people. I've been pressured more than once to try to enjoy being hurt while the man gets his rocks off but I'm a fairly tough cookie and nobody gets that past me.

But what about all those girls and women who aren't as tough as I am, what happens to them? How is their experience of sex twisted, shaped because not only is her lover pressuring her to say yes to whatever he wants, the wider culture is discouraging her from saying no, discouraging her from staying true to her own inner voice, her own needs?

Yes, yes. I know that there are women who like to be hurt and who (as that fellow Frank had said) need to feel the "pain that gives pleasure" but there are many more who don't and yet they're pressured all the time to stop being a "prude".

What I find so tiresome is the slick marketing of sadism to a gullible public. Look, the Marquis de Sade was put in jail not because of what he wrote but because of what he did. Yes, Hollywood tried to make him out to be a martyr for "freedom of speech" but the fact is he was jailed because he sexually tortured young women. He was viewed as so depraved that even the French aristocrats locked up one of their own (and how often did that happen?). The media never remind us that after being sentenced for sexually torturing his maids, the Marquis de Sade complained that "There's not a woman on earth who'd ever had cause to complain of my services if I'd been sure of being able to kill her afterwards."[viii]

Nowadays, hurting young women for sexual fun has become somewhat *de rigeur*. It's generally not middle-aged women like me who are being psychologically affected by it because that sort of thing wasn't beamed into family homes when I was growing up. It's mostly girls and younger women who are suffering because cruelty to the female form has even seeped into Mommy Porn. Isn't it about time for society to sober up and say, "OK, then, what the HELL is going on here?"

If you took all jolly references to sadism in our culture these days and instead replaced the word "women" with "dogs" being tortured for someone else's pleasure, civil society would be outraged.

Our bodies are beautifully designed to be adored and loved. Our bodies are the place from which we offer our souls and our frail humanity to one another. You're not supposed to "almost" get to heaven, you're supposed to get there! It is magical, mystical even. Angels envy us this wonder. I am sure of it. Norbert can't get there when he needs to do it with handcuffs and nipple clamps and blindfolds and tightly knotted rope around someone's neck.

In England during the latter part of the 20th Century, the House of Lords had to wade into the subject of sexual sadism. A legal challenge had been brought forward by a group of men who'd been caught putting fishhooks into each other's scrotums (as well as inserted into their penises) and hanging each other up by their testicles. They claimed that because it was consensual, it was legal.

The House of Lords decided it is not entirely legal to inflict bodily harm even if it is consensual.

Sure, you can say "but it's their choice" and this is what the men's lawyers kept claiming. But the House of Lords, after careful consideration, made it clear that society sometimes has to protect people from themselves and extreme sado-masochism is an act of violence, not an act of sex.

Eros is not the god of fishhooks in the scrotum. Eros is the god of sexual *love*. Whatever one does with fishhooks during a sexual interchange cannot be called 'erotic'. It's something. It certainly is.

But it is not in the spirit of Eros.

∞

"I don't know why I'm telling you all this," continued Norbert. "People usually only know one part of my life, or the other, and here I'm telling you everything." He peered at me. "So, you've never tried it, the clubs?"

Here with Norbert on a sunny day in Luxembourg Gardens, it had become depressingly clear that it was unlikely I'd find a lover, let alone my love, on a French Internet dating site.

"Norbert, I'm really not interested. What is it with you guys? I just don't want to go and have sex in a public place with perfect strangers. And I really, really don't want to be hurt by anyone. I'm too sensitive for that." He continued to look at me, hoping. "Norbert, I mean, look. Men here in France always want me to go into clubs with them – I'm their ticket to a good time. In those places, you know darn well that the men trade and barter women's asses, for gosh sakes. That's why a man can't get into one of those clubs without a woman. How liberated is that? Ha. It's no different than all those queens, those statues around the duck pond for God's sakes, Norbert. Being traded."

"Well, you should never go to any club, not here in Paris or anywhere, unless you trust the man you're with and he can protect you, look out for you. You don't want to get into a trap…and there are lots of those," Norbert counseled. "Just be careful about that."

Traps?

He explained: A nice girl wants to 'try it' (oh, just once, see what it's like, might be fun) and she goes to one of these clubs – which aren't run like Church Socials, by the way. They're run by mobsters and if they're not mobsters, they're ... well, just don't cross them, that's all. So the 'nice girl' she goes to the club. Let's say, let's just say, that her boyfriend or husband or her new date is a nice guy, not out to trick her or anything, but isn't too big and strong or, like Norbert, doesn't have the right connections 'in there'. So they go, and somebody sees her as the innocent she is and so warms up to her husband, starts chatting him up and, sure, that sounds like fun – they'll do an exchange -- and then in no time she's in a torture chamber being filmed naked, clamped, roped, whipped, raped by a few men (hopefully 'just' that) then the night's frolicking is done and the nice couple get to go home. Her man didn't protect her. That was his job, to protect her ass and he didn't know what he was doing.

He'd seen it, Norbert had. Sometimes, the husband would be forced to watch. Gives the rapists more of a thrill, he pointed out.

Sadists, he explained, enjoy inflicting emotional pain, too.

Then, after it's all done and her clothes are back on, what is the woman going to do? Call the French police? "Hello, I went to an S&M club where I only wanted to try out some light sado-masochism and they filmed me being tortured and then raped me and I was forced to smile but I kept saying no (which means "more, more, more" in a Torture Chamber) and I'd like you to press charges, please and thank you?"

No, the woman keeps it to herself, tries not to remember, and certainly doesn't bring it up at dinner parties back home.

There are plenty of women walking this earth, especially here in Paris, with these memories. Norbert knows. He shook his head, remembering. "So, be careful about who you go with."

The Count had given me the very same warning, remember. "Norbert. I'm not going to one of these places. It doesn't interest me. At all. Someone might as well ask if I'd like to have sex in a pile of fresh pig manure. The answer is 'no' and I won't even add a 'thank you' to that."

Norbert shivered and made a bit of a scowl at the thought of sex in pig manure.

"Anyway," continued Norbert, "The clubs, they're part of my past, mostly. Nobody wants an old stallion like me, and, anyway, I'm getting older, too. It's not so easy for me, anymore. I just like the feel of a woman next to me, her body close. In the morning, especially."

Life has its mysteries. Norbert and those two French women who'd earlier French-lady-stomped their way past us in the Luxemburg Gardens had each arrived at the same destination, the same place in life.

Norbert had just taken the scenic route.

∞

"Ah," he looked up brightly at a statue tucked into a corner of the garden just east of the *Senat*. "There's Murger."

"Murger?"

"The poet who brought me to Paris. The one I wanted to meet, who was already dead or about to be dead when I was imagining meeting him. It's a shame, really, that he's forgotten now."

We stopped to take an espresso together and parted on friendly terms. I didn't have to say *peut-être* to Norbert, just a friendly *au revoir*.

As I walked through the gates at Luxembourg Gardens to the tiny street next to the French school, I kept asking myself what was wrong with me. Why was I drawing such a string of very, well, let's be polite, very unfortunate men?

When I was in my late teens, I read and re-read Carl Jung's work and his understanding of how humans are drawn to each other seemed to make a lot of sense. We are, at some level, responsible for the people in our lives because something in us is drawn to them and vice versa. The people in our lives are reflections of our inner selves and it is only when we make the effort to grow and change that the people or behaviors of the people around us change and then the kind of life we lead changes, too. That's why so many people keep repeating the same mistakes with different people (pointing a finger at myself here, given that I've been married three times) and that's why it is so important to dig deep inside and undo whatever it is that is drawing people you don't want to be with into your life.

Why did I keep attracting men who just wanted to use me as a sex toy? Had the world really changed so much? While the world has always had some creepy men who wanted to do creepy things, there also have always been really very nice men who not only want sexual love but the full presence of a woman. So much of the world's greatest love poetry is written by men so I know I'm not imagining things. Why was I getting stuck with all these weirdoes?

I didn't care what the answer was at that moment. After class, I went straight back to my apartment to get my profile off the Internet. Just as I was about to shut down my profile for good, I received an email from a very handsome, younger man.

"I think you will want to meet me," wrote the young Italian man. People often miss the subtleties when writing in English when it's their second (or in his case, third) language. Eduardo was fluent in Italian, French and English.

I looked at his profile again. Thirty-eight. Older than Robert.

I looked at his photos again. Curly salt and pepper hair. Kind eyes.

I looked at his height. 181 cm. I translated it to feet. Oh, six feet tall. That's lovely. As I was pondering the young Italian wrote again. "Perhaps a coffee tomorrow? Or a glass of wine?"

Pourquoi pas?

CHAPTER TWENTY

False, and Not So False, Friends

Eduardo was stunning in person. His green eyes seemed wise and his curly hair made me just want to reach out and touch them, run my fingers through those curls. But I didn't. Instead, I listened to the handsome young man speak in perfect English touched with a delicate mix of both French and Italian accents. Ladies, this is a delightful accent. I would swoon just listening to a man like that read the phone book.

"I was born in Sees-e-lee," he said as he sipped his coffee, "But my parents moved us to Paris when I was seeks-teen."

He worked for the family – or The Family, I could never tell exactly – as an accountant "monitoring the investments." His aunt owned clubs in Paris and I began to suspect he worked for The Family because he'd talked about how he had to audit family businesses throughout Sees-e-lee, Ee-taly and France and the way he referred to his aunt, she sounded like a mighty force, one who was never to be disappointed. "In The Family," he explained, "One says 'yes' to my aunt."

Eduardo asked me a few polite questions and then said, "So, I knew when I read your profile that you would most certainly want to meet me."

That's a bit cheeky, I thought. True, any red-blooded heterosexual woman would want to meet a tall, very fit and
handsome tri-lingual Italian who spoke with a slow confidence
that made you want to find out how skilled he might be naked
but if he had any sense, he wouldn't be so forthright about it
before even finishing his coffee.

"You see," he said calmly as he took a sip of his espresso
and then ever so delicately licked his full lips, "I speak Italian,
French and English perfectly and when I read your profile, I
thought, 'Oh, poor dear. She doesn't know what she's just
done'."

"What did I do?"

"And worse, the French men reading this would not understand, either, for there are false friends between English and
French but not so much with English and Italian, no I don't
think so much with English and Italian."

"False friends?" I asked.

"Yes, *les faux amis*. A 'false friend' is a word that seems to
be the same in both languages but in fact has a completely different meaning in each language. People easily misunderstand
one another."

Les faux amis, yes. False friends. I'd run into it before, with
my French-Canadian ex-husband. It has to do with the fact
that the English language is littered with French words. It all
started way back in 1066 when William the Conqueror (from
Normandy) came across the Channel to claim England as his
own. The French language became the language of the court
and of much of the countryside.

Plenty of French words got absorbed into the English language and over the course of hundreds of years, these words
sometimes took on completely different meanings. They still

sounded mostly the same and looked mostly the same when written, but without knowing it, you could easily insult someone else because they'd 'hear' the same word differently. André and I had experienced *les faux amis* phenomenon when I learned that he'd broken a promise to me, again. I said, "You violated me!"

He instantly got furious, became red in the face, and yelled back, "I did not rape you!"

"Don't be crazy!" I yelled, "I said you violated me!"

And so we went on like that for a few minutes until I started to laugh because I finally clued in to what was happening. *Viol* in French also means rape. When André heard 'violate' he kept hearing *viol* (rape).

At the café with the lovely Italian man, I put my espresso down and turned to him. "What did I do?"

"Do you know what the word *aventureuse* means in French?" he asked.

"Adventuress," I replied.

"Yes, it does. But do you know what it *means*? In French, that is."

I shook my head.

"It means, and I'm sorry to say this, but it means 'slut'."

Slut.

I had been announcing to all of Paris that I was "strong and feminine, soft and kind, a bit of a *slut* . . ."

"And when I first read your profile, I thought, "Oh, look at this: an educated adventuress" but then I read this again and understood, no, the poor woman is English and doesn't know what she has written."

True.

Eduardo and I exchanged telephone numbers and he said he'd take me for dinner but every time we had sort of arranged something, he would have to go help his aunt with something or the family (The Family?) would send him to Italy to audit one of their companies and when it came right down to it, I don't think Eduardo was as taken with my physique as I was with his. Disappointed, I was, but in a way, I was OK with that because Eduardo was a man who had never been married and we didn't have much in common, really. Besides, in addition to announcing to all of Paris that I was a "slut", my online dating profile made it clear that I was "looking for the right man for the rest of my life." Eduardo, as beautiful and as elegant and as sexy as he was, wasn't the "right man" and we both knew it.

∞

Did I correct my profile? No. The day earlier I had taken it down and wasn't about to put it back up. Paris would have to offer me a man the normal way, in person. I was wasting too much time on the Internet and some of that twiddling away on the computer was so that I could avoid writing. Between avoiding writing, going to French classes and sitting around at cafés with a few people in Paris I could now call new friends, life was getting pretty busy for me.

Hemingway had once said, "In every port, you will find one Estonian."

Sometimes, you'll find a few more, even in Paris.

One set of my new friends were Estonians, people my age with my ethnic and cultural heritage who had grown up not in the West but on the other side of the Iron Curtain during the

Soviet Occupation. In fact, I'd befriended both the journalist wife of the Estonian Ambassador as well as the Ambassador, himself. This might sound impressive but at any given time, there are probably 12 Estonians living in Paris and they all make a point of knowing each other.

One breezy early spring afternoon, as a few of my Estonian friends and I sat around a table at an outdoor café on the *Champs-Élysées*, the Ambassador said, "You know, in Soviet Times we knew there were Estonians outside of the country, the ones who escaped. Most families, by some years after the war, were able to keep in touch with their loved ones through letters even though the Soviets censored them. But as a nation, we knew nothing as a whole about where our people were. Nothing at all. The Soviets didn't gather information on Estonians outside of the country as a group. They knew where the Estonians were in the West – the KGB watch some of you quite closely. When we finally formed our own government, one of the first things we did was try to understand where all our people were. We found them mostly in Canada, yes, Germany, England and Australia, also. About 200,000 now," he said proudly. Even more proudly, he leaned back and asked, "And do you know what we discovered? We learned that all our people outside the country had done very well. Very well for themselves."

Estonians who had escaped the Soviets didn't start mafias, build black markets, go on welfare. No. They arrived penniless in countries with languages and cultures completely unrelated to their own and survived by working hard and being honest. Most had expected to go back to Estonia one day. That's what they wanted, to go back home. While waiting for the day that never came for them, they figured out how to make their special form of black bread (a form of rye bread) in their adopted countries.

Wherever there are Estonian immigrants, there are information exchanges about where to get the best black bread in that city. This particular rye bread information exchange had just happened that afternoon in Paris and we were now all on to our agreeable second round of wine.

Another fact about Estonians: we are only fully at ease when we know where our next sauna is coming from. It was as true for me as it was for the rest of the Estonians around the table. The Estonian Embassy in Paris was being rebuilt – with a large sauna, of course – but we all missed our own saunas "back home".

When an Estonian builds a new home, the sauna is always built first, before the house. A sauna had once been considered a sacred place, a place where the _maarahvas_ (Estonians) had cleansed the night before the holy day, Thors Day (Thursday). It was also the place where children were born and where people were taken to die. Saunas are always clean, warm, dry. They provide a measure of peace and comfort. While the Catholic Church did put a stop to preparatory Thors' Day bathing, no one at any point in history has been able to keep Estonians from our saunas no matter where on the planet an Estonian lives. Not even Singapore, which is a bit ridiculous given how hot it is there. A friend's husband explained that the group of Finns and Estonians living in Singapore got together and ordered a portable sauna from Finland and set it up on the roof of one of the apartment buildings. Everybody was excited but then, standing around the portable sauna on the roof up there, they realized there was one little problem. Where in Singapore could they possibly find wood for the fire?

The answer?

IKEA.

They scooted off to the IKEA in Singapore, bought a few very cheap tables and chairs, and, *voilà!*

∞

The other Paris friends I'd made were from my French class. A young Russian boy named Roman decided to adopt me. Technically, he was a man because he was 21 but he was the same age as Anneli, my youngest, so to me he will always be a boy and I don't think he minded that.

When I first started these afternoon French classes, Roman would always come in late, looking like he'd just woken up or was drunk, or both. Pascal the Rascal would glare at him as he walked to the far corner of the class and slump down in his chair. Each of us had selected our own 'spot' and so no one else ever sat in Roman's chair.

Being a compulsively punctual person, I always got to class at least five minutes early and one day, as I walked into class, I was surprised to see Roman sitting there, not in 'his' chair but in the chair immediately next to mine. His face was washed and his hair combed and he smiled warmly as I put my books down.

"So you're Estonian," he said brightly.

"Yes."

"I can speak some Estonian."

"Really?"

"Yes, I had Estonian friends." He was proud of himself.

"Ah, well, you see, I don't speak any Estonian."

This startled him. After all, I had announced in class, "*Je suise Estonienne.*"

"I was born in Toronto, to Estonian refugees."

We spoke in a mixture of English and French and, besides, Roman wasn't looking for another Estonian friend but a mother figure, someone older and hopefully wiser who would make time for him.

He had been orphaned at the age of 12. His mother had managed to get him out of Belarus to Germany at the age of 3 but soon after his 12th birthday, she died of breast cancer. "I woke up on my 12th birthday," said Roman, "And knew I would spend the day with my mother in her room."

Here in Paris, Roman was stateless, paperless (as they say in French), and struggling to make sense of his life.

His great fortune had been that in Germany as a teenager he worked as a laborer for an archaeology professor. The archaeologist went out of his way to help the boy, first by giving him that job and a place to stay and then, in the midst of a serious emotional breakdown when he was 18, by finding him a dad.

When Roman couldn't get out of bed, refused to eat and could hardly speak he was so listless and depressed, the German archaeologist said, "Let's call your family." When the man discovered there was no one to call, he said to Roman, "That's not right. Everyone deserves a family." The professor then explained to Roman that he'd adopt him but Germans were unable to adopt an adult, and Roman was 18 so they'd have to look for someone in France. "The French," he said, "are legally permitted to adopt an adult."

After a few months, the German professor of archaeology found a childless French man who was Vice President of an organization that worked to protect the rights of political prisoners. The French man explained he'd love to have a son since none of his girlfriends had ever wanted a child of their own. The German professor paid for Roman's train ticket to Paris. At the train station in Paris, Roman met Michel, the man who would be his new dad.

As Roman told me his story, I didn't say, "Oh, poor you!" No, I kept saying how lucky he was that his mother got him out of Belarus. How lucky he was to have met the German arche-ologist and how lucky he was now that Michel had adopted him and here he was living right here in Paris. "Congratulations", I said to him, holding my espresso up to his cup of coffee in a toast, "You got here. To Paris! Here we both sit in the same café in the same magical city that most of the world wants to visit one day. And here we are, Parisians!"

Roman looked at me over the top of his wee espresso cup.

I continued. "I spent my whole adult life trying to find my way to live here just for a little while and you get to call Paris your home forever."

Roman took a sip of his coffee, still looking at me, trying to read my face. Then he said, "You've had a hard life, haven't you?"

"Why would you say that?"

"Because, every time I've told my story, people feel sorry for me, are so surprised at my bad luck. But you said I was lucky."

"You're a very perceptive young man. Yes, I had a hard start to life, a really hard one at times. The point is, life can be hard. It's hard for a lot of people. We need to look at where we are, now, and if we don't like where we are, we should look at where we want to be and try to get there. Never just crumple in on yourself and complain. That gets you nowhere fast."

"Nowhere fast?"

"It's a saying."

We finished up our coffees. I hadn't realized he'd decided, right then and there, that I would be his new mom.

Roman had a lot of things going for him but he didn't have a mother and so he decided to tag along with me whenever he could, invited himself over to my apartment for company using the excuse that he knew it was hard for me to bring large bottles of water up the stairs so he'd drag a dozen or so enormous bottles of water up the stairs to my apartment. I'd sometimes make him pasta with olive oil and fresh basil or sometimes an omelet with *crème fraîche* and chanterelle mushrooms or we'd sit out at a café with our mutual friends from class and soak in the sounds and the smells and the wine that Paris offered us.

From that point on, he was always on time for class and never again did I see him looking hung over. In fact, based on a motherly talk I had with him – only once – he severed friendships with some dangerous, drug-driven young men who I could tell were on the road to big trouble if they hadn't already arrived there.

"Roman," I said to him one night after meeting those men. "God gives you 24 hours each day and we never know how many days we really have. You need to ask how you want to spend each day of your life. With friends who are doing nothing good? Who could dangerous? Or do you want to spend time with people who trying to make a life for themselves? How you spend each of those 24 hours each day matters, you know."

He instantly made the right choice right then and there but didn't tell me until months later.

When Roman's birthday came around, I threw a little birthday party for him. He was born the day after Anneli and so it was easy to remember his birthday. I made everyone wear a silly birthday hat and put candles in a wee chocolate cake, made a light dinner, and offered plenty of champagne and a few small gifts. He cried a little that night.

The next day he told me that this had been his first birthday party in over ten years. His mother had died 3 weeks after his 12th birthday but she was so very sick toward the end, there was no birthday party. Not even cake.

"Now I have a new birthday memory," said Roman brightly.

Many things were changing for Roman – with the help of his adopted father, he got busy reaching for that brass ring as his life spun from heartache to hope to wherever his life would take him now.

Roman became one of the lovely, lovely gifts that Paris gave to me, and I will always thank Paris for that.

∞

Another gift from the French class was the Nicaraguan-Italian woman, Istmania, and her Nicaraguan-Italian-French family who would have me over for dinner in their cozy little Parisian apartment where we'd share wine and laughter. Istmania was the same age as Kaia, my eldest. She'd only recently moved to Paris – to recover from a devastating divorce – and the two of us spent many hours at the mid-point between where we both lived, which happened to be smack dab in the middle of the Seine on Ile St. Louis at a little café not far from where I did my morning yoga across the river from the Notre Dame Cathedral. This little café was both a tourist spot and a spot for the locals. One day, when the waiter, Arthur, distract-edly gave us our wine and some potato chips, Istmania lifted the bowl of chips, flicked back her hair indignantly, and said, "We're not tourists."

"Oh, excuse me," said Arthur good-naturedly. He brought back a bowl of complimentary olives and chunks of cheese.

"What impresses me, Istmania," I said one day as we shared some more olives and cheese and a *pichet* of wine and then an-other *pichet*, "is that you're never afraid to use the 'F' word."

"The F word?" asked Istmania, sitting back with her glass of wine in hand. "The 'F' word . . ." She looked at me.

"Feminist."

She laughed and looked at me with curiosity. "In English, this is the 'F' word?"

"Well, it seems to be as profoundly offensive as the other 'F' word in the English language."

"Yes, the same in Nicaragua, only worse because of the Spanish macho attitudes." She took a sip of wine and added, "But this word, it has such a simple meaning, no? How can a woman not believe she should have the same rights to men? It was not so long ago that a woman could not have a good job and women still do not earn enough money, no?"

For centuries, laws were enacted to prevent women from earning a decent living. If women were 'naturally' inferior to men in their capabilities, you wouldn't need laws, would you? In North America, right up until 1968, there were school boards that refused to let a married woman work as a teacher. If she was single and got married, bam. She was out of a job. Married male schoolteachers were permitted to keep working, of course.

All sorts of laws have been established over the years to block women from having enough money to survive without a man. In fact, Istmania and I were sitting there wearing jeans, unwittingly breaking another law that had been put in place specifically to keep women from working in key professions.[ix] Until 2013, women in Paris who wanted to wear pants had to apply to the police for permission to do so.

Obviously, French police officers were no longer enforcing this ridiculous law. The "no pants on a woman without police permission" law had been put in place in 1800 when women and even some men were pushing for women's equality, all the way back then. This law had been put in place to prevent women from being able to work in professions that paid a living wage rather than those that required she take her clothes off.

Istmania and I spent lots of pleasant evenings at that bar on *Île St. Louis* across the river not far from the Notre Dame Cathedral, talking about history and progress and the lovely determination of so many people in the past who helped us have the right to sit here without a male guardian and drink wine that we could afford on our own.

I needed to write about it, though, and I wasn't. Wine by the Seine with friends was so much more fun than sitting in an apartment – even a lovely little apartment in Paris – writing all alone. But, I said to myself, it was time to buckle down. When I told both Roman and Istmania that this would be my last series of French classes, they worried they'd never see me again.

"I'll still be in Paris," I said. "We'll still be friends, won't we?"

"Always," said Roman.

So far, this has turned out to be true.

CHAPTER TWENTY-ONE

Routines and Revolutions

Yes, it was very much time for me to start working properly on that book about the feminists – male and female – who had made Paris or France their home. My recent conversations with Istmania had confirmed this for me. She was born in the late 1970s and so very little of this turning point in the world's history – the time when women burst out of the boxes they'd long been forced into – is talked about or understood.

It wasn't until the 1970s that the world started opening up for women, and well into the 1980s before married women had the right to build a credit rating independently of her husband or, if single, without a male co-signer. Laws had to be enacted to force banks to demanding that women have male co-signers.

In the late 1980s, my ex-husband's sister asked him to co-sign for a loan. It wasn't that she didn't have the money. She did. She actually had more money than we did tucked away in the bank. What she didn't have was the right set of genitals.

I pointed out that it was finally illegal for companies to make women come to their brothers and fathers and husbands like this and she was happy to make that point clear to the car company. She got her car, she bought a house, she bought lots more property and she's doing very well, thank you. But what would it have been like for her had she lived just a few years earlier and didn't have a brother or father to sign for her?

It was tough, very tough, for a woman to make it on her own and not because she was incapable but because the laws had been lined up to block her way. It was like this everywhere and many people, men and women alike, tried to justify it by claiming the real reason women could hardly earn a decent wage was due to innate differences between the sexes.

I remember when socio-biologists in the 1970s and 1980s were even trying to explain away rape – men had a biological "instinct" to spread their seed and so rape was only a natural "behavioral adaptation".

I have too much respect for men to believe that nonsense. There are so many men who are impressive, compassionate people. Look, there isn't a gene for cleaning toilets and yet it is almost exclusively women who clean toilets. You can't tell me that because it's almost exclusively women who clean toilets that this is a 'behavioral adaptation' and perfectly natural.

Look, I'm hopelessly heterosexual so I well know there are differences between men and women, but so many of the justifications for cornering women into poverty are based on very flimsy "science".

There are all sorts of strange justifications around why women generally don't like sex as much as men that keep popping up, too. At this stage in the rebuilding of our cultural mores, who really knows what goes on in the minds of mating females so why would we women bow down to groundless theories? One journalist who seemed to already understand the problem of justifying gender differences said it well when writing about penguin sexuality:

Adelie penguins build their nests with stones, a rare
commodity in Antartica and one for which they are
willing to pay . . . When their partner's back is turned,
they trade intimate favours with other single males in
return for bigger, better stones . . . Zoologists specu-
late that the female may be trying to improve the
genetic variability of her offspring. Or she could just
be having fun.[x]

∞

Maybe, I thought, I'd been behaving too much like an Adelie penguin, spending too much time trying to find my 'fun',
and that's why the Universe had prevented me from meeting
the right man, or any lover at all (other than Robert) while here.
The Universe, knowing how writers (and wannabe writers) behave also knows that if I had a man around to distract me, I'd
never actually get to my writing, ever.

All my notes were piled up on the dining room table but I'd
never managed to get around to actually writing anything – anything of value, that is. There'd been school (French classes),
the afterschool drinks and pot-luck student parties now and
again (almost always at my apartment). There were the relentless series of first "dates", there had been shopping, going to
the market on Thursdays and Sundays, taking long walks, doing yoga by the Seine, sitting around thinking, going to a couple
of Estonian events in the city . . . in other words, there had been
a lot of avoiding I'd been doing and it was time to face it, to sit
down and write.

244 · MARET JAKS

Just as I decided to do that, I realized it was Thursday, market day at the Bastille Market. I needed some exercise and I needed some fresh eggs and yogurt and so I decided to start my morning by taking the long route to the market, walking up toward the metro *Filles du Calvaire* to honor a heroine of mine.

By a coincidence, and only a coincidence, I lived down the street from a memorial to one of the women I'd wanted to write about, a near forgotten revolutionary, Olympe de Gouges. On my way to market, I would sometimes take this route to *Filles du Calvaire* and around back to the Bastille so that I would pass by the small little plaque that had been put up to remember her and take a moment to honor her spirit. She had been brave and bold enough to imagine a world where women could enjoy full human rights alongside their menfolk. Not even writers like Rousseau could imagine that. In fact, he wrote that women belonged in the home and her only job should be to serve her man. Who widows and spinsters and any other woman without a man were supposed to serve just wasn't even a consideration for Rousseau.

I wonder: would Rousseau be considered such a great thinker if he'd said that slavery was "natural" for Africans and that their role on this earth was to serve?

When I was a child, eleven or twelve, I sat in class learning about the French Revolution and *Les Droits de L'homme et du Citoyen*. I knew my French well enough to know that this document spoke about the rights of men, not women.

"Why didn't women get any rights?" I asked.

"Oh, it was a different time, then. People didn't think about things like that," said my teacher.

The teacher was dead wrong. Decades later, I learned that revolutionary women fought alongside their men – and sometimes, like during The October March on Versailles, up in front directly in the line of fire – and they had fully expected to share in the victory. Instead, the male revolutionaries enacted laws restricting women's lives even more severely than they had ever been under the King. The men didn't like the fact that women were flexing their political muscles and so they made it a capital offense – yes, a capital offense – for women to gather in groups of more than five.

Six women knitting together and they could end up on the guillotine.

Mary Wollstonecraft, the British author of *A Vindication of the Rights of Women*, had lived in Paris during this revolution and wrote her book, published in 1792, in reaction to what she had witnessed. In fact, so many people had started to advocate on behalf of human rights for women that the French revolutionaries invented the word *feministe*, which then gave birth to the English word, feminist.

∞

In response to the injustice that revolutionary men had foisted on women, the *feministe* Olympe de Gouges wrote *The Rights of Woman and the Female Citizen* in 1791. She promoted a form of equality between the sexes two hundred years before the West changed to laws in the 1980s so that women finally had the right to equal property in marriage, the right for children born within or outside of wedlock to be treated equally, the right to practice any profession including legal and government roles, the right to speak freely. Probably the most surprising right that Olympe claimed for women was the right to name the father of her children. Until some point long after the French Revolution, a French woman had no right to name the child's father. If she was married, her husband was legally considered the father. If she was not married and had a child, the child's father could only be identified if he, himself, wished to step forward.

Imagine how convenient this was for the masters of the house to ensure that no maid of his could ever claim paternity.

Rousseau could only imagine human rights for less than half the population and yet he is considered a great man. Olympe knew that human rights belong to all humans and she is mostly forgotten.

Olympe's treatise on rights closes with a challenge, three simple words: "Woman, wake up."

Wake up.

On November 3, 1793, two years after writing *The Rights of Woman and the Female Citizen*, Olympe de Gouges along with another outspoken *feministe*, Madame Rolande, were guillotined.

Her death was reported in one paper as follows:

> Olympe de Gouges, born with an exalted imagination, mistook her delirium for an inspiration of nature. She wanted to be a man of state. She took up the projects of the perfidious people who want to divide France. It seems the law has punished this conspirator for having forgotten the virtues that belong to her sex.[xi]

A kinder Parisian who was witness to her death anonymously wrote:

Yesterday, at seven o'clock in the evening, a most ex-
traordinary person called Olympe de Gouges who
held the imposing title of woman of letters, was taken
to the scaffold . . . She approached the scaffold with a
calm and serene expression on her face, and forced
the guillotine's furies, which had driven her to this
place of torture, to admit that such courage and
beauty had never been seen before...

Under the small blue plaque with Olympe de Gouges' name
are the words, "*une femme de lettres feministes*". Nearly 150
years after she advocated for women's rights, French women
got the vote.

The women's revolution has been the longest, most important revolution in human history and yet few know much
about it, not even kindly sixth grade teachers.

∞

My efforts to write about all of this had been exhausting and
perhaps I've already bored you with these facts, so you see how
the writing was going (or not going) for me. Each morning I
would wake up already feeling too tired to write and not know
what to put down on paper so I did what every writer does: I
mostly avoided writing. I did a lot of online searches and read
through various websites and what do you know?

I stumbled upon a lover. A real lover. One who stayed the
night, had breakfast with me in the morning, took me to art
shows, taught me interesting historical facts about France,
kissed beautifully. His name was Günther, a German novelist

who made Paris his home. He was younger, tall and quite handsome, and a pleasure to be with.

I was finally able to exhale.

CHAPTER TWENTY-TWO

Something in Common

While enjoying free olives and cheese and a *pichet* of wine, Istmania asked why I wouldn't ever fall in love with Günther. "He's a sadist," I said.

Her eyes widened.

"But," I added, "He's pretty damned good in bed." I realized how that must have sounded. "Oh, don't worry," I explained. "There are two basic kinds of sexual sadists: those who can have an orgasm only if they're hurting somebody and those who would prefer to hurt somebody during sex but can also pretty much enjoy themselves without doing that."

"You know all this?" laughed Istmania, studying my face to see if maybe I was joking.

"Sadly, yes," I said. We both laughed.

After finishing our wine we walked through *Île St Louis* toward *Rue de Deux-Ponts*, at which point I would turn left and she would turn right. Before parting, Istmania confirmed, "You are coming to our Friday drink after class?"

Each Friday night, the students from class went around the corner to a cheerful café that served very well priced wine. I continued to join in on Friday nights and we'd each have only one glass – mostly because that's all the younger students could afford – and then we'd all be on our way to the weekend which is a universally welcomed time of the week even if you're just a French student in Paris with nothing much to do. I didn't really have a 'weekend' per se because I just wrote whenever I could and when I met Günther, I worked my so-called 'writing' schedule around his very structured writing day. It helped.

Günther, oddly enough, was a Baltic German. Estonians are rare, only a little over a million in the world. But Baltic Germans are from an even more exclusive group. Ever since the Livonian Brothers of the Sword were sent in to crush the spirit of the Estonian 'heathens' back in the 12th century, German Barons had been the ruling class of the Baltic States, forcing 7-day work weeks and collecting taxes. It was the Barons who actively kept the Baltics in bondage for all those centuries because no matter which of the many countries invaded over the centuries – Sweden, Poland, Tsarist Russia – the German Barons always obliged the victors by fulfilling their role as overlords and tax collectors.

The Soviet Union changed all that. Stalin's invading soldiers caused most Baltic Germans and many Estonians to suddenly share a common history. In 1944, Günther's once wealthy family fled the Baltics and became refugees when his mother was just a little girl, like my own mother.

While Estonian refugees had lost everything as a result of the invasion, the Baltic Germans lost even more: their status. They'd always fancied themselves aristocrats and were a bit startled to discover that their own people – the Germans back in Germany – considered them little more than country bumpkins with funny accents. Try as she might, Günther's mother could not reclaim an aristocratic title of her own so she leaned heavily on Günther to 'marry up' and find a countess or some other such female with a title. It wasn't about the money. She had married a banker and had enough money. Besides, many aristocrats who still cling to their ancestral titles have very little money. No, it was about reclaiming faded glory.

Alas, since Günther had neither title nor money, most of the available countesses whom he managed to meet snubbed this poor but tall and very handsome Baltic German author.

I met Günther through an online bulletin board. I'd been busy avoiding writing and answered his ad. I'd sworn off the dating sites but distracted myself by perusing the English language versions of online bulletin boards and when I read that this particular man was looking for someone to go to art shows and concerts with, I was up for that. I also hoped he was handsome and single and I was absolutely not disappointed.

∞

We'd agreed to meet for the first time in the middle of *Place des Vosges*, the park around the corner from where I was living. It was a sunny spring day, the park was filled with people enjoying that sun, and it was as though we had both entered the park from opposite gates at the very same moment because we met right in the middle, had walked up at the exact same time. As I walked to the middle of the park, the wind swirling my long skirt around and caused the scarf I'd wrapped around my waist to blow gently in front of me and then behind me. Just as I arrived at the center of the park, my hair blew in front of my eyes and so I pulled it back, looked up and saw a tall, very handsome man in his early 40s standing there. Dark hair, blue

252 · MARET JAKS

eyes, big white smile, lovely dimple in the chin. In a sophisticated, elegant voice tinged with a light German accent, he said,
"You look like you stepped out of a movie."

"Are you Günther?"

"Yes," he said and reached out to gently kiss my hand, the
back of my hand. "*Enchanté, Madame.*" And like any well
brought up German (Baltic or not), he bowed straight from the
waist ever so slightly.

Very charming.

That's the thing. Günther was charm, itself. He was a novelist – had actually published a few books – and on the side
wrote full feature art and culture reviews for a newspaper in
Berlin. That's where he made most of his money, actually, and
it wasn't really very much. He knew a tremendous amount
about art history, the classics, and classical music. He'd written
books on art history and a biography of a German novelist from
the 18th Century that I'd never heard of. He was ultra-sensitive
about music – I had noticed this when we were at my apartment
having a glass of wine. I had put some soft jazz on and he
rubbed his ears now and again and would then catch himself
and smile at me. I asked if he would like me to change the
music. Most music other than classical hurt his ears he explained apologetically. There was nothing he could do about
it. He was very sensitive.

This was true.

He was the most sensitive, sweetest sadist I'd ever met.

∞

We started off as art exhibit buddies, Günther and I. Then
one day I surprised myself into having sex with him. We were

at the museum next to the French *Senat* at the Luxembourg Gardens. The gardens were in full bloom and French police dress sharply in blue walked around close to the *Senat*, always watching.

We were strolling through the exhibit of Titian who was, as Günther explained, considered the greatest Venetian master during his time, the 16th century. The paintings were all portraits, images of the wealthy; the power brokers of Europe. To look at this master's work, to see how he made a fleck of paint put a sparkle in the eye, the luster in the hair, to see a slight bit of worry but mostly pride in the faces of these men, the sense of who they were, was humbling. You felt yourself to be in the actual presence of this master's subjects, feeling the spirits of the people he painted the way he saw them – or the way he knew his patrons wanted to be seen. Through his work, he had somehow kept alive the spirits of those he served nearly 500 years earlier. You could look at a Titian portrait and feel that you could almost start up a conversation with the painted image.

The portrait of an Austrian who had been the Emperor of the Holy Roman Empire in the early 1500s drew me from across the room. Günther told me that this particular Austrian emperor, Charles V, is famous for having said, "I speak Spanish to God, Italian to women, French to men and German to my horse." Günther admired that Austrian.

As we walked out of the museum into a beautiful sunny day into Luxembourg Gardens, Günther turned to me and said, "Well?"

"Well, what?"

"What do you want to do now?"

"I want to take you to bed."

"Oh," he said shyly, and smiled. "Oh, that would be . . ."

God, I thought. What did I just say? We'd not even kissed yet and here I was, ready to grab him by the tie (yes, this German author living in Paris wore suits and ties to art exhibits) and haul him to my bedroom. Which was across Paris, about a 45-minute walk away. That was embarrassing. We'd have a long walk back to my place and all that time we'd be thinking about getting naked together even though we'd never actually done that yet, not with each other. And the walk back to my place would take us over cobblestones that look romantic but are downright treacherous to walk on and then across a bridge and through throngs of tourists by Notre Dame and, in spite of what it might sound like from afar, none of that was sensual, except the view over the Seine. That's always sensual.

I'd embarrassed myself.

"I'd like that, yes," said Günther with a polite formality that felt it came out of Victorian Britain.

That's just how he was, extremely tender and polite.

Look, by this point I already knew he was a sadist. Given my unfortunate encounters with people like Frank and The Count and The Stallion, I'd learned to appear casual about whatever the fellow said on the first date, not look surprised or disgusted so that the man wouldn't hide his preferences. I wanted to know what he really wanted, not what he thought I wanted him to say. Günther had let it slip (I lured it out of him, actually, by talking about The Stallion) that he liked going to sex clubs – as The Dominator, he was quick to add. He said that in this regard, the Japanese were 'way ahead' of the West, had made a whole art of it.

Art?

Yes, he'd done a great deal of research on Japanese bondage techniques for a novel he had written but couldn't get published.

"Why not?" I enquired.

"My publishers insisted I, how did they put it? Yes, they insisted I 'disentangle' some of the sex scenes from the violence, but I refused to do it."

"They what?"

"They found it too sexually violent, wanted me to change it," he sniffed.

It must have been pretty gruesome, I thought, and he must have had a hard-on the whole time he was writing it.

That's when I made it clear that there was no way I'd be into anything but what dating websites listed as "conventional sex" with the options such as "lips / tongues" and sure "with the lights on", but that's all I needed to have a good time.

Plus a condom.

The nice thing about younger men – even just a few years younger – is that they come with their own condoms and don't make a baby face and such a fuss about putting them on. That's one of the reasons I like younger men. They're still able to function quite well with these mandatory sexual accessories. Older men whine and complain, claim they forgot their condoms hoping that I'll not have mine handy (hah!) and let them just go along for the ride, condom-less. When I whip out a condom from the drawer at the side of my bed or from my purse, it's not uncommon that we end up reverting to a night of cuddling. These poor older guys just didn't get enough condom training when they were younger, whereas the young men know how to do it properly sheathed.

Günther had explained to me, more than once, that he wasn't "one of those men" who are trapped in a routine, that he didn't always have to "play" (which is code among sado-masochists for consensual sexual violence). He found me luscious, he said.

He was so damn handsome, his hands so beautiful and his eyes so blue and bright and his smile so soft that I will admit I was thrilled to learn he didn't always have to "play" to have a good time.

As we rather awkwardly trudged along the streets of Paris back to my apartment, I tried to make small talk. "Hungry?" I asked.

"Only for you," he said politely, looking at me from the corner of his eye, smiling slightly.

"Well, you'll have to keep your strength up, won't you?" I said. "We could pick up these curried chicken pastries I know on *Île St. Louis*. It's on the way."

Sex with curried chicken breath.

Wasn't thinking.

Exhaling

Günther's breath, curried or not, was soft and light against my skin. He explored all of me as though I were a precious work of art, kissed each inch of skin on my shoulders, my neck, my face, each eyelid, down the center of me to my toes, and then half way back up. He was gentle and powerful – my favorite combination in a man, a delicious mix of strength and tenderness. He was also very skilled and I was so ready to offer myself up to him.

There are always exceptions to prove the rule and Günther was an exception as a lover. By this I mean that Günther had never been married and his girlfriends lasted three months or so and yet he was a tremendously good lover and understood a woman's body more than your average man. His lovely penis stayed rock hard even though it was tucked in that condom and when I felt him press against me, asking, inviting himself in and then gently pulling back so that we could extend our pleasure, I couldn't contain myself. Twice. I was so available to him, so ready despite the fact that I'd sometimes be thinking, "too bad he's also a sadist, he's so damn handsome" and when I opened my eyes and saw his blue, blue eyes gazing into my face in that deeply pleasured, distracted way and I'd open up to him.

"That was so easy," whispered Günther in my ear gently.

"You're so good," I whispered back. My hand stroked him, rubbing the hair on his chest and feeling down his belly to his very hard, very inviting manhood. It was big and firm and uncircumcised. I love that, an uncircumcised penis. I don't know why. Novelty, I suppose. North American men are generally circumcised and with this extra flap of skin, the 'little house' as some men have called it, there was more of an animal connection. Most male animals have little houses for their penises, don't they?

When it was Günther's time to offer himself to me, he stalled and mumbled something tenderly in German. Yes, German sounds as beautiful as French at those moments, soft and gentle and sweet. He repeated himself, again in German.

"Pardon?" I said.

"Will you be my sex slave?" he asked.

I wasn't up for that. I stayed silent. The answer was "no" of course. Not only no, but *never*.

He repeated himself again. "Will you be my sex slave?" This time, he sounded more urgent, struggling.

Oh, what the hell, I thought.

"Yes."

Wham. All his strength and power was released all at once. It was done. That's all he needed from me, a simple "yes" to his question and he was able to find his own peace with God.

"Don't, whatever you do, put that condom in the toilet," I said to him as he got up to remove it. "Really, I mean it. That toilet comes with a warning."

"Yes, I've seen that," he said calmly. "What kind of toilet is this, anyway."

"A dangerous one," I shouted as he walked down the hall. "It can't be trusted."

∞

That awful toilet with its threatening personality seemed to have its own presence in my space. I had to mention it to every guest who came to the apartment the way you'd warn someone about a roommate's preferences. "Don't leave your shoes by the door" or "please remember to hang the towels" or whatever peculiarity the particular roommate had.

Instead, I had to talk about what the toilet did and didn't like. This proved to be especially tiresome on those nights when I hosted parties for the French students. Whenever I noticed the toilet door open, I'd call out "Remember, nothing but a small bit of toilet paper . . ." and always crossed my fingers. It was uncomfortable.

Yes, in an odd sort of way, the toilet was like a roommate and now me and my toilet also had some lovely company on a fairly regular basis. Günther was careful to mind its special needs and never, not once, did he toss a condom down that toilet.

I felt I could get along with a man like that for the rest of my stay in Paris, a man who could be tender and loving and powerfully masculine during sex without being threatening. It was odd and I don't think he actually noticed, but he'd given me all the power because he could absolutely never ever have his orgasm until I simply said "yes" to that question of his. That's all I'd have to do, and sometimes I'd say "yes" right away and at other times, I'd playfully delay my answer, making him ask again. And again. I'd never say "yes" long term to a man like that, though. He was to be my lover, never my love. He couldn't be my love. We'd never be able to fully satisfy each other's deepest needs. But, sadist or no sadist, I had finally managed to land a highly skilled, attentive, polite, well-educated and very sexy younger man in my bed.

What I didn't realize at the time, though, was that sadism can be contagious.

∞

The doorbell kept ringing and the floor kept squeaking. There were already too many people packed into the place but at this point, I had no control over the situation.

"Thanks," I kept saying as people arrived with their potluck dinner contributions.

We were having a going away party for The Bulgarian (Marija was her actual name) because she was heading off to Spain. I'd told her to invite her friends from the school.

She had a lot of friends.

It made sense, really, because everyone loved Marija. She was just a down-to-earth, decent and kind person and when she looked at you she always smiled a very big smile, her eyes shining. Marija spoke no English and I spoke no Bulgarian so we muddled through in our pretty mediocre French on those Friday nights out with the class. She had been a bit of a mystery to everyone. We couldn't exactly tell her age, we didn't know why she was in Paris or anything about her other than she was quite a lovely person.

"Yes, I am married," she answered to my question one day. "And I have two babies. One aged two and the other 9 months." She could tell what the next question would be from me so she answered. "They are in Bulgaria with my husband and his mother."

They had lived together in a big house in Sofia, the capital of Bulgaria. Her husband owned a winery. Yes, Bulgarians make wine. That was a surprise to me, too, but I later learned that just before the collapse of the Soviet Union, Bulgaria was the second largest winemaking country in the world. As well, it has a long, long history of winemaking dating back to the Thracians which means Bulgarians were making wine long before the French ever got around to it.

Being much younger than her husband, and speaking only Bulgarian, Marija felt out of place when his friends would arrive and speak in French while they sipped his wine. But she didn't come to Paris to learn French. She came to Paris because she wanted a divorce.

"Please," her husband had pleaded. "Please go to Paris, live with my sister and think about things. If, after a while, you really know you want a divorce, I will accept that. But please think about it, go to Paris."

So here she was. She'd been here for five months and for some reason blurted out her whole story to me all at once, nearly all in one breath.

"I had owned a design shop in Sofia, made dresses and hats and things. Then I got married. My husband is thirteen years older than I am. His friends are so much more sophisticated. I always felt, I don't know, a nothing when all of them were at the house. There I was, living in the shadows, twenty-four years old with two little babies and I thought 'My life is over'."

"Over?" I asked.

"Yes, I felt it was time to wear a babushka. What was left for me in life? I had a baby so young. Then I met you and you had a baby even younger and your life is not over."

God, I hope not, I thought.

"You wear such nice clothes and you laugh and you're funny."

"Oh, I don't always laugh," I said, "But, sometimes, what else is there to do?"

Marija smiled, knowing the truth of that. "Yes, well, you are older than my mother and you still wear short skirts."

See? Robert's advice to keep wearing short skirts had inspired someone else, too.

"Marija, life is never over until you close your eyes for the last time," I said. "It's true that lots of people end their lives long before they're actually dead but it doesn't mean you have to do that. I refuse to do that." I paused to see if she wanted to say something but she seemed to ache for more motherly advice from a woman who still wore short skirts. "Just remember this: live your life like you own it. Because you do. I think everyone should take Auntie Mame's advice: 'Live, live, live!'"

"Auntie Mame?"

"From a movie."

"Oh." Marija thought a moment but I could tell she didn't know what movie I was talking about. "My mother," she continued, "Had children, put on her babushka, got fat and, well, all she did was be a mother. I've never seen her happy, not really happy. I don't want that."

"Then don't do that," I said. "Do whatever you want. That was the whole point about the Women's Revolution. Do what you want, not what you're told to want. Anyway, Paris is a magical city. Have you noticed that? It has a gift for each of us if we look for it. Any idea what Paris is giving you?"

"Time to decide," she said, "whether I want a divorce."

∞

Put a whole bunch of people from around the world who don't know each other – some Estonians from the Embassy, all those young people who were learning French, Luz the Argentinian cleaning lady and her husband who brought his marionettes – add in the various international dishes they've cooked up for the party and a few bottles of something (including just plain orange juice) and what do you have?

A bit too much fun.

All of them were squatted in a circle and dancing to Lebanese music with their arms crossed and kicking out their legs like a bunch of Russian dancers. No one was drunk but absolutely everyone was happy. Quite a number of the people – for example, the man who brought the Lebanese dance music – were Muslim and they'd been drinking only the orange juice but were dancing with just as much uninhibited bouncing joy as everybody else.

The whole floor was heaving with each bounce.

"Quite a party," said Istmania. We were the only two people not bouncing up and down on the floor. Even my cleaning lady, Luz, and her husband who had already done his marionette show for us earlier in the night, were squatting and bouncing and kicking out and laughing.

Fortunately, the music was so loud that I couldn't hear the doorbell ring when my Neighbor Below came pounding up the stairs. Only much later did I learn, from the partygoers who were also smokers, that every time they walked down the stairs to go for a smoke she'd burst out from her apartment and scream at them. It had startled them at first but, after a while, they did the French Shrug.

"People! People! People!" I shouted over the din. "I want to make a toast before the Last Metro."

The last metro in Paris triggers a sudden end to a party. It was really the only way to get home for most of the students as well as for Luz and her husband and those puppets. None of them had cars or enough money for taxis. Lots of them lived on the outskirts of Paris where the rents are cheaper and it was too far to walk.

"It's the Last Metro?" someone asked frantically. A few looked at their watches.

"No, no, there's still time," somebody said with relief and poured himself another glass of wine.

"I just want to make a toast to Marija." Everyone looked over at Marija and held up a glass if they could find theirs or an imaginary glass if they couldn't. "Here is to love and luck and happiness."

"Here's to love and luck and happiness," everyone chimed in.

We were celebrating because Marija had finally understood something.

"I love my husband," she'd told me a week earlier. "I want to go home. We talked last night and I'm going to start my store again, just part-time. His mom agreed to look after the boys when I'm in the store."

They'd decided to meet up again in Spain, where they'd spent their first honeymoon, and have a second honeymoon and a second start to their shared life.

That's why we absolutely had to have a party and why we were all so happy.

It was going to be worth the massive amount of grief I'd get tomorrow from the Neighbor Below.

∞

I woke up after the party and realized that my time in Paris would be coming to a close soon, too. My flight back was two months away and it was clear that my book about the famous feminists haunting an apartment in Paris was not going to be done. It wasn't even close to being done. I'd kept rewriting it, trying to get into the 'groove', to find a technique that would work, make the characters come alive but I couldn't. The book so far was boring and flat and, besides, who'd want to read it? Who was my audience for the book? It embarrassed me to think that I'd spent so much of my life imagining that I would be a writer and here I was looking at a pile of nothing. I'd be going home man-less and book-less. Not quite the dream fulfilled that I'd been hoping for.

The morning after the Bulgarian sendoff party, I woke early as usual and continued my 'avoid writing' techniques by wading around the online bulletin board ads in the section 'Men Seeking Women', sort of wanting to see if Günther still had an ad in order to satisfy the sadistic side of his sexual needs (he didn't), and then got distracted and began looking at ads from all over the world. One, posted in London, made me laugh out loud:

Seriously insane, venal, Nigerian hustler seeks harem -
Age: 106

I clicked open the posting.

> Not really. Not at all. Tonight I've been surfing
> through lots of these online ads. Holy shit! There are a
> lot of spooky, deranged, or just depressed people
> around. I am actually living on an island in the Medi-
> terranean, having moved here from London two years
> ago. I write for a living, I've got a couple of ex-wives
> and some kids. I'm 58 years old, have published
> books, edited magazines, written columns, won liter-
> ary prizes, been around the block. It's seriously hard to
> take myself too seriously. I'll swap pictures - or jokes.
> Oh yeah, my height requirements are blah blah blah, I
> am dying to hear from American women living in Kan-
> sas who would like to meet Hugh Grant, and I like all
> kinds of alternative hotel music, particularly Coco Ro-
> sie.

I felt compelled to write him, thanking him for the laugh, gave him a quick summary of the weird encounters I'd been having with men in Paris and said it was so comforting to see that a man had actually noticed how weird things had gotten in the dating world, from an online perspective. I also sent him a joke – he said he'd swap jokes, so why not? Then I wished him well and went out to a flower shop that opened early.

I left some bouquets at the doors of the Neighbor Above and the Neighbor Below with a little note of apology – explaining that I was sorry for the noise the night before and tried to sum- marize it all by saying simply: "It was the Bulgarians."

CHAPTER TWENTY-FOUR

The Ultimatum

After dropping off the flowers I went as usual to meet up with the Seine on *Île St Louis*, and do yoga next to my chestnut tree. This time, something was off. I was in that 'bend over, touch your toes, breathe, and then hold that posture' pose, looking through my legs at an upside-down Paris. Yes, something was off. First, there was that homeless man who lived under the bridge. It wasn't unusual that I would see him in the morning from this upside-down angle, sweeping the walkway in front of his little hole under the bridge where he lived. I often did this pose and often saw him upside down in the morning. No, that wasn't what was unusual. What was unusual was that he was sweeping the walkway wearing flowing pink harem pants, a blue bolero jacket and an orange turban. I could see the curly white hair on his chest from here. I continued to hold that posture, trying not to let his fashion sense distract me.

But why was he wearing harem pants, I wondered.

Often, there just aren't reasonable answers to things. We move along through life doing our best but what does it matter? What does it matter?

268 · MARET JAKS

Then I began to cry. My life felt upside down and I didn't
know what to do. In a little over two months I would be on a
plane back home. I knew I would be leaving without love
(Günther, remember, didn't count) and without a book. Yes,
I'd been writing. Sometimes just a little snippet of something,
sometimes a whole boring chapter. But did it matter?
Shouldn't I just give up and become a tourist? I had two
months to do something with. Yes, maybe I should be a tourist,
hit a whole bunch of museums and take in the sights outside of
Paris, go to Burgundy or Bordeaux or just hop in a rented car
and take a road trip anywhere at all.

While doing yoga by the Seine a few weeks earlier, a small
poem seemed to float up from the river, itself, and land in my
heart. I'd quickly noted it down and went back to doing yoga.
It was now repeating itself in my head:

> *Let go your tiny anchor.*
> *It won't hold you anyway.*
> *The river has a job to do*
> *and you can't keep your life*
> *at bay.*

I kept hearing this as I stood there bent over in the forward
bend pose and a tear rolled up my face and fell off my forehead.
Was I holding on too hard to the idea of writing? Did it mean
I should give up? Is that why the little poem kept repeating
itself in my head?

I stood up and wiped the tears from my forehead, looked out
over the River Seine and asked her to help me, to give me a
sign.

The French have a story about how the Seine was formed. The Seine was originally a beautiful young woman but her beauty caught the attention of the old sea god and he chased after her, to rape her as so many of those Greek and Roman gods enjoyed doing back then. She wanted nothing to do with the horrible man so she ran away as fast as she could and when the old geezer nearly caught up with the beautiful young woman, another god took pity on her and made her into a river so that just as the would-be rapist caught up with the girl, she slipped through the old man's hands and became a river.

The Seine is still affected by that old sea god. Each day, as the sea god keeps trying to reach her, she moves further inland and when the sea god gives up for the day, she relaxes and flows to the sea.

Even this far inland, the waters of the River Seine move back and forth with the tide.

Today, the Seine had nothing to offer me. Police divers were doing their morning swim practice next to the police boat that chugged along slowly. People fall into the Seine and the river police rescue them, so on many mornings, you'll see these police keeping in shape this way. The seagulls were swooping over the river looking for breakfast. The pigeons marched along and pecked at the gravel between the stones. The chestnut tree by my side watched it all, as usual.

I had come here to maybe find love and to write a book. I'd accomplished neither. I'd come to Paris, gotten on an Internet merry-go-round, tried to grab that brass ring, but I'd missed it and time had raced by. What had I done here? Not what I'd expected to do, not at all.

Writing is 'a peculiar form of torture' said the novelist, E.A. Markham, and it's lonely, very lonely, too. I'd locked myself away trying to get that book out of me but it was no use.

There by the banks of the Seine, I knew I wanted something to break, something to give – to get a signal from Life, a sign that would tell me to go on writing or give up. I felt a fury building in me despite the fact that I was doing yoga, which is supposed to calm you down. A rage began to burn and I was tired, damn it. I was tired of all my own foolishness and this wasted effort. I'd given up on the man thing. There was nothing I could do about that. But what about writing? I'd been writing all my life, hoping for the day I'd come to Paris and put it all together and it wasn't working. It just wasn't working.

I stood up and yelled toward the sky, "Damn it! I want a sign and I want it *today!*" I stomped my way over to the stairs, past the man in what I now realized were see-through pink harem pants (he was wearing underwear, thank heavens) and as I marched up the stairs, wanting to know if I should bother writing any more or if I should just go off and enjoy the last several weeks of Paris rather than struggle so hard, I gave an ultimatum.

"Look," I said out loud because it was still the morning and all of *Île St Louis* was sleeping except for the man in harem pants and what did I care what he thought. "Look, if I don't get a sign – and get it *today* – I quit. I'm not writing anymore. I want a sign, and I want it *now!*"

Who was I shouting at?

Life. The Universe. Everything.

With that, I stomped past that strange man there by the Seine, stomped across the bridge, and then stomped all the way back to the apartment. I went straight into the bathroom and used the monster toilet and I only tell you this because it was the monster toilet that gave me a sign.

It heaved, roared (yes, roared and threatened me) and then belched everything back up.

Disgustingly so.

"Oh, no, no, no!" I pleaded out loud with the toilet. "No, please!"

It didn't matter. Stuff got on the floor, oozed around the bottom of the useless bidet and inched its way toward the tub. It didn't really matter how disgusting this was, how really horribly creepy it was to have to call the plumber, I had to.

Despite the fact that the bathroom walls had notices posted in two languages, the plumber spoke only one: French. Turns out, my French classes had paid off. He understood and came right away.

∞

I'd already opened the bathroom window and wiped up as much of the toilet belch off the floor that I could manage using rolls and rolls of paper towels and stuffed it all into a few plastic bags before Pierre the Plumber arrived.

"It's an old toilet," he said.

"Yes," I said, nodding. The two of us stood there in the bathroom facing the toilet, feeling a bit cautious because that thing seemed to be threatening to belch again if we came any closer.

"We have to empty it," said Pierre the Plumber decidedly.

"We do?"

"Yes."

Sorry, but he was the trained professional, not me. That's what he was paid for.

I had lived in terror of this toilet for months now and, finally, the toilet had spoken. If you go around asking Life for a sign, it's important you be prepared for the answer, know how to read the signs. I'd asked for a sign and this was it: My writing was full of shit.

Give it up.

Oh, God, I thought. A lifetime of dreams gone, just like that.

I'd asked for it. It was my own fault. I'm superstitious and a person really shouldn't threaten The Universe like that without expecting something in return.

Just standing watching as Pierre emptied the toilet made me go into the kitchen and wash my hands some more.

"Here you go," said Pierre the Plumber cheerfully, holding three more plastic bags but this time, instead of being full of paper towels it was full of liquid and goo and yuck.

"What am I supposed to do with this?" I asked.

"Put it in the garbage. And then I will turn off the water.""

"Turn off the water? Wait. Wait until I get back."

I raced down the stairs with the bags of liquid stuff and placed them in the big garbage bin in the courtyard and was never able to look at that garbage bin again the same way. Then I ran back up the stairs and scrubbed my hands some more.

"OK, Pierre," I said. "You can turn the water off now."

He tried to fix it. He really did. But after an hour or so, he gave up and called the landlady using my phone. I sat at the dining room where I'd struggled to write all these months and thought glumly, "I'll have to scrub that phone when he's gone."

"Yes, Madame," said Pierre courteously but firmly, "It is finally dead. No, it's not her fault. No, it was an old toilet and

I told you it would die soon and now it has. It should have been replaced when it broke again last year. No, I can't let you blame her. It was not her fault." He nodded in agreement to something. "And, yes, she understands every word I'm saying right now. Yes, she does understand French. Yes, I know, she didn't understand so well before but now she does . . ."

Pierre the Plumber smiled with kindness looking over the phone toward me.

Then he began to speak rapidly. I've no idea what he said and he nodded a few times and hung up the phone.

"That's it," he said happily. "A new toilet."

"How much?" I asked nervously. With the way that rental agreements are written in France, the fact that the toilet had died on my 'watch' while I was renting the place probably meant that it was *usagée* and I'd now be stuck paying for it.

"A lot. It's a lot of money, these electronic toilets. When people put bathrooms into apartments without the right kind of plumbing, you see, it's a lot of money. Right here," he walked me over to the bathroom, pointing at something along the floor and behind the tub. That empty, fowl-looking monster toilet had had one last laugh at me but now it was dead. Dead, empty. "Along here, the toilet has to push, push hard, to get everything moving along when normally a toilet just needs to use gravity, but here, along the wall and up to over here," Pierre kept pointing out things I didn't really want to know, "the toilet must push, not drop, and so it needs strength to do that and the electric motor must do the work and, well, it becomes tired and breaks."

The toilet sat there in silence with not even a drop of water or anything else in it. Just an emptiness. It was dead.

"But how much do I have to pay?"

"Nothing," said Pierre. "Your landlady has to pay. It's her toilet, not yours." Then he winked at me. "You know, in truth, it was you or someone you know who put a tampon down the toilet and these toilets, they can't take anything but a little bit of toilet paper. But . . . to my mind, Madame Catellini has made so many people pay for her plumbing problems that I thought it just wasn't right. No. You broke the toilet, yes, but it is still her toilet. She will pay me, not you."

It had to be one of the French students, I thought. Sure, there were signs all over the bathroom warning people about the monster toilet but who reads bathroom walls at parties?

Pierre the Plumber began to putter with the landlady's toilet, unscrew things, and I went back to my computer. I could hear him whistling cheerfully, loving his stinky job.

I opened my laptop and, since I'd already gotten the message from the toilet, there was no way I'd even think of writing. Nope. It was over.

My heart felt dead, stunned into silence. Is the heart the seat of dreams? It must be, because my heart felt like a clump of lead, heavy in my chest. I wasn't even sure it was beating.

Enough, already. I'd asked for a sign and I'd gotten one. I'd mourn later.

∞

I went into my email account. There was only one email for me and it wasn't from Günther. It was from the writer I'd emailed earlier that morning, the writer living on a Mediterranean island who'd written that posting about how weird so many of the men's dating profiles are. He really was a writer. He'd replied with quite a lengthy email about his life, the books he'd written, his featured articles in *Vogue* and other major magazines, and a bit about his next project. He wrote so much that it seemed to me he was avoiding writing . . . like any good writer does! But what he didn't know while he was distracting himself by writing this email was how very important his opening paragraph would be to me, how life changing. It jolted my heart, restarting it. I gasped and Pierre, who was crouched over the toilet, peered out of the bathroom to see if I was all right. I smiled at him. Beamed, even.

You see, it wasn't only the toilet that had given me a sign that day. The writer had unwittingly sent me two additional signs. First, he helped me believe that someone in this great big Universe of ours had heard me wail out there by the Seine. Without knowing it, the writer had confirmed for me that there was magic in the world, something bigger to life than just working and eating and sleeping, a force that not only connects to us all but also connects us all. My body felt like it was sparkling, shining even.

The second sign he sent along was the opening paragraph. I read those three opening lines over and over again.

I hadn't told this man that I was writing anything. No, I would never have said that to an actual writer, to someone who made his living doing what I was still puttering around with. I was too embarrassed about that tedious, boring book I'd been scribbling at to have admitted it. The writer had said something that inspired me to see what I needed to do. The toilet, it was right about my book. I'd read that sign right and I knew I had to throw that first book aside. The second sign I got that day from the writer was that I had to write a different book. He didn't even know he'd said that because all he said in his first paragraph, a paragraph I read over and over again, was:

Your social adventures since you arrived in Paris are
worthy of a feature film. Funny and terrifying at the
same time. You write extremely well.

"You write extremely well," he'd said. "You write extremely well."

I write extremely well! Me!

Each time I read those three sentences from this highly accomplished writer, I felt so grateful to Life, to The Universe, to
Everything.

Of course, I'd written only one paragraph to him about my
life in Paris, but he liked it! It was funny, he'd said. Terrifying,
too. That's good, I thought. Good!

"Yes!" I shouted and jumped up from the chair, slapping
down the lid of my laptop in victory.

"*Pardon?*" asked Pierre as he peaked out again from the
bathroom.

"Nothing, nothing," I smiled, shining.

"Well," said Pierre as he hauled the dead toilet to the door.
"I'll order the new toilet and you should have it in two or three
days."

"*Pardon?*" It was my turn to be surprised. "What am I to
do?"

"Oh, I'm sure your neighbors will let you use their toilets."

Oh, I thought, I'm pretty sure not.

"You can use the shower now and also the kitchen. The
water's back on," said Pierre as he lugged the toilet to the hallway. "And," he said as he called back while shoving the dead
toilet into the little elevator, "I'll call you when the new toilet
arrives."

I was forced to learn that people can, indeed, live in Paris for days without a toilet in their apartment. When Hemingway wrote about *Place de la Constrescarpe* just after World War I, none of the apartments around the *Place* had indoor plumbing. At least, here in the 21st century, I'd still be able to have a warm bath and brush my teeth and wash dishes. I figured out how to use a bucket for most urgencies (all you need to do is carefully drain the bucket down the bathroom sink and then scrub out that sink) and I walked down the street to the café for the other situation. Then, after three days, the new toilet arrived. I figured that this was cause to celebrate, so I woke up the morning after the toilet had been installed and decided I'd spend the whole day writing and nothing else. It was time to focus on what I'd really come to Paris for. I came to Paris to reclaim my life, to prove that just because life sometimes takes you on a very wiggly, very long scenic route with the occasionally terrifying moments that make you race along in the wrong direction, you can always keep trying to drive in the direction of your dreams.

George Eliot once said, "It is never too late to become what you might have been."

My transition day toward who I might have been and who I might become was today.

Today.

New toilet, new life.

That monster toilet, now sitting on a heap of other dead toilets somewhere on the outskirts of Paris, was right and I'm glad I listened to it. In its last gasp of life, it did its best to send me a message. I still hold a strange sort of affection for that thing. It had been my roommate in Paris, after all. But it was right. The other book wasn't what I was supposed to be working on.

It wasn't other people's lives I needed to be focused on but my own, the magic of my own life, the magic that each of us can touch by living, really living, in this world with all the privileges and fun and responsibilities that being a fully engaged citizen entails.

It was thanks to the efforts of those *feministes* I had come to love that I could do what I was doing now, live life as I wanted to live, earn a good living while keeping my clothes on and keep my baby with me even though I was single and just a teenager. Yes, I was able to have sex without a signed marriage license and still be permitted to hold a job and not be shamed or, as in some countries still today, stoned to death.

In short, it was because of their efforts and the efforts of so many millions of wonderful women and men through the years that I could, as my stubborn little seven-year-old self had decided, now live as "a Woman and be whatever I wanted to be and do whatever I wanted to do."

Writing with a new focus, shifting gears, was what I now had to do to become what I wanted to be: a writer.

After opening the windows both to the street and to the courtyard to let the sounds of Paris and the sunny breeze swirl around the apartment, I sat down at the dining room table and turned on my computer.

∞

Günther was impressed with my determination, my focus. He had work to do, too, and so we each wrote on our own during the days and spent time together at night and had breakfast together before going back to our writing routine.

"There's a movie I thought you might like to see," said Günther one Sunday morning as we were having our usual breakfast of mangoes and coffee and croissants and toasted *tartines*. I'd taken to buying a full baguette the night before and using the leftover for breakfast. The moment you cut a baguette down the middle and slather something on the top (in this case, butter and lavender honey), it's called a *tartine*. Any open-faced sandwich is a tartine, actually.

"Another Film Noir?" I asked trying not to sigh. Günther was doing an article on the many Film Noirs at the various little movie theatres scattered all over Paris and between my own spurts of writing, I'd tagged along until it got too predictably boring. A lonely detective or a down-and-out writer, a femme fatale, a few hard-boiled criminals, some murders and many cups of black coffee – that's all I can remember of the half dozen or so Film Noirs I'd seen with Günther. He was drawn to these films, they were his 'favorite'.

"No, a different sort," was all he said. "I don't remember the title."

I really should have pressed Günther for details because when we were three minutes into that film, I really wanted to hurt that man in a way he'd never forget.

CHAPTER TWENTY-FIVE

Does Mild Sadism Hurt?

The theatre was built into the bowels of Paris, an underground theatre cut from the limestone under the city. We'd gone inside, bought tickets and then went down, down, down a very long, narrow flight of stairs to the theatre. There's no popcorn in Paris theatres. No popcorn, no whispering, no drinks, no candy. Here, nothing threatens the velvet silence that is a Paris movie theatre. In this sacred darkness, you must never utter a sound or shift suddenly in your seat and you must certainly never, ever giggle or groan or breathe too loudly, not even if you're watching a porn musical.

Which is what Günther had brought me to see.

Inside my head I screamed "Günther, I'll get you for this!" I seethed – silently and to myself, of course – as we sat watching a skinny little girl who was roughly the same age as my youngest daughter wander around an apartment and wiggle on command, naked from her waist down for much of the film. The male character was fully clothed.

Until he wasn't. Which is how I then found my way to get back at Günther.

The director, I learned later, wanted to provoke the British rating system so he made sure that all of the explicit sexual acts (and there were many) were done with a very young woman smiling at the camera or outright "asking for it". This way, the filmmaker could claim the explicit sex was consensual and could now be called "art" and shown in regular movie theaters rather than just porn houses.

The young woman, just barely out of her teens, had been a Southern Baptist and agreed to do the film just to strike out at her ultra-conservative mother. She immediately regretted it and asked, then begged, the director not to use her real name in the credits.

He didn't consent. He used her real name.

As we began watching this horrible excuse for a film, I kept wondering how I'd get back at Günther for this. I also wondered, "Isn't being paid money for sex actually prostitution?" Prostitution isn't legal in Britain where the movie was filmed. Yet here we had an illegal activity that was filmed and then distributed to movie theaters, and respectable reviewers sat watching this, scribbling notes, and then wrote their reviews. Oh, and another reason this thing could be loosely called art was because between the sex scenes, the girl would put her clothes back on and go to a loud and pretty awful grunge concert.

It would have been mildly less shocking to be sitting there watching a porn musical had my lover and I not – at breakfast the very day before – talked about what I have in common with the great writer D. H. Lawrence: we both deeply loathed pornography.[xii]

This fact had startled Günther. For some peculiar reason, porn-lovers equate porn-haters with sex-haters. So, you're either 'for' sexual oppression (pornography, sex clubs, strippers) or 'for' sexual oppression (no sex at any time for any reason)?

That doesn't make any sense.

The two of us had stumbled upon the subject of pornography when this lover of mine had told me how wildly uninhibited I was compared to other women.

"I am?" I said shyly, a little flattered. "I wouldn't know. I don't sleep with other women, so I wouldn't know. I just do what I want."

"And I like what you want," he smiled. "You're so pornographic."

The word pornographic sounds oh so very much worse when it's said with a German accent.

My face tightened. Darkened, really. My lover noticed.

"Pornographic? What the hell does porn have to do with me? I'm just being a normal woman. And I can tell you it's damn hard these days to be a normal woman with pornography shouting obscenities at us all the time. Why insult me like that?"

"I didn't mean to insult you."

"Don't consider me pornographic! A good lover? Thanks. A 'wildly uninhibited lover?' If you think so. But pornographic? That's just, well, that's just, that's just sad."

"Sad?" said Günther, still awfully surprised that what he considered to be this wildly uninhibited lover of his could hardly keep from spitting when the word 'pornographic' came out of her mouth.

"Pornography's not real. It's just business. It just sells your own orgasms back to you."

"That's an interesting thought," said Günther, hiding his shock at my reaction by rubbing his chin like an old man, pondering.

"Do you think you and I 'do' pornography? That disgusts me. I mean even D.H. Lawrence hated pornography, you know." I thought that it would appeal to the writer in Günther to bring up D. H. Lawrence. "He's probably rolling, no writhing, in his grave right now, poor man, the way the porn industry – and it's only an industry, not a sacred right -- used *Lady Chatterley's Lover* to prop up all sorts of exploitive lies. He wrote that pornographers 'diddle' the masses, making porn users unable to tell the difference between what they want and what the exploiters want them to want." I stuffed half of my croissant in my mouth to shut myself up for a moment and he sat there sipping his coffee, still thinking (probably scheming, I realize now). "Günther, you and I have fun in bed because you're a really good lover and you care about how I'm feeling with you," I said, touching his lovely hand. "With you, I can't help but answer your 'call'."

He smiled, getting the allusion to one of D. H. Lawrence's poems about the 'call' and the 'answer' between two lovers.

I passed my lover slices of sweet mango and poured us some more coffee. Normally, Günther would have insisted on doing these small graces but today he was different, distracted.

"D. H. Lawrence said that porn lovers hate sex as much as the 'greyest Puritan' – his words."

Günther looked at me, kept drinking his coffee and kept listening quietly. This had impressed me at the time. I really thought he was listening, paying attention.

But I had been duped.

∞

He and I were now sitting in that theatre built into the lime-stone under Paris and I couldn't believe what was happening. It felt surreal. He'd tricked me. The bastard. I blinked. I hardly breathed. Now and again Günther looked over to see my reaction, but I didn't move. Not at all. Yes, I wanted to leave, to jump from my chair, to slap Günther hard across the face – no, to punch him right in the nose, actually – and yell out, "How dare you! How dare you!"

But no. I was smart enough not to do that. Why? Because getting upset would have given him pleasure. Remember, a sadist takes pleasure in other people's suffering and I was not about to let Günther get a millisecond of pleasure from what he'd just done. He would never know how I was really feeling right now, my heart thumping too slowly, dark and bruised, as the two of us sat side-by-side watching these kids do their best to sell erections.

Occasionally, Günther would look over at me to get a reaction and I'd look at him and smile gently. No, I'd never let him see what was really going on inside me. Never.

Oddly enough, or perhaps not so oddly, it was during this film that I discovered my own inner sadist. I can honestly say that I have never before – ever – taken any pleasure from an-other person's pain but during that movie, something snapped. when I noticed that Günther had started to suffer. He would look my way uncomfortably, rub his ears, try to smile and then face the screen again. Oh, how I enjoyed those moments and especially when, periodically, the girl would get dressed and she and her man would go off to a raunchy grunge concert.

Günther wouldn't actually call that music. It was screech-
ing noise blasting from electric guitars and drums and, oh, how
wonderfully Günther suffered through each second of those
songs. Günther suffers when he hears a single wrong note at a
Beethoven concert, so imagine how much he rubbed his ears
whenever the grunge guitar squealed and shrieked at full blast.
First one ear, then the other. At one point, he was rubbing both.

That wasn't enough for me, though. I wanted him to suffer
more and I wanted his pain to come from me directly. I wasn't
sure how, but I was going to get him. Oh, just you wait, I
thought.

Every time Günther flinched, I smiled inside. The elegant,
polished writer, the passionate reviewer of classical music and
Wagnerian operas, so hated rock 'n' roll let alone grunge that
that the pain must have been ricocheting about in that clueless
head of his. At times, he held his nose, bracing against the pain
as though holding his breath would lessen the intensity, like
when you plug your nose on a plane to relieve the pressure as
it lands.

"Take that! Ha, ha!" I thought as I shot sharp mental arrows
at him in the darkness, hoping the rancid music would get even
louder and make it worse for him.

Now, if you think that I might have been wrong about Günther's sadistic interest in taking me to a film like this, think
again. He'd once let me have a glimpse of his extended version
of sadism when he told me about a roommate of his, a woman
who'd learned of his particular interest in S&M clubs. She was
a masochist, she'd hungrily explained to him, and asked more
than once for him to take her to one of those clubs. He didn't.
So his roommate would wander around the apartment always
half dressed, thinking that would convince him. Günther said

he made a point of pretending not to notice that her bosom (as he called it) was nearly always falling out of her loosely tied housecoat and he watched with increasing pleasure as her sexual tension kept building throughout the weeks.

"Well?" I asked. "Did you finally give in?"

"Oh no," he smiled. "Never. And I don't think she understood that I was helping her out, really. Giving her a taste of it."

"Helping her out?"

"She said she wanted to experience S&M and so you see by not ever, not even once, acknowledging her womanhood, no matter what she did, even though she was quite a beautiful young woman . . ." he grinned slyly, remembering back. "I made her s-u-ffer." He said the word 'suffer' slowly, softly, as if the word itself deserved affection. Then he smiled brightly and looked me straight in the eyes. "Now, that's a bit sadistic, don't you think?"

I actually had to laugh. It was funny, really. It's like the old joke but it's not so much of a joke, is it? "A masochist says please beat me; a sadist says no."

He knew what he was doing back then, and he knew now.

What he didn't know was that I was going to get him.

Yet the more I watched of this porn musical, the more elusive seemed the revenge. So far, we'd not seen the male actor naked.

And then we did. I won't go into the details but let me tell you, when I finally saw that young man's glory I sighed, for this was the mightiest, most beautiful penis I'd ever seen in my life. A work of art in itself. Wow. Whoever did the casting for this porn musical had done a very, very good job for the male lead.

The music continued to be perfectly awful so I knew that Günther was still suffering in silence. I practiced whispering the word 'suffer' in my head, mentally saying it with the same breathless affection as Günther when he'd told me how he'd made his foolishly curious roommate s-u-ffer. Slowly. Say it slowly. S-u-ffer. Günther, I'll make you s-u-ffer.

At long last, the rock and roll shrieked to its merciful end, the kids put some clothes on and caught a cab. Over. Done. Thank heavens.

The credits rolled and the lights slowly started to light up the porn cavern. Günther looked at me, probing my face, seeking a reaction. "Well?" he said, forcing an innocent curiosity, foolishly unprepared for what I was about to say.

I smiled brightly. "All I can say is . . ." I leaned into Günther's shoulder and gave a breathy whisper, my lips lightly touching his ear, "I want a cock like *that* for Christmas!"

At this point, I should say that I'm ashamed to remember how very much this startled Günther, how much it hurt him to hear me speak of another man's glory in such a greedy way and how much I enjoyed seeing how much it hurt. Yes, I should say that I'm ashamed.

But I'm not.

As it turns out, though, two sadists don't really do so well together. One of you has to enjoy being hurt and no self-respecting sadist I know likes to feel pain.

CHAPTER TWENTY-SIX

Surprises and Then Some

Günther took me to a café and bought me a coffee after the film. We sat there together but things would never be the same. He was unable to stop thinking about what I'd told him. "It interested you, did it?" he asked.

"What?" I replied innocently.

"The . . . the look of that man?"

"Oh, no, he wasn't so handsome. You're very handsome."

"Yes, but I'm not really a comparison to how he looks."

"No, you're much more handsome. The actor's face wasn't all that good looking but he was very fit, wasn't he?" I waited a moment. "And you know, I've never seen a penis that big before, and so beautiful, too. It was really beautiful, don't you think?"

"I don't know," he sighed and rubbed his ear again. Was it a coincidence that he rubbed the ear that I'd whispered into? "I don't actually think about the size of things."

You could say that my plan backfired because after that, no matter how hard he tried (and he did try, poor boy), Günther was unable to get an erection. Well, with me, anyway.

"This isn't normal," said Günther.

"I know, really I do. You're usually so 'up at the ready' and everything."

"Yes," he sighed and lay back on the pillow. "It's just that I can't really stop thinking about what you said." I let him think about it some more. "I keep thinking that you're thinking about what you want for Christmas."

It was a nasty thing Günther had done to me. Nasty. Before taking me to that awful film, he'd read one of my papers on the effects of pornography and how it had gotten mainstreamed.

Over our breakfast of mangoes and coffee the day before our visit to the porn musical, I had explained that just because lots of people feel more comfortable imagining that pornography has no effect on any of us, that it's just good 'fun' or a release valve of some sort, doesn't mean they're right. They're misinformed. A picture says a thousand words, we all know that, and a lot of what pornography is telling us is not only wrong, it's dangerous.

Back in the 60s, when pornography was quickly becoming mainstream, people heard what they wanted to hear. When Denmark decriminalized pornography and prostitution, a year later it was announced that a minor miracle had occurred -- sex crimes had gone down in Denmark. But it wasn't true.

Not at all.

It was just the opposite, only worse.

∞

These are the facts: prior to the change in the laws, Denmark counted pornography and prostitution as sex crimes. When the laws changed, the number of sex crimes only appeared to go down because all the numbers relating to pornography and prostitution had evaporated. They were no longer counted as sex crimes. When another study[xiii] was commissioned, this is what was discovered: when pornography and prostitution were decriminalized, the number of violent rapes increased.

This new, more scientifically sound study was never widely reported by the media.

Beyond the rape effect, the fact that pornography commercializes the most precious part of our humanity – our ability to share the deepest part of ourselves – is what bothers me (and, by the way, bothered D. H. Lawrence) the most. It re-shapes our way of being, robs us of what we own outright at birth: the right to experience our precious bodies with another human being without external interference.

It's true that the government has no place in our bedrooms. But neither does big business or organized crime.

I had explained all of this to Günther so I still feel a bit justified in claiming my isolated moment of sadism.

Sadism. You know, when I was being bullied at school as a little girl, my mother would take me aside and explain, "Happy people don't try to make other people unhappy." It was her way of asking me to feel compassion for people who were trying to hurt me. When I think of sadism these days, I just think it's really sad-ism. Something in Günther was sad, sad about being lonely, sad about never finding his countess, sad about being a novelist and never making quite enough money to comfortably support himself, sad about not keeping his mother happy, sad about not being able to genuinely, easily connect with people. He was such a very polite man, normally, that it threw me off to imagine him having to hurt a woman for fun. Thankfully, though, with the exception of that horrible porn musical, he never took his sadness out on me.

Our weeks together as lovers had been exactly what we both needed but now we shifted to being only friends of a sort, getting together for dinners. Sometimes, we'd nip out to a museum or he'd come over for one of those potluck parties that I kept hosting for the French students. The kids did all the work, anyway.

"I don't really like him," said Istmania looking across the room in Günther's direction at a party one day. "Especially taking you to a porn musical."

"Oh, he's not so bad, really," I laughed. "You have to feel sort of sorry for him, don't you? I mean, feeling like you have to hurt other people . . . he must be very isolated inside, very lonely. That's probably why he likes Film Noir so much. The lonely writer, the isolated man."

"I don't care about that," said Istmania. "But I do think you're very funny!"

Funny. It means so many different things, that word. It can mean you're amusing or that you're very odd or that you're just eccentric. At this stage, after my merry-go-round in Paris, I felt funny. Yes, I did. I felt all three funnies plus uncomfortable at the same time. I could never quite determine why I still liked the sadist so much, but I did. Up close and perisonal, before he'd encountered his difficulties in bed with me, Günther had been very tender, really. In bed, he was commanding and comforting and gentle and strong and, most importantly, present. When it was good with Günther, it was really, really (and I could add a third *really*) good and I was grateful to have shared a bed with him in Paris.

∞

"So you fly home soon?" asked Istmania as she passed me another drink.

"Two weeks."

Two weeks left as a *Parisienne* and then I'd revert to being a Torontonian again. Just doesn't sound as lovely, does it? It now frightened me to go home. I didn't have that book written and, besides, what was I really going home to? The future was pretty much a blank canvas.

What do you do when you look into your own future and you see mostly nothing of interest? That had never happened to me before. I'd always had Paris waiting for me in that future of mine, and now what? Yes, I looked forward to seeing my daughters again, but they wouldn't be filling my life up anymore. They were grown women and had their own lives to get on with. We'd still be having the occasional Sunday supper to enjoy together but I refused to be the sort of mother that invades an adult child's space. My parents didn't park themselves in my life and I wasn't about to park myself in my children's lives, either. I'd have to get on with things, too. I knew that. I'd have to become a Torontonian again, search for another contract – my mortgage would be waiting for me, after all. I'd have to try to get back into the rhythm of my old life.

Nothing I could think up about going home felt like a future that I wanted to step into.

Strangely, a dream you give up and a dream you live out each leave a gap in your life, an emptiness. I had nothing to spin around in my mind. As I got ready to leave Paris, I kept wondering what I could let my mind wander into, conjure up as a goal, now that I no longer had Paris to plan for.

I didn't know and I tried not to think about it even though I felt that question keep poking around at my insides. Just get it done, I told myself. Just pack up the suitcases, give stuff away that you can't fit in those suitcases or you can't take back (like my speakers that plug into European electrical outlets), walk around the neighborhood one last time and call for a cab.

"I'd rather not come with you to the airport," Günther had said with genuine sorrow as he helped put my luggage into the taxi. "It will feel too much like good-bye."

It is good-bye, I thought, though I still expected we'd email.

"I am coming to the airport," said Istmania, "even if you don't want me to."

I had no choice about that. Italians, as she pointed out (and she was half Italian), take their entire extended family to the airport even if only one of them is actually leaving and I can attest to that. I've been stuck in line behind dozens of Italians, worried I'd not catch my plane, and then discover that there were only two Italians who were checking in and I was next up. The rest were there to socialize and, it seems, makes as much happy noise as possible.

Roman had said his good-byes the night before. The morning I was scheduled to fly out, he had a meeting with a French government official on the long road to becoming a French citizen, a person with a state and the right to a passport.

"We'll always be in each other's lives," I promised. "I'm only an email away. And," I added while looking directly into his sad blue eyes, "I'll be back for your next birthday."

∞

Istmania and I had left for the airport with plenty of time to make a few toasts together over a glass of breakfast champagne but the young man at the counter couldn't figure out how to charge me for the extra bags. He kept going back and forth to the head agent. "I am sorry, *Madame*, but the machine does not like your credit card." The machine didn't like any of my credit cards it turned out and so he went one more time to speak with the agent, checked the luggage, gave me the tags and a little note to take to the agent in the other line.

I watched the bags roll away and down the chute to the baggage sorting machines, held the little note up to Istmania and said, "There's a hole in the system." Istmania didn't understand. "My bags are on their way to the plane and now the system can't force me to pay." I saw the look of disappointment in Istmania's face. "Don't worry. Don't worry. I'm nothing if not honest. I'll pay for my extra luggage even though, technically, there's no way I really have to. Anyway, I wouldn't want to get that unbelievably handsome young man in any trouble."

Istmania giggled. I had seen how she'd been watching him.

We walked over to the line with the head agent and waited. And waited. When it was finally my turn, the woman turned to me rather gruffly and asked in French, "What do you want?"

"Um." Gosh, I thought, she didn't even say, "*Bonjour, Madame*." I'd become so accustomed to these small, polite gestures. She'd surprised me and I couldn't find any French words in my head. "Um," I hesitated again and now everyone behind me was listening. "I want to pay."

"Pay for what?"

"The luggage." I turned to look over at the young man who had been having so much trouble with my bags and credit cards.

"*Madame* Jaks?" smiled the agent politely. "Oh, I told the young man you didn't have to pay."

"Pardon?"

She brushed me away with a smile. "Have a very nice flight, *Madame.*"

"Yes!" I said and held up a fist in victory. "Now I can afford the champagne!"

Everyone within hearing range laughed.

"Have a glass for me, will you?" the agent asked.

The fact is, I should have paid hundreds and hundreds of dollars for all this excess luggage, which is probably why the young man couldn't get anything to work. Few people severely overdo their luggage allowance the way I had done that day.

Istmania and I had that glass (or two . . .) of champagne together, saying very little for once. We would see each other again. Just exactly when, we didn't know, so we sat together in the silence of our friendship. She would soon be heading back to Nicaragua to face her life there. We all have to do that, don't we? Face our own lives.

"Good-bye," I said.

"Non," said Istmania wagging a finger at me. *"Au revoir."*

"Until we see each other again", she'd said in French, which is a more accurate translation of *au revoir.*

Au revoir, friend. *Au revoir,* Paris. *Au revoir* to all those little hopes I'd held for a while. Or was it good-bye?

Do we ever really know for sure?

On the plane, I discovered quite happily that the airline steward seated me in First Class. No, the nice agent who didn't make me pay for my bags hadn't upgraded me. I sneaked a peek at my ticket hoping not to draw attention to myself in case someone had made a big mistake and then felt obliged to boot me out of First Class . . .

Nope. No mistake. Months ago, I'd unknowingly booked myself into First Class – using only economy airline points.

"There's a hole in the system," I smiled to myself as the stewardess gave me a glass of champagne. Those of us in First Class then waited for the rest of plane to board.

CHAPTER TWENTY-SEVEN

A Door Opens, Deliciously

At border control, the normal routine for me is this: I state with complete honesty how much I've spent and then get directed into the special customs area to pay taxes on the difference between what I shelled out on the trip and the miniscule allowance that the government allows us to bring back into the country.

Often, the greeting from Canadian customs agents is downright hostile because they're trained to be suspicious, trying to understand, for example, why I go to Paris sometimes for just four days (using points, for gosh sakes, and booking early for the best deals). "Is she a drug mule?" they obviously wondered. One official even demanded to know what I did for a living, how I could afford going to Paris "all the time." This, in my opinion, was none of his business. Some people buy second homes, some people gamble all their money away, some people go to Paris all the time. So I said I was independently wealthy. OK, so technically I lied but as a citizen of two free countries, I'm allowed to go anywhere I want without apologies. Search me, if you'd like.

Which they often did, by the way. Actually, they usually put Julie the Sniff Dog up to it and she's gotten me more than once, wiggling around the luggage area wagging her tail and then coming straight over to my carry-on bag and sitting down, kerplop, right next to it. That was the signal from this little canine customs agent to the human one. Signal for what? Julie the Sniff Dog, a cute little beagle, has gotten me twice for bringing an illegal substance into Canada. The third time, as I saw her come sniffing my way, I raised both my hands in the air like a common criminal and confessed, "I have an apple in my backpack!" It had happened before. Again I was hauled to the special customs room. On that occasion I was told that if it happened one more time, if they found just one more apple on a return trip, they'd have to fine me $200 and they would be forced to go through every inch of my luggage with a fine tooth comb.

Did I want that?

You can imagine, then, how thrilled I was to be walking up to the customs official dragging back thousands upon thousands of dollars of shoes and clothes and lavender honey.

"You spent what?" asked the agent.

I repeated the amount.

"That's a lot of money," she said as she circled a few things on my re-entry card and scribbled a few codes in large red ink.

"Yes, well, I was living in Paris for several months and I always spend too much money on shoes. But they're used, now. Don't I get a little credit for that, like have them marked down or something?"

"Afraid not," she said, making a red mark and then a secret code on my customs card as custom agents do, and handed me back that card so I could go and claim my luggage and all those shoes before going off to pay those taxes.

After I heaved all that luggage onto a cart, put my backpack on, and arranged the big blue hockey bag (with wheels, thank heavens) that so that I could drag it behind me, I made my way to the next customs checkpoint, mentally calculating how much I would have to pay in taxes.

It was a lot. A lot.

Oh well, I thought. That's the deal. You buy stuff, you pay taxes on re-entry.

I showed the next agent my card covered in red circles and secret codes. At this stage, you're either pointed left to exit to meet your family or told to go to the right to the special customs room and pay up. I automatically started to turn right toward the customs room.

"Whoa," said the agent. "You go that-a-way." He pointed left – to the exit.

"But, I . . . I have to pay taxes. I was out of the country for several months and . . ."

"Ma'am," he grinned looking at my cart with the ridiculously high pile of luggage leaning precariously to one side, looking more like it belonged in a Dr. Seuss book. "You seem just a little too busy to be paying taxes today." He tapped his hand to the side of his forehead in a sort of salute. "Welcome home, ma'am."

∞

Life is a series of circumstances and along the way there are decision points and detours and then, usually, more detours. The good thing is, none of us really knows where we're going, not really. What I didn't know then as I pulled that awkward hockey bag along behind me and pushed the hefty luggage cart up to the 'Exit' door of the Customs area was that this door was really the Entrance door to a new life. I stood looking at this Exit door not wanting to walk through, stood there with a bit of a sigh stuck inside my chest and waited for that sigh to release itself. I didn't want to go through those doors, go back to my life, because I didn't have that beautiful dream of living in Paris buried inside me, though I did want to see my daughters. But here's the thing: I was about to enter a new life, a life that no longer included one of my dreams because it was now a part of me, a part of my past. I had been a *Parisienne* for seven months. In a small way – very small and invisible to anyone else, I know – I had contributed to the spirit that is Paris, blended part of my soul with hers, and was now part of her history and she mine.

What I also didn't know when I walked through those Entrance doors was that I was needed back home. My daughters, my adult children, needed me. I still had some more mothering to do and I was glad of that.

Kaia, the eldest, had a surprise for us. She'd recently discovered she was about to make me a grandmother. We were soon to welcome a little boy into our lives, a very blond and bright blue-eyed sweetheart looking like any good little Estonian boy would. I thought of my grandparents, his great-great-grandparents, and knew that he and I would one day make the journey to Estonia together to visit with the spirits of our ancestors, to celebrate *Jaanipäev* and The Perfect Kiss, to celebrate life itself and dance around a fire to honor the strength of those who fought for our survival, his and mine. Our ancestors had held us in their hearts, as I hold my own children and grandchildren – and even future generations – in mine.

My youngest daughter, as it turned out, also had a surprise for me. Anneli wanted to abandon her school plans. She needed a long walk by the Lake Ontario along with somewhat stern motherly advice as she tried to sort her life out. What was she to do? She was about to get an apparently useless Latin degree and felt trapped. After being interviewed for a graduate program in the Classics Department at Stanford in California, she realized something. "I don't want to be a Latin professor," she said. "I don't want to get my PhD."

"Well," I pointed out, "You'd better think of something because right now all you've educated yourself for is to get a job where you say 'Would you like fries with that?'"

"I could be a baker, there's a job at a café near the university that needs someone to make croissants. I always wanted to learn how to make croissants."

"I don't accept this," I said as she worried through her future. "I accepted you wanted to take Latin because that's what you loved even though it's not the kind of expertise that gets you very far in the 21st century! I accepted that you wanted to go to a little nothing school that nobody's heard of because it was the place you really wanted to be. [For the record, she could have gone to a toney Ivey League school but passed it by for the "little nothing school" and, yes, I wholly supported her choice.] But I don't accept that you want to be a baker of croissants back in that little university town, hovering around because you don't know what else to do. Not at all. You're afraid and you're curling in on yourself. Find something you love and then I'll trust what you want to do."

"But I can't get into medical school with a Latin degree," she blurted out. "That's why I studied Latin in high school, remember? I wanted to be a doctor. But now I can't get in."

"Can't?" I challenged. "Can't? Never say never and never say can't. You know that."

"Live! Live! Live!" is what she'd always heard from me – and witnessed me trying to do, for God's sake. Live your life doing what you love to do, find a way to do it. Don't let the Serpent of Fear crank itself so tightly around your chest that you live your whole life holding your breath!

"Follow your bliss" is and always will be, sound advice. It's not an airy-fairy "do all your affirmations and you'll be happy" sort of thing. Joseph Campbell had spent a lifetime studying other cultures and their mythologies stretching back thousands of years. The collective wisdom of the human spirit is this:

> Follow your bliss and don't be afraid, and doors will
> open where you didn't know they were going to be.

It takes courage to live like that. It takes courage to live with the Twin Serpents. It takes courage to move forward in the direction of your dreams when it looks like you're headed straight for a brick wall.

Both of my children had grown up with that message, had witnessed me doing my best to try to live it. Hadn't it been baked into their deep subconscious?

My insistence that Anneli face down her "can't" and "never" worries seemed to have snapped my daughter back into herself because a year later, she was studying medicine at one of the world's premier medical schools.

She also baked croissants – at home, for fun.

∞

Sometimes, in a quiet moment when I'm all alone, I think of what I call 'that little girl', the teenager who made a promise to her baby and then became basically a frightened girl in a business suit with one single computer course under her belt trying to make ends meet, trying to pay bills, trying to make day care arrangements and figure out how to be a good mom and a good breadwinner, trying to find that next contract. On occasion, I still tear up in gratitude to this person who is no longer me but who got me here thanks to all that trying. No, she is no longer 'me' but, thankfully, she's still a part of me because at this point in my life, I very much need her innocent courage, her ability to question the status quo. I'm looking 50 squarely in the eye and I don't know how to 'do' 50 just like I didn't know how to 'do' single teenaged mom.

At times, I try to honor 'that little girl' and do my best to look forward into my old age. I even sometimes say to myself, "I'm going to grow to be an Older Woman and do whatever I want to do and be whatever I want to be." There's some wisdom in that thinking, even if it's not so easy here at this stage of my life. In this culture, women seem to evaporate at a certain age. We're made invisible, unnecessary. Women over 40 are pretty much non-existent on the Internet and TV, never mind women over 50. When it comes to the Internet, some of this is because women just aren't stepping up to the plate, I know. Some of it is because women aren't claiming – even embracing – their old age.

But if she (that little girl) could face down the odds and give me, the woman thirty years into her future, a pretty good life, then I owe the woman I will be in thirty years a pretty good life, too, don't I?

Back then, at the very beginning of my womanhood, I'll admit that terror fueled me, terror and the love for my baby. Yes, those twin serpents – Love and Fear – can do so much for you if you're lucky enough to harness their energy just right. Maybe, just maybe, loving life and being afraid to waste a single minute of it will harness those twin serpents so that I keep dancing with this thing called Life -- wearing high heels and short skirts until Zack tells me I'm beginning to look tragic -- well into my 80s.

I must keep reminding myself to 'age well', not grow old.

But how do we age well?

Many, though not all, French women know how to do this. First, get a good hairdresser. When the hairdresser I'd found in Paris – a slender, confident, beautiful young woman – gently suggested that I change my hair cut, I blurted out, "But why?"

We spoke only in very simple French together, she knew no English, and sometimes we used gestures to get our points across. Looking at me in the mirror as she fussed with my hair a bit and thought about it, she nodded in the direction of what I would call an old lady. This woman was getting her hair cut in a style she must have worn since the 1960s, almost a beehive. It was died jet black which looked just wrong against her old skin. "You see," said my hairdresser softly, "There's nothing wrong with getting older. There's just something wrong with becoming an old lady."

I surrendered and let her do whatever she wanted to do with my hair. The new cut livened up my face, even made me look younger without trying to pretend I was still in my twenties.

Beyond the haircut, how to grow old gracefully? Wait, I don't think I even want that. I don't want to grow old gracefully! 'Growing old gracefully' feels like I'm supposed to take a back seat, become sheepish and quiet, not bother anybody, to wear pearls well and to sip my gin-spiked tea in polite silence. To become invisible.

I want to grow old well. I want to stay alive and engaged and active and "Live! Live! Live!" till the day I close my eyes for the last time.

There are so many things we don't know, and most of them – I learned as I settled in back home – are actually better than we could possibly have imagined.

∞

When I walked through those 'Entrance' doors into the rest of my life, what I didn't know was that I was about to meet someone who had been transferred from Europe to Canada, arriving in the country the very same week that I'd stepped back into my regular life.

He had arrived at the international airport and walked through those very same 'Exit/Entrance' doors.

We didn't meet right away. Life kept happening. I was busy looking for another contract, busy catching up with friends and, yes, busy writing. But one day, to my great surprise, I found him.

He was sitting alone at the bar one night, looking out the window at the dark lake. Over the course of more than a decade, I'd walked into this very bar hundreds of times and never once had I seen such a breathtakingly handsome man sitting at the window. Not only that, he was sitting in what I considered to be 'my' seat.

I liked this place because of the narrow table that stretches across the length of the ceiling-to-floor, wall-to-wall windows.

It has a panoramic view of Lake Ontario and I used to sit in the bar of the restaurant, Canoe, at that window in that very seat just to enjoy watching the changing mood of the lake and wide expanse of sky at the end of the day. Sitting there when it was night, I'd have a glass of something and look out into the dark empty spaces, spaces of what seemed like deep pools of nothing, places to let your dreams take hold, pools of darkness edged by the flicker of lights from homes that dotted along the edges of the small islands that hugged the bay, islands that offered not only shelter but shape to the night.

This is the bar where over the last fifteen years I have often taken a client or two but as it was, I was alone this night. I had come to read some notes I'd written for this book and because I didn't have to dress up to impress anyone, I didn't. I'd been writing all week and the only reason I'd dropped by on this night was to take in some of the elegant, soothing bar music and to have a glass of champagne, a reward for sticking with it, for working alone at home for hour upon hour all week just to meet a silly, self-imposed deadline. That particular morning, I woke early and had reached into the pile of crumpled clothes next to my bed to pull on yesterday's jeans.

I had tossed on the same blue sweater I'd worn the day before and I knew as I stood there that I hadn't washed my hair – hopefully I'd brushed it, I suddenly thought. I froze at the entrance to the bar and ran my fingers through my hair, trying to fluff it up, but I couldn't be sure – had I brushed it? Certainly I had no makeup on. Deodorant? I couldn't remember. Did I at least squirt on some perfume at some point during the day? I couldn't be sure about that, either.

I'd been absorbed at the computer all day and here I was and there he was and … I stood there, not knowing what to do.

Several chairs on either side of him were empty. Was I brave enough to go and sit next to him?

No.

But I did finally manage to screw up enough courage to sit just a few chairs away, close enough for him to notice me, if he wanted to.

I immediately pretended to read my notes.

"Oh please, please," I whined inside my head, irrationally. "Talk to me."

But he didn't. Why would he? I sat there like a lump with my glass of champagne, pretending to read, giving off an air of being completely self-contained because it would have been too embarrassing to let him see what I was really thinking. Not once did I even have the courage to look up at him except at those moments when I could tell from the corner of my eye that he was looking out over the lake. That's when I'd sneak a peak. Oh, my, his hands were stunning. I liked his profile, too. He had a nice line to his nose, a delicious line from his forehead down his nose and down his lips to a strong neck. He swallowed and I watched his Adam's apple go up, then down. I wanted to touch that neck. His jaw line was strong and I so wanted to stroke his face along the line of that jaw. A man's profile, how he looks from the side, is what you see when you lie next to each other in bed and my mind had already started to imagine that we were lying together warm and naked and I was looking at him from the side. Oh, stop that, I told my mind. Spend time figuring out how to get him to talk to you first. That would be a start. But I didn't know how. It turned out that I had no idea know how to pick a man up in a bar. Not a clue.

Anyway, he didn't even seem to notice I was sitting there.

The two of us sat like that for a while, drinking alone and silently looking out over the lake but never once at each other. Two solitudes. I put my hand to my forehead – now pretending to concentrate while still pretending to read. How foolish, I know. That would really put anyone off trying to talk to me. My whole body had started to sparkle at the sound of his voice. He was speaking with the waitress. I was feeling faint. How privately embarrassing.

What was going on? This had never happened to me before.

Then I heard him ask for his bill.

"Oh! Oh no! He's getting away!" I screamed inside my head.

He handed the waitress his credit card and said, "I'm leaving for Paris tomorrow. Business."

The waitress walked away to process the bill.

"Now's your chance," I thought. But no, I was too afraid, too embarrassed. I had no idea how to pick up a man in a bar, how to chat him up. It had always happened the other way around and at the age of 48, well, I couldn't bring myself to do it for the first time.

Just couldn't.

∞

The waitress was back in a flash – too fast, too fast, I didn't have time to think – and he signed the bill and took his card and thanked her.

"Have a nice time in Paris," she said.

I sat there and watched as he put away his wallet.

Ole tubli, ole tubli for Christ's sake, I thought. Live bravely, live bravely, oh please do something, just something!

As he stood up to go, I saw he was very tall as well as being very handsome, tall with broad shoulders and that jaw line of his that I wanted to stroke. I swallowed hard, clutched at my glass of champagne as if it would keep me from falling off the bar stool and leaned way over in his direction. In a feeble voice, a voice I hardly recognized as my own it was so squeezed and tight, I squeaked, "I used to live in Paris."

He smiled politely at me.

How embarrassing, I thought. Who cares? What does he care that I used to live in Paris? What would a man, oh such a deliciously handsome man as that, want with me? Especially today. Of all days to sit here and look like crap.

He quickly adjusted his tie and then adjusted his suit jacket as if to make sure his wallet dropped down into his breast pocket. He patted his right-hand pants pocket to check for his keys, perhaps, and pushed his chair in.

He was leaving.

He began to walk to the door which was just behind me. There was something about him, something. He was so beautiful, so tall, so very very very . . . .

"I'm sorry," he said warmly. "I couldn't hear you."

I looked up and felt a part of me, something precious from very deep inside, float up and fall into his kind, blue eyes.

"I . . . I used to live in Paris," I squeaked again.

"In Paris?"

"Yes," I said, still white-knuckling my drink.

Leaning down toward me just a bit and touching the chair next to mine, he said softly, "Would you like another glass of champagne?"

As anyone who knows me knows, I never say no to champagne.

He pulled up a chair and I tried to stay centered, stay focused. All parts of me were tingling, sparkling with excitement. I'd never felt this sort of instantaneous, deliciously irrational passion for a complete stranger ever in my life.

"My name is Stefan," he said in his beautiful voice.

"Nice to meet you, Stefan," I said and here's a fact: I don't think I've ever spoken a truer sentence in my life.

After our glass of champagne, Stefan walked me halfway home, careful not to make me feel uncomfortable by walking me all the way to my door. He handed me his card.

"Thank you," I said, thrilled that he wanted me to know how to reach him.

"I've enjoyed meeting you," said Stefan. "You're a very interesting woman."

"Thank you," I said again.

"Perhaps when I'm back from Paris, we could have dinner? I'm still new to Toronto and . . ."

"I'd be very happy to," I interrupted.

We stood at the corner of Spadina and King Street in Toronto, not wanting the lights to change.

"Have a nice evening," he smiled. Had he been French, not Austrian, he would have kiss-kissed me on each cheek but instead we shook hands. I enjoyed feeling the warmth of his hand and we stood there for just a moment, not letting go.

"I used to live in Paris," I smiled, "and helloes and goodbyes just don't feel right anymore without doing this." I stood on my tip toes and kiss-kissed him on each cheek. Of course, I took the opportunity to breathe him in, to smell him up close as I like to do when I meet a man. He smelled so damn fine, so unreasonably delicious. My entire body felt like it was starting to sing. At his neck, I breathed him in again. He did the same on my hair. I wanted to kiss that neck of his but instead I stood back and smiled a naturally warm, inviting smile. Perhaps I was beaming, I don't know.

"Thank you," he said awkwardly. I could tell that he had liked breathing me in, too.

Oh, this was going to be good I thought as I walked the rest of the way home on my own. This man and I are going to be very, very good together.

Ole tubli.

ACKNOWLEDGEMENTS

I would first like to thank my second husband, whom I have called Mel in this book, for always believing I could actually write something. Then, of course, I very much thank my family and friends who listened politely as I endlessly yakked on and on about what I was one day, in some far-off distant future, going to do in Paris. Thank you for always going along with it and for encouraging me. Also, I owe a very big thank you to Cathy Bamford who looked after my home, my car and my pets while I traveled.

At the end of the day, this book could not have happened without the ongoing support including many rounds of excellent criticism and advice from friends who are writers: Keltie Thomas, Christina Tari, Sydney Clark, Dr. Wendy Stross, Claudia Balon-Perin, Mark Jones and Kate. For years, they worked with me through the often very tedious task of reading and rereading bits and pieces of this book.

I also had support from some men who read snippets of this book: Ted Carrette, Al Routh and Michel. Thanks for your interest and your feedback.

Alan Teder went through the last round with a fine-tooth comb and found all those little missing words and slight (but important) grammatical mistakes I'd managed to slip in when I was supposedly 'fixing up' the book after the editors had already been through it. Thanks so very much, Alan.

To Jana Schilder, Shawna Kaufman and Tracey Black: Thanks for that last read-through and pointing out where the boring bits were still lingering. I hope you caught them all.

About the Author

Citizen. Writer. Entrepreneur. Mother.
Sister. Daughter. Memm. Ex-Wife. Friend.
Human. Humane. Aunt. Dog-Servant. Neighbor.
Seeker. Soul. Lover. Traveler. Opinionated.

Believes in miracles.
Don't you?

318 · MARET JAKS

Maret Jaks spent her early years as part of a community of Estonian refugees in Canada, which means she's a bit on the crazy side about saunas, kringel, and a certain type of sauerkraut that only Estonians make. She has two biological daughters and has raised a few foster daughters. Thanks to her time in Paris, she now has a Belarussian foster son, too.

Although Maret has lived in a few countries and in many cities, towns, and townships, she never lives alone. There's always a dog or two at her side, especially when she's writing (they have their own writing chairs next to her).

With a high school degree under her belt, Maret became a technical consultant with a specialty that allowed her to command fees that provided well for her family. She was told it couldn't be done. But "Never say never and never surrender" is her personal motto – along with Auntie Mame's message to "Live! Live! Live!"

Hoping she'll be able to wear high heels right into her 80s, and beyond, Maret plans to continue to dance with Life right up to the moment she closes her eyes for the last time. She hopes you do, too – in high heels or clunky workbooks or even sneakers with orthotics, it doesn't matter. What matters is that we live bravely, as bravely as we can.

Ole tubli.

To learn more about **Maret Jaks**, please go to her website or sign up for her substack.

https://maretjaks.com/

https://maret.substack.com

End Notes

---

[i] When this chapter was first reviewed by some writers in 2009, they balked at this sentence, challenged me, said I was exaggerating. I held firm – because right up to the 1980s throughout the Western world, women who were not married were shamed, coerced or forced by circumstance or family to give their babies up for adoption. People seem to have completely forgotten about this!

Just as I completed this book, the BBC ran this story: "Australian PM Gillard sorry for 'shameful' forced adoptions." From the 1950s through the 1970s, hospitals had developed policies to coerce and force unwed mothers to sign papers giving their babies away to "meet the demand for adopted babies." It is estimated that this happened to 300,000 young women. In the video accompanying the article, Duncan Kennedy of the BBC said, *"Generations of women were punished for having sex outside of marriage and have spent their lives recoiling from its cruel consequences."* March 20, 2013 http://www.bbc.co.uk/news/world-asia-21872919

[ii] Mark Twain's Notebook.

[iii] Lee, Jennifer (Editor), *Paris in Mind: Three Centuries of Americans Writing About Paris*, Vintage Books, New York, 2003, p. 213.

[iv] Sadly, it's been shown that in racist societies, children absorb the negative messages from outside the family but at least, within the home, the parents love their children without reference to their race.

[v] Anderson, Bonnie S. and Zinsser, Judith P., *A History of Their Own, Volume II*, Harper & Row, New York City, 1988, p. 258.

[vi] When I was president of a group that helped women in prison, a number of our clients were women. The board decided to host a forum on the plight of prostitutes, both for and against legalizing it. We wanted women who had experienced being a prostitute to speak, not only theoretical academics.

Interestingly, we could find many, many women who had been prostitutes who felt that under no circumstances should it ever be made legal, but none of them would speak in public. In private, they spoke very eloquently, very touchingly, about why they opposed making prostitution legal. But in the end, our forum featured only academics and a single prostitute (a 6' 2" trans-identified male) in favor of making it legal. Despite our best efforts, we could not convince any of the former prostitutes who opposed legalizing prostitution to speak in public.

So, our debate was missing an important perspective – just like in most of the public forums you hear about these days – because women traumatized by prostitution were trying to get on with their lives and wouldn't go public.

[vii] Happily, in 2013, France also passed legislation similar to the Swedish prostitution laws that target the men who pay money for sex.

[viii] Daniels, Sarah, Masterpieces (Modern Plays), Methuen, London, 1986

[ix] "Parisian women now legally allowed to wear trousers. Yes, you read that right," Jill Mahoney, *The Globe and Mail*, February 4, 2013.

[x] *The Globe and Mail*, "Social Studies: A daily miscellany of information", Sneaky Penguins, Kesterton, Michael, Sept 27, 2007, page L8.

[xi] Scott, Joan Wallach, *Only Paradoxes to Offer: French Feminists and the Rights of Man*, 1996. Harvard University Press, Cambridge, Massachusetts. p. 52.

[xii] Lawrence, D.H., *Pornography and Obscenity, No. XIII* - The Outcast Chapbooks No. 13, Lincoln Press, Yonkers, New York, July 1942. a-*"The mass is forever vulgar, because it can't distinguish between its own original feelings and the feelings which are diddled into existence by the exploiter."* p. 9. b-*"This is the great pornographical class . . . they have as great a hate and contempt of sex as the greyest Puritan . . ."* p. 14-15.

[xiii] *Criminal Neglect: Why Sex Offenders Go Free* by Dr. William Marshall and Sylvia Barrett, in the chapter, "The Link to Pornography". Doubleday, 1991.